SAND TO SILICON

GOING GLOBAL

RAPID GROWTH
LESSONS FROM DUBAI

SAND TO SILICON

GOING GLOBAL

RAPID GROWTH LESSONS FROM DUBAI

JEFFREY SAMPLER & SAEB EIGNER

MOTIVATE
PUBLISHING

To our friends and families.

Published by **Motivate Publishing**

Dubai: PO Box 2331, Dubai, UAE
Tel: (+971 4) 282 4060; fax: (+971 4) 282 7898
e-mail: books@motivate.ae   www.booksarabia.com

Office 508, Building No 8, Dubai Media City, Dubai, UAE
Tel: (+971 4) 390 3550; fax: (+971 4) 390 4845

Abu Dhabi: PO Box 43072, Abu Dhabi, UAE
Tel: (+971 2) 677 2005; fax: (+971 2) 677 0124

London: Acre House, 11/15 William Road, London NW1 3ER
e-mail: motivateuk@motivate.ae

Directors:	Obaid Humaid Al Tayer and Ian Fairservice
Consultant Editor:	David Steele
Editors:	Moushumi Nandy
	Albert Harvey Pincis
Assistant Editor:	Zelda Pinto
Senior Designer:	Cithadel Francisco
Designer:	Charlie Banalo

General Manager Books: Jonathan Griffiths

Cover Design by Cithadel Miclat Francisco

ISBN: 978 1 86063 254 9

British Library Cataloguing-in-Publication Data. A catalogue record for this book is available from the British Library.

Printed by Emirates Printing Press, Dubai, UAE

CONTENTS

PREFACE

Imagination is the beginning of creation. You imagine what you desire,
you will what you imagine and at last you create what you will.

George Bernard Shaw

In many ways this project is a microcosm of Dubai – people from
different backgrounds and experiences working together to achieve
something that would have been impossible without true collaboration
and the merging of skills.

Saeb has an intimate knowledge of the Middle East, especially the
Gulf, and has been travelling there on business for over twenty years.
Jeff has been visiting the Middle East region for the past few years to
lecture at economic forums and corporate strategy events. Jeff's lack of
familiarity with Dubai's history showed when he asked Saeb about a
series of photographs he saw hanging on the wall of the Dubai World
Trade Club, while attending an event together.

The photos showed what appeared to be a small village of tents and
mud houses, with a few traditional dhows moored in the muddy water
of a modest creek alongside them. When Jeff discovered that the
photos depicted Dubai not of a century ago, but of the 1950s, the
degree of growth the area had experienced became immediately clear.
Jeff shared his sense of astonishment with Saeb, and the two began to
flesh out the building blocks of what would become *Sand to Silicon*, the
first book (published in London by Profile Books in 2003) of which
this book *Sand to Silicon – Going Global* is its sequel.

The simple question that motivated the books – how was such growth
achieved in such a short period of time? – proved to be the beginning of
an extremely interesting quest. However, much like Dubai, the answer
was more subtle than the obvious achievements that are visible to the
naked eye. To help us understand these subtleties we were fortunate to
have access to many of Dubai's leading businessmen and government
officials. In the process, Jeff learned that Saeb's cell phone contains the
telephone numbers of the "Who's Who" of the region. We were both
humbled by the graciousness and time provided to us by many
incredibly busy and important people, all of whom wanted the story
told, as if it was their own. Such a sense of pride and achievement.

This kindness is perhaps best illustrated by our first interview with

Dubai's visionary then Crown Prince and now Ruler, His Highness General Sheikh Mohammed bin Rashid Al Maktoum (who is referred to hereafter as Sheikh Mohammed, as he is more commonly known to everyone in Dubai). We were told it would be impossible to see him on this trip, but a few phone calls were placed while we were interviewing Mohammad Al Gergawi, head of Sheikh Mohammed's Executive Office and Sheikh Mohammed agreed to see us at his desert farm on a Saturday night. We were relieved that the meeting could take place early in our research, as how better to get the insights into an organization than talk with its CEO.

About an hour into the desert from central Dubai, we arrived at Sheikh Mohammed's retreat, where he keeps his cherished stable of Arabian endurance race horses, many of which have been ridden to victory in international competitions by Sheikh Mohammed, his wife and his sons. We arrived just after sundown and were shown into a large trophy room displaying all manner of equestrian art, trophies, and photographs from competitions, where we waited patiently while Sheikh Mohammed finished his meeting with a prominent European CEO at the other end of the room. We expected a similar fifteen minute meeting, but once his other guests had left, Sheikh Mohammed invited us to relax with him and have dinner around a great fire outside, in the open air, surrounded by the desert, where the story of Dubai began.

We were shown to a bonfire surrounded by pillows and bolsters on Persian rugs. There we were joined by Sheikh Mohammed and two of his most senior officials, Mohammad Al Gergawi and Sultan Bin Sulayem. We relaxed and talked long into the desert night. While we enjoyed a healthy meal of fresh-grilled lamb, flatbread and salad, Sheikh Mohammed answered our questions honestly and candidly, without any of the guardedness or detachment one might easily expect. He was genuinely interested in our project and, to gain a solid understanding, asked thoughtful and probing questions – it was a genuine two way dialogue.

By the end of the evening, we had completed an incredibly interesting interview with the man clearly responsible for the exceptional success Dubai has been experiencing. But some of our most important insights from the evening had nothing to do with what was spoken around the fire. We experienced first-hand the remarkable presence of the then Crown Prince that seems to affect nearly every area of everyday life and work in Dubai. His ability to make us feel at once welcome and relaxed while engaging us in an active and challenging dialogue was a unique experience that stayed with us throughout our visit and beyond. This initial interview truly helped us understand what nearly everyone we spoke to meant when they mentioned the leadership of Sheikh Mohammed.

What was evident was Sheikh Mohammed's energy, drive and total belief in what he is trying to achieve, albeit not at all costs. He naturally understands the need to balance Dubai's growth with its culture and traditions, and seems concerned that the social infrastructure keeps pace with his business vision – for without this balance he feels that the growth may be difficult to sustain at such a pace without loss of identity that would be unacceptable.

Indeed, these views of balanced growth were shared in many of our interviews outside of Dubai. For example, Sir Richard Branson, Chairman of the Virgin Group and The Earl of Home, Chairman of Coutts & Co, and previously Chairman of Merchant Bank Morgan Grenfell, an early financier of Dubai, both spoke of how they admired Dubai's open approach to business. In particular Sir Richard Branson was highly complimentary of Dubai's open sky policy. Both commented how, remarkably, business success had been achieved bearing in mind the additional worries and duties not normally the concern of a CEO, such as the social responsibilities of education, hospitals, infrastructure and the environment, to name but a few, including managing Dubai's role in the federation of seven emirates. One of the noticeable differences in our discussions with Dubai's leadership over the last five years is the effort at tackling environmental/green concerns and also a wide range of social and related issues.

In our quest to capture the perspectives and efforts that have led to the rapid growth and success of Dubai, we sought, at the same time, to develop a model for balanced corporate growth in which both business and social responsibilities work successfully together. Indeed, as business and its role in society evolves, this will be one of the main challenges to 21st century senior management. We think that Dubai provides a wealth of insights on these topics – and we hope that after reading this book you will do so too.

Going Global

As soon as the first book was written in 2003 and sent to the publisher, we realized that it was rapidly becoming out of date, and it was only a matter of time before we had to write its sequel. We knew that interest in the story of Dubai was only continuing to grow, because at one point when the first edition of the book was out of print, copies were selling on Amazon for $1000![1] This only motivated us more to update the growing, and increasingly global, story of Dubai.

However, we are undoubtedly aware that this book will also become out of date just as quickly, because Dubai never seems to slow its pace of growth. Thus, while we have made every effort to document many of the amazing new developments in Dubai, as well as Dubai's increasingly global impact, the reader should always remember the purpose of the book is not just to document Dubai's latest achievements, but to explain a strategy for achieving this amazing growth. We feel that a number of these insights are transferable to other countries and companies and are the real jewels behind Dubai's ever-increasing display of success.

ENDNOTES

1   Amazon 30.07.08

ACKNOWLEDGEMENTS

Sand to Silicon – Going Global, published by Motivate Publishing in Dubai, is the updated, revised and expanded version of the first book, *Sand to Silicon*, published by Profile Books in London in 2003.

We would like to begin by thanking Sheikh Mohammed, not only for the wonderful evening at his desert retreat back in late 2002 that galvanized this story but also for being so easily accessible thereafter. We have met him and bumped into him many times, in Dubai and London, where we live. We have also been fortunate since the first book to have met a number of Sheikh Mohammed's sons when they accompanied him, and saw first hand how the drive, energy and wisdom is being instilled in the next generation.

We could not have completed either of the two books in such short periods of time (which we now refer to as "Dubai time") without the help of so many people, most of whom we hope to have listed here, but there are surely others, and our warmest thanks go to them as well. There are some who asked to remain anonymous and we have, of course, respected that wish and thank them too.

Many of those originally interviewed back in 2002/2003 have moved on in their respective careers, with most taking on more and bigger responsibilities; we have been fortunate to witness first hand the insightfulness, hard work and sheer energy of many of them. Some early interviewees such as Mohammad Al Gergawi, Dr Anwar Gargash and Sheikha Lubna Al Qasimi became part of Sheikh Mohammed's first cabinet embodying the new energy of the UAE's drive. Sultan Bin Sulayem of the Ports, Customs & Free Zone Corporation and Jebel Ali Free Zone and Dubai World, with its varied and diversified subsidiaries and JV's went on to complete Palm Jumeirah and to launch two other massive palm projects plus The World islands development as well as acquire P&O – an important milestone in Dubai's going global strategy. Mohammad Al Gergawi launched Dubai Holding with its now recognized subtle but effective logo (with a red "tick" next to the company names). Dubai Holding contains many well known subsidiaries – each in their own right a major player both in developing Dubai and taking the message globally. Sheikh Ahmed took Emirates from strength to strength with the airline now flying to 100 destinations, exporting Dubai's reputation to many of the new cities to which it flies opening new routes for trade and opportunity. He opened the amazing new airport terminal (increasing capacity to some 70 million passengers and serving 120 airlines) while simultaneously constructing the massive Dubai World Central in Jebel Ali (with a capacity of 120 million passengers and the first of six parallel runways already complete in record time).

Our research was assisted by an array of government and industry figures at all levels who have generously shared their thoughts with us. They include Mohammed Ali Alabbar of Emaar Properties (builders of Burj Dubai, the world's tallest building) and head of the Government of Dubai's Department of Economic Development, Khalid Bin Sulayem of the Department of Tourism and Commerce Marketing; Khalid Al Kassim of the Department of Economic Development; Abdul Baset Al Janahi of the Dubai Development and Investment Authority and the Mohammed Bin Rashid Establishment's Young Business Leaders; many past and present members of the Dubai International Financial Centre (DIFC), most notably its Governor Dr Omar bin Sulaiman and his staff, and Essa Kazim Chairman and CEO of Borse Dubai and the Dubai Financial Market (Dubai's stock exchange). Abdul Rahman Al Owais, Minister of Culture, a most knowledgeable driver of the cultural agenda, and Reem Al Hashimi (UAE Minister of State) a new member of the UAE Cabinet embodying the growing number of aspiring professional women in the UAE.

There are many who believe that the "wave" of the future can be seen beyond the city centre, reaching to the Dubai Technology, Electronic Commerce and Media (TECOM) Free Zone and now well beyond that. We are grateful to those who helped us gain a close understanding of this important and highly successful area, including the Zones' then Director General and now Chairman Ahmad Bin Byat who has since been tasked with the new strategic role of Secretary General of the Dubai Executive Council, and TECOM's Deputy Director General Abdulhamid Al Juma who now also runs the growing Dubai International Film Festival (DIFF); to Microsoft's Abdullatif Al Mulla for his "tenant company" perspective. There are many others, some of whom were not interviewed for the book but in meeting them new perspectives were given (at times inadvertently!). Our thanks go to them too. They include Fadel Al Ali of Dubai Holding, Helal Al Merri of the World Trade Centre, Soud Ba'alawi of Dubai Group, Samir Al Ansari of Dubai International Capital, Hashem Al Dabel of Dubai Properties, Farhan Faraidooni of Sama Dubai, Saeed Al Mountafiq of

Tatweer and Nabil Al Yousuf of The Executive Office (TEO).

Travellers throughout the world who have yet to experience the delights of Dubai may have, nevertheless, passed through its airport or flown on its airline, Emirates, if fortunate enough they may have even flown on its new amazing A380. Our thanks go to those who provided perceptive thoughts into the challenges of maintaining and growing these facilities: Sheikh Ahmed bin Saeed Al Maktoum ("Sheikh Ahmed"), President of Dubai's Department of Civil Aviation and Chairman of Emirates Group (which includes Emirates airline), Maurice Flanagan the airlines' founding CEO and now Emirates Group's Executive Vice Chairman who is always so very generous with his time, never turning down a request); Mike Simon, the Director of Corporate Communications for the Emirates Group; Dr Mohammed Al Zarouni of the Dubai Airport Free Zone Authority; and Anita Mehra Homayoun, Director of Marketing at the Department of Civil Aviation.

We are grateful to many representatives of the private sector, including: Abdullah Majed Al Ghurair and Avi Bhojani of Bates PanGulf, Raja Easa Al Gurg of the Easa Saleh Al Gurg Group, Kito de Boer McKinsey's Managing Director for the Middle East and Tim Breen at McKinsey in Dubai, Anis Al Jallaf of Union Properties, Shehab Gargash of Daman Securities, Mike Stevenson from PricewaterhouseCoopers, Ziad Galadari of the law firm Galadari & Associates, as well as many individuals from the banking sector both within DIFC and in the UAE in general.

We also thank Jumeirah in Dubai for always looking after us so well during our stays at their splendid hotels and their Executive Chairman Gerald Lawless for his and his teams' time and effort.

We are also grateful to Dr Anwar Gargash Minister for Federal National Council Affairs and Minister of State for Foreign Affairs, a key driver in holding the UAE's first and successful elections, an invaluable source of local knowledge and most generous with his and his family's time for giving us much logistical support and advice during our stays.

We are indebted to all those at Sheikh Mohammed's Executive Office in Dubai (TEO), particularly its Chairman Mohammad Al Gergawi who was always accessible and most generous with his and his family's time. All members of TEO's most helpful team – where no question was too difficult to answer nor a task too great to handle, and where the word "done" (i.e. getting something done) was used literally and results were always delivered with quick turn around. They include many – most notably the Chairman's executive assistant Wafa Al Khatib, TEO director Maryam Kalban (who followed the story from its early days having unbeknown to us also been involved with statistics research for the first book), and Shatha Banihashim (who worked on updating the appendices).

Also, many thanks to our many friends and others in the Gulf region who have given their advice, time, and thoughts freely – providing a perspective of how Dubai is viewed by its neighbours.

In London, we are grateful to the Earl of Home for sharing his early experiences of Dubai since the 1960's; Geoffrey Bignell for having kindly read and amended the introduction and who, too, knew the area during the early days. We should also like to thank Sir Richard Branson for his interview and views on Dubai, his most helpful Strategy Director, Gordon McCallum, for having made that possible and Apurv Bagri for his Asia perspective and our friends in Singapore for their insightfulness and perceptive comments. Thanks too to Lisa Ellis for her patience and professionalism in dealing with so many different parties and two demanding authors.

Thanks too to the publisher of the first edition, *Sand to Silicon*, Stephen Brough of Profile Books in London.

Thanks go to Andrew Conway, our research assistant, whose flexibility and efficiency with the first book made it possible for us to have completed it in "Dubai time".

Special thanks go to our publishers Motivate. Notably their managing partner and group editor, Ian Fairservice who embodies the success story of those who arrived in Dubai early on, having created the region's largest publishing house. We are grateful also to Ian's excellent team, including the head of books, Jonathan Griffiths, who is always enthusiastic and encouraging as well as Moushumi Nandy, who has worked tirelessly to check that we have all of our facts correct.

Thanks too, of course, to all of those who have reviewed and/or commented on the book, some of whose comments are quoted on the back cover. Also thanks to our friends and colleagues in academia for their views and insights.

We close in thanking, again, Sheikh Mohammed for having not only galvanized our quest for what lies behind the story but for the pleasure of having seen first hand a world leader in action, with a style of his very own.

We hope our book can play a humble part in bringing Dubai's amazing story of rapid growth to the attention of the world and record what has been done in such a short period of time. We now feel part of this story, even if we play a very small part indeed.

We hope that, if nothing else, people will enjoy reading the book, even if it is a management book!

Finally, we would like to thank our families for their patience and support while we were immersed in the creation of this book, compiled during our "free" time at all hours of the day and night, weekends and holidays too, since we both have demanding day jobs.

*Our children, Timmy, Sean and Serena, thank you;
we love you very much.*

CHAPTER 1

INTRODUCTION

Our business story is about courage . . .

Sheikh Mohammed

This is a book about Dubai and how the lessons of its successful, large-scale, rapid growth can be applied to organizations. Today it is almost impossible not to be aware of Dubai. Over just three generations and mostly within the past half century, this very small emirate has raised its profile globally through a range of bold developments, corporate acquisitions, strategic alliances and clever ideas. These include free zones for business that have made it a regional centre for many leading international firms, a biennial air show, Dubai International Airport, Emirates airline, Jebel Ali and Rashid Ports, the Dubai International Financial Centre, Dubailand, Dubai World Central, the Dubai World Cup horse race, and its development as a tourism centre with some of the most stunning hotels in the world out of their collection of over 300 hotels, including the now iconic Burj Al Arab (which at the time of its opening was known as the world's only 'seven-star' hotel). Dubai has grown both up and out, with the construction of Burj Dubai (the world's tallest building) and the metamorphosis of the coastline with the construction of three massive palm-shaped peninsulas and 'The World', another mixed-use luxury development of islands designed to resemble, from the air, a map of the world. Dubai seems to be growing in all directions – up, out and in. "Up" with the construction of Burj Dubai (the world's tallest building). "Out" with the metamorphosis of the coastline through the construction of three massive palm-shaped peninsulas and 'The World', another mixed-use luxury development of islands designed to resemble, from the air, a map of the world. And "in" with many of the latest developments expanding into the previously undeveloped desert. These developments are partially enabled by expanding the Creek and bringing the sea inland.

Many attribute much of the emirate's recent growth to its being run

1

like a corporation, hence the much used metaphor of Dubai Inc. Sheikh Mohammed, Dubai's Ruler, and his father, the late Ruler of Dubai, Sheikh Rashid Bin Saeed Al Maktoum, before him, have been fond of saying that 'what's good for business is good for Dubai', and the reverse is also true. The government's structure has more in common with that of a private-run company than a public one. The ruling family appoint senior government officials and, together, they start and manage most of the big initiatives in Dubai, while the government does step back when it judges the moment right to leave matters to market forces. Dubai's success owes a lot to its openness: it has opened itself to the world through its free zones and lines of communication and access from top to bottom and bottom to top are remarkably open. There is a strong bond between the people of Dubai and the ruling Al Maktoum family; business is largely done on the basis of trust, regulations introduced when they are felt necessary to reinforce trust and confidence. As Dubai's Ruler and the Vice President and Prime Minister of the United Arab Emirates (UAE) since January 2006, Sheikh Mohammed runs a lean government machine and is loath to slow it and the UAE/Dubai down by adding layers of what he considers (and many in the emirates tend to agree) to be unnecessary bureaucracy. At the same time as becoming Dubai's Ruler, taking over from his late brother (Sheikh Maktoum), Sheikh Mohammed also became UAE's Prime Minister and Vice President. His first step was to form a new government, seen by many as embodying the new future, infused with a cadre of young, professional and progressive ministers on whom he can rely to implement his agenda for openness, new initiatives and a streamlined government.

However, just like the world of corporate or organizational change, the new agenda often takes longer than originally anticipated to reach its full fruition, because of the many constituent factors, including many different and varied stakeholders. Sheikh Mohammed's charisma, determination and history of getting things done bode well for him in achieving this transformation. However, it should be noted that the dynamics of change will be different than those prevailing in Dubai, of which he is the ruler (the President of the UAE to whom the Prime Minister reports is the Ruler of Abu Dhabi, the federal capital). Just over a year after he formed his initial cabinet a reshuffle was announced, not unlike many organizations' senior management restructure; this is all new to the UAE which had not been accustomed to such rapid change, at least not in government. The point was being made that Sheikh Mohammed was on a mission and wants to ensure everyone is rowing hard and in unison to steer through the waters ahead.

This book appears at an important time in Dubai's development. Its rapid growth shows no sign of slowing down, and some say that it is in danger of creating a bubble that can only end up bursting. They point to the endless construction of residential and commercial property, hotels, theme parks and luxury retail shopping centres, wondering if there can ever be demand for that much. Such scepticism is not new in Dubai: most projects undertaken by the government have had their critics when they were announced. But still the superlatives show no sign of abating – ever larger retail complexes are being announced, and one developer is already considering developing an even taller skyscraper than Burj Dubai, which is currently the world's tallest building.

Since the first edition of this book was published in 2003, the face of Dubai has been transformed once again, and many of the developments announced early in this century have been built. Perhaps even more important, some of Dubai's leading businesses have stretched their reach beyond the emirates' borders, leveraging their local experience and using their growing wealth and liquidity to move into markets around the world. This has presented an additional set of challenges and risks, as the highly-publicized acquisition by DP World of P&O, which included the management of ports in the USA (DP World later disposed of these ports), has shown. But now that Dubai's global visibility is at an all-time high, the stakes are perhaps higher than ever before. This was highlighted, again, in late 2007 by Borse Dubai taking significant shareholdings in NASDAQ, the London Stock Exchange, and its move to acquire the Swedish Stock Exchange (OMX). These deals and many others will undoubtedly be part of a continuing trend as Dubai increases its global economic footprint. Recent, well publicized deals only highlight the broader trend (to which Dubai has brought further international attention) of the increasing importance of nation-state or sovereign wealth funds in today's complex and interconnected global financial markets.

Chapter by chapter

In Chapter 2, a brief history of Dubai sets the stage and introduces the basic concepts behind its rapid growth.

Chapters 3 and 4 examine two models for growth: Silicon Valley and Singapore. Silicon Valley is a bottom-up, organic growth model, in which dynamic R&D and technology businesses have developed with little intervention since just before the Second World War. The growth of Singapore, by contrast, has been driven from the top down. Since the country became independent in 1965, Lee Kuan Yew's government has created a huge portfolio of projects designed to create a good standard of living for Singaporeans. During 2002–2003, when the first edition of this book was being written, Singapore was cited by many in Dubai as a source of inspiration and there are indeed many similarities between the two of them, from their early prosperity as entrepôts, the success of their government-owned airlines and other industries, to the excitement with high technology and the recent press coverage on their sovereign wealth funds. Although lately some in Dubai feel that Dubai has arrived and Singapore may have slowed down during a crucial short period, during which Dubai has been going through one of rapid growth; albeit in a different relative scale to the slower reaction of its immediate neighbour(s) and competitor(s) where by the time they realized what was happening, it may prove to have been too late to react in an effective manner. However, many in Dubai still look with admiration at Singapore and in particular at aspects of its governance and related government best practices.

But despite the overt similarities, Dubai's growth model lies somewhere between Silicon Valley's bottom-up and Singapore's top-down approaches. Dubai is compared and contrasted to these models in chapters 3 and 4, and the details of the Dubai model are examined in the following chapters.

Chapter 5 considers the first phase of what we have called the strategic trajectory model, which explains how Dubai has achieved its large-scale, rapid growth. Called the **asset creation** phase, it starts with the development of the Creek, which set the emirate off on a strategic trajectory, building on existing capabilities, which would continue over the following decades.

Chapter 6 examines the next phase: **asset acceleration**. Once Dubai had created a basic portfolio of assets – ports, airports, airline, hotels, manufacturing plants and so on – their utilization was ratcheted up several notches to act as a springboard for future asset creation – even greater shipping and airport capacities, free zones, hotels, the creation of the Palm Islands, Dubai International Financial Centre, Dubailand and Dubai World Central. Each new asset helped build momentum.

Chapter 7 looks at the third phase: **asset leverage**. This is when all the components of the business ecosystem or strategic vortex combine to create further value. Increasing numbers of visitors and competition among hotels drive innovation and growth in the hospitality industry. The early success of Dubai Internet City, a high-tech industrial park inside a duty-free zone, attracted more companies from around the world and spawned similar free zone developments. Building on and reinforcing the assets that currently exist drives future development along the same strategic trajectory.

Chapter 8 moves on to **asset harvesting, reinvestment** and **reinvention** – three of the four potential phases that can follow on from asset leverage. Assets that have outlived their usefulness can be harvested and their resources redeployed (returning to the asset creation stage). Assets that continue to be useful and productive may need reinvestment. Others may need adjustment, closing down or reinvention to maintain their momentum, or completely new ventures may spring out of established ones.

Chapter 9 has been added for this edition. It addresses **asset globalization**, the fourth and final alternative path following asset leverage. In the five years since the first edition was published, several leading firms have taken the giant step of expanding outside of their local market to compete with the best the world has to offer – on the competition's turf. But with the opportunities afforded by this potential, additional and different types of challenges and risk often appear.

Lastly, Chapter 10 considers what lessons can be drawn from Dubai's success and applied to corporations and other organizations both in the public and private sectors.

CHAPTER 2

DUBAI IN PERSPECTIVE

What is good for business is good for Dubai.

Sheikh Rashid

There are many spots to sample the contrasts of modern Dubai. There's the Gold Souk, no longer an open-air market but a seemingly endless row of storefronts selling all manner of jewellery and trinkets made from the metal that's been a mainstay of the local economy for decades. There's a walkway alongside Dubai's Creek, where traditional dhows moor in the shadow of gleaming skyscrapers. If one is feeling more adventurous, there's always the slopes of Ski Dubai, one of the world's largest indoor ski slopes, which offers a frosty alpine experience year round, even as the thermometer outside often tops forty degrees Celsius. Or for something more relaxing a stroll along Dubai Marina's new development or Palm Jumeirah as it gets ready to set the standards for a new lifestyle experience in Dubai.

But probably one of the best vantage points to take in all that is modern Dubai is the lobby of the Emirates Towers hotel (the authors' favourite business hotel in Dubai) and its adjoining office and shopping complex. Usually buzzing with activity, it mirrors the bustling business environment in Dubai and the diversity of the people who do business there. Some wear traditional Middle-Eastern clothes, though most are in Western business or casual attire. While English and Arabic predominate, numerous other languages are spoken. Most people are likely to be involved in trade or services rather than oil-related transactions, as oil now accounts for less than eight per cent of gross domestic product (GDP) (see appendix 2).[1]

There will also be many women, both Gulf nationals in traditional dress and foreigners, most wearing the latest fashions. Women are free to work, drive and come and go as they please in Dubai with no fear of harassment. It is not only in business that Dubai enjoys more liberal attitudes than other parts of the region.

From Vu's restaurant on the 50th floor of the Emirates Towers hotel can be seen the sail-shaped Burj Al Arab hotel built on its own man-made island. Perhaps the emirate's best-known landmark, as a result of the marketing of Dubai as a tourism destination, its image once graced many of Dubai's car licence plates. Further man-made islands are also seen stretching out towards the horizon, some taking the shape of tremendous Palm trees, others forming a map of the world – all of which are starting to support luxury residences, hotels, dining, and other amenities. Also visible is the constant flow of cargo into Port Rashid, a reminder of the trade that has underpinned much of the emirate's growth.

In the foreground, the view includes the high-rise hotels, apartment buildings and offices along Sheikh Zayed Road constructed in the past decade. Many have helipads in anticipation of things to come. Adjacent to the hotel is the brand new 110-acre campus of the Dubai International Financial Centre (DIFC), with a vast array of modern office, residential and hotel buildings in various stages of completion and its now iconic gate shaped main building, known as 'The Gate' (see photo in chapter 6), and just beyond this area you can see the slick and impressive shape of Burj Dubai.

Beyond the hotel, looking across the busy eight-lane Sheikh Zayed Road and high-rise glass buildings towards the sea, are blocks of low-rise housing, some old, some new. A mosque is within walking distance of most dwellings, underlining the importance and prevalence of Islam in Dubai. As another indication of Dubai's diversity and tolerance, all this can be taken in while enjoying any chosen beverage, which is not an option in many states in the region. It is this tolerance and sense of freedom and openness that underpins the lifestyle choice of many expatriates who come to Dubai, while maintaining a respect for local and regional cultures. Interestingly much of the respect afforded by both the local and foreign population is self imposed rather than legislated. This reminds us of something that Einstein once said, "Laws alone can not secure freedom of expression; in order that every man present his views without penalty there must be spirit of tolerance in the entire population."

Vital statistics
One of the seven emirates comprising the United Arab Emirates (UAE), Dubai lies on the eastern coast of the Arabian Peninsula. It covers 3,885 square kilometres, or five per cent of the total land area of the UAE (excluding islands), the majority of its population is concentrated in and around Dubai city, which is rapidly expanding inland into the once desert areas as well as outwards towards Jebel Ali, which is on the border with Abu Dhabi.

Ruled for generations by the Al Maktoum family, Sheikh Maktoum Bin Rashid Al Maktoum, became ruler in 1990 upon the death of his father, Sheikh Rashid, and five years later, he signed a decree appointing his brother, Sheikh Mohammed, Crown Prince. Sheikh Rashid had personally overseen the development of Dubai's significant infrastructure and industries since becoming ruler in 1958, and the involvement of his sons made them well-equipped to pick up where he left off. Following Sheikh Maktoum's death in January 2006, Sheikh Mohammed became ruler, and soon thereafter, was appointed the Vice President and Prime Minister of the UAE.

In terms of geographic size, it falls between Luxembourg and the US state of Delaware. Compared with Singapore, Dubai has less than a quarter of the population living in an area over five times larger. With its natural harbour opening into the Gulf and the Indian Ocean beyond and its location midway along major east-west and north-south shipping routes, Dubai has long been a regional trade centre. As traders and business people have been drawn to the area, both the population and economic output have grown markedly.

At the beginning of the 20th century, about 3,000 people lived in Dubai. By 1947, the number had grown to 25,000.[2] In 1975, following the discovery of oil and the start of large infrastructure projects, the population grew to 183,200. By the end of the century that number increased fivefold, reaching 1,071,000 in 2004, and is currently approximately 1.5 million and rising fast, with expectations of reaching four million by 2020 being mentioned (see appendix 3). Fewer than 20 per cent of Dubai's population were UAE nationals in 2001, with expatriates from the Indian subcontinent making up a large part of the foreign population.

In the last quarter of a century, Dubai's GDP grew from $2.2 billion in 1975 to $17 billion in 2001 (at current prices). And by 2004, it almost doubled to $30.1 billion (at current prices), further increased to $38.2 billion in 2005, reached over $46 billion in 2006 and stands at just under US $54 billion in 2007. At the same time, dependence on oil revenue has declined, from 46 per cent of GDP in 1975 to only 7.1 per cent in 2004. GDP per head has increased to over $30,000 in 2004. Thus Dubai has one of the highest GDPs per head in the world, and it has already surpassed the government's 2001 goal of reaching $25,000 by 2010 (see appendix 2).[3] To understand what lies behind this growth, it is helpful to look back at Dubai's history.

A brief history
Until 1833, the area now known as Dubai was inhabited by a few pearl divers and fishermen and their families living at the mouth of the Creek. That started to change with the arrival of an offshoot of the

Bani Yas tribe from Abu Dhabi. Led by Sheikh Maktoum Bin Buti, the Al-Bufalasah group brought 800 new settlers to Dubai, and Sheikh Maktoum became the first of many Al Maktoum family rulers of Dubai (see appendix 1).

Early traders

During the decades that followed an increasing amount of trade was attracted to the Creek, and by the end of the century many merchant families had prospered.

The growing importance of the region became apparent to the British, who, at that time, were not reluctant to establish footholds wherever they could to secure their shipping routes. Between 1820 and 1892, the rulers of Dubai, along with other Arab sheikhs, signed a series of treaties that gave the British increasing powers of policing and dispute arbitration. These agreements ensured safe passage along the shipping routes and prevented other powers from encroaching, while leaving internal rule to the sheikhs. Following the agreements of 1853, the area became known as the Trucial States, a name that would remain until the British withdrew in 1971.

At the end of the 19th century, Dubai's fortunes were boosted when many traders decided to forsake Lingah, the most prominent trading port in the lower Persian side of the Gulf, after new regulations and taxes were imposed. The then ruler of Dubai, Sheikh Maktoum Bin Hasher Al Maktoum, taking advantage of Lingah's decline, helped establish Dubai as an entrepôt and set a direction that Dubai has since followed. Persian merchants began to flock to Dubai, and merchants from elsewhere in the region followed. By 1906, there were around 2,000 houses around the Creek and 350 traders in the souk, making it one of the biggest in the region.

The depression of the late 1920s and 1930s, combined with competition from Japanese cultured pearls, sent the Dubai economy into decline. Trading continued nevertheless, with the gold trade as a mainstay. Determined as ever, Dubai's traders found in the period after India's independence a particularly lucrative market for grey-market goods among closed economies such as India, Pakistan and Iran.

But trade was hampered by the limitations of Dubai's natural infrastructure. By the 1950s, traffic in the Creek was almost at a standstill. The merchant ships and fishing vessels often had to moor three abreast, and silting reduced the width of the navigable lanes as well as their depth, which in places was only two feet.

A port and an airport

The traders who depended upon the Creek for their livelihood complained to the then ruler, Sheikh Rashid, who, mindful that infrastructural modernization of the Creek would enable new shipping companies with larger vessels to use Dubai, decided to proceed with a costly expansion project. It was a bold move; the projected cost represented several times Dubai's annual gross domestic product. To raise the necessary finance, a tax was imposed on imports; there was a bond issue, which was taken up by the major trading families who depended on the Creek; and Sheikh Rashid borrowed the remaining funds from the Emir of Kuwait, effectively mortgaging the Emirate of Dubai in the process.

With finance secured, the project went ahead in 1959 and was completed in 1960. As a result, trade increased by 20 per cent to nearly $17 million (equivalent to about $103 million today). Furthermore, the income from import taxes enabled Dubai to repay its loan from Kuwait much earlier than expected.

The project provided Dubai with a much-needed boost in trading capacity, and set the tone for many more speculative projects. The Creek improvements were viewed with scepticism by others in the region, particularly in light of the risk posed by the loan arrangement with Kuwait. This scepticism would re-emerge many times over the coming years (indeed, you hear it even today) as similarly ambitious and risky projects were undertaken, and each time the government's gamble would pay off.

While the Creek was dredged and modernized, an airport was built with the aim of further developing Dubai's business potential. Dubai International Airport was opened by Sheikh Rashid in 1960. With an 1,800-metre runway, a small terminal building, control tower, firehouse, two duty-free shops and a parking lot for 500 vehicles, it bore little resemblance to today's busy and much larger hub, although the original terminal building still exists. Today some 105 airlines use the airport to connect to over 250 destinations worldwide with annual passenger throughput of over 35 million passengers.

From the start, an 'open-skies' policy was adopted. Any airline was allowed to use the airport without the restrictions or protectionist tactics that have proved so limiting to other international airports. This policy was originally intended to help Dubai become a major international hub, and, combined with seemingly constant improvements and expansion, it has proved immensely successful. The launch of Emirates airline and its growth in tandem with the airport and the economy of Dubai have also played a major part in the airport's development.

The size of the airport can be measured by its yearly passenger numbers. In 1980, it handled 2.8 million passengers; by 1990, that number had almost doubled to five million. In 2001, 13.5 million passengers used the airport; in 2002, the number increased to 16 million; almost 25 million passengers used the airport in 2005, with this number exceeding 35 million in 2007. In 2010, 60 million passengers are expected (see appendix 6). And the airport isn't all just about growing the numbers. The original two duty-free shops have grown into a major shopping experience, with a worldwide reputation among travellers, and the airport has won many international awards for its service and facilities.[4]

The existing Dubai airport is expanded by the 2008 opening of the new terminal expected to handle some 50 million passengers and will soon have company in the form of the new Al Maktoum International Airport. Planned to be ten times larger than the current airport, it will have a capacity of 120 million passengers a year, two terminals, six parallel runways, and extensive facilities, including a large logistics hub, residential and commercial areas, a golf resort, and a business park.[5]

These early steps set an important precedent that Dubai continues to build upon today. By developing this capability to transfer people and goods in and out of the emirate long before its neighbours, Dubai established itself early on as an efficient and open transport hub – a move that would prove essential as oil reserves dwindled.

Oil and Dubai
While the airport and Creek were being developed, the search for oil was in progress, as many of Dubai's neighbours had already struck it rich. Some of their wealth had trickled down to Dubai as they bought goods that were easily available there. In 1966, oil deposits were discovered offshore; and in 1969, oil revenues began to flow into Dubai. However, Dubai's oil reserves were known to be a mere fraction of those of neighbours such as Abu Dhabi and Saudi Arabia. The government resolved to spend the oil money carefully, using it to fund a variety of major infrastructure projects. It is keen to reduce its dependence on oil, knowing that it may not last long into the 21st century. In 1990, oil accounted for 35 per cent of GDP; by 2004, this had decreased to just 7.1 per cent. The aim is to reduce oil's share of GDP to just one per cent by 2010, after which reserves are expected to be largely depleted.

As Dubai was gearing up for oil production in the late 1960s, the UK announced its intention to withdraw from the area. This provided a fresh incentive for the ruling families of the Trucial States to discuss forming a federation. The rulers of Abu Dhabi and Dubai led the discussions, realizing that coming together as a federation would provide them with substantially increased political and economic stability, strengthening their position in the region.

In 1971 the British left and the United Arab Emirates came into being, made up of the emirates of Abu Dhabi, Dubai, Sharjah, Ajman, Umm al-Qaiwain and Fujairah. Ras al-Khaimah joined the following year.

The UAE is governed by a Federal Supreme Council consisting of the rulers of each of the seven emirates, with a president elected from within the group who serves for a five-year term. Each emirate has its own political and judicial powers, but foreign affairs, defence, healthcare and education are managed at the federal level.

Democracy and Election

As we discuss in the book, Dubai as well as the UAE in general, practises a traditional system of consultation in its decision-making process. Working in tandem with the rapid growth that this book discusses, the UAE government initiated a political plan to create greater participation by its citizens. Since our first book was published, elections were held in December 2006 to elect members to the Federal National Council (FNC) members, the FNC is maturing and evolving as its results manifest itself, ushering in a healthy debate of public policies, among its constituents and stakeholders. The elections were heralded as a great success and resulted, a first for the region, in a woman being elected to a representative body. This process and its success is a very important constituent part in building a participatory culture, where everyone feels able to be part of the story. Again, as we will see later in the book, there are similarities here with Singapore, where each of the two countries has adopted a system that best suits the needs of its own constituent parts i.e. it is not one size fits all.

Dubai is the second-largest emirate after Abu Dhabi, which is also the capital of UAE. Although Dubai enjoys the outward benefits of being part of the federation (such as in international relations and a shared defence strategy), it is seen by some to be in the shadow of the much richer Abu Dhabi. Moreover, in recent years Dubai appears to have struggled against some of the federal regulations, such as business ownership laws. Part of the reason for its creation of free zones was to overcome some of these restrictions. But since January 2006 with Sheikh Mohammed becoming the UAE Vice President and Prime Minister there is a sense that he is succeeding in bringing the various emirates closer with a clearer alignment of federal strategies and deliverables.

Developing the infrastructure

The years following the discovery of oil and the formation of the UAE saw some of the most dramatic development of Dubai's infrastructure. Based on its traditional strengths in trade, the government built two ports and developed several heavy industries during the 1970s. These facilities have led to Dubai's position as one of the world's largest shipping centres.

A new port

In just a quarter of a century, the increases in trade have been dramatic. In 1975, imports were worth $1.93 billion, exports $2.45 billion and re-exports $1.52 billion. By 2004, imports had increased to $40.6 billion, exports to $2.6 billion and re-exports to $15.5 billion. In 2004, the main import sources were China, India, Japan, the USA and Germany; and the main re-export destinations were India, Iran, Iraq, Switzerland and Pakistan.[6] As an indication of the diversity and volume of this trade, Dubai has purportedly been among the world's leading exporters of wristwatches since the 1970s, despite the fact that not a single watch is manufactured in the UAE. Watches come from all corners of the globe and the majority go straight out again as re-exports. This would almost certainly explain the presence of Switzerland among Dubai's top five re-export partners.

The booming business in the Creek convinced the government that a larger deepwater harbour was needed to allow Dubai's growth as a port to continue. Much of the sea-going traffic then, as now, was in the form of dhows, traditional wooden cargo vessels used in the Gulf and neighbouring waters. With their distinctive raised bow and stern, and often seemingly overflowing with all manner of goods, these ships have changed little over the centuries. By 1966, around 4,000 dhows were arriving each year; larger ships were arriving too, but they had to anchor offshore and shuttle goods to the port on smaller boats.

Initial studies were based on four berths, but the design was modified during construction to include 16 berths. The port was completed in just five years and opened in 1972. Once again, the ambitious plans had been viewed by some with scepticism, but by the time the port opened there was a long line of ships waiting for berths. Early successes led to immediate expansion, and by 1978 a further 19 berths had been added.

Soon after the completion of the first phase of Port Rashid, the government announced its intention to develop an even larger port 35 kilometres from the centre of Dubai. At the time, there was spare capacity at the existing port, but the government believed that the new port would eventually be needed and it had a budgetary surplus with which to finance it.

In 1976, while the expansion of Port Rashid was under way, construction of Jebel Ali Port began with an initial investment of $2.5 billion (1976 prices). It opened only three years later. The first phase with 66 berths was completed in 1983, making it the largest man-made harbour in the world.

The management of Port Rashid and Jebel Ali was merged in 1991, and in the same year the combined ports handled one million TEUs (20-foot equivalent units, a standard measure used by the shipping industry) for the first time. In 2000, the ports were handling three times as much, and in 2004, they handled 6.4 million TEUs. Another reorganization took place in 2005 to integrate management of all port operations into a single entity, DP World. At the same time, a new regulator for the ports was created. The growth of port capacity continues, with a four-phase expansion project under way that is planned to increase it to 21.8 million TEUs by 2010. At the end of 2004, the additional capacity created at Jebel Ali amounted to more than seven million TEUs. The majority of DP World's revenue comes from outside Dubai with global gross throughput starting in 2007 at some 43 million TEU.[7] The global expansion of DP World is a good example; others will be discussed throughout the book.

Heavy industries
As well as major infrastructure and ports, the government developed a series of heavy industries during the 1970s. With an initial investment of $1.4 billion (including share capital and long-term loans) in 1979, the Dubai Aluminium Company (DUBAL) was established near Jebel Ali and is now the largest single-site aluminium producer in the West, and one of the world's most profitable smelters, generating some 900,000 metric tonnes of quality hot metal in 2007. Excess heat from the smelting process is used by a nearby desalination plant to produce around 25 million gallons of fresh water every day. Other industries hatched by the government during this time include a gas plant, dry dock and cable manufacturing plant.

Although these investments were intended to generate foreign currency revenue, they were also meant to send a signal to potential investors. As Mohammed Ali Alabbar, DUBAL Vice Chairman from 1992 to 2003, explains:

> *Heavy industries are confidence-builders. Their development was a strategic move for Dubai, but it was also driven by solid investment criteria – it had to be commercially viable. At first, they may have underestimated the effect of building credibility; it's done much better than anyone expected.*

DUBAL has done very well indeed. In 2006, it was serving clients in more than 44 countries and contributing around five per cent of Dubai's GDP. And after 25 years in operation, DUBAL started expanding internationally with partnerships to develop a plant in India (2005) and one in Abu Dhabi (2006), each featuring DUBAL's proprietary technologies.[8]

Promoting travel and tourism
With the flow of trade continuing through Dubai's ports and airport,

the government embarked on a series of projects that would continue throughout the late 1970s and 1980s, geared towards attracting visitors for business and pleasure.

The construction of the Dubai International Trade Centre was the first of these. When it was announced, it was viewed with reservation because it was to be located on the outskirts of the city (essentially in the desert) and there wasn't a perceived demand for a 39-storey office building at that time. But the project went ahead as planned and was completed in 1979. What would later become known as the World Trade Centre became home to a range of international businesses and consulates, as well as exhibition and conference facilities and the Dubai Stock Exchange (Dubai Financial Market). It was also the first of many iconic building projects, with its distinctive silhouette visible for miles. Today, however, it is dwarfed by many taller towers in what is fast becoming Dubai's business and financial district. The Dubai World Trade Centre has reinvented itself many times to become an important hub of international events and exhibitions – from computers and technology (GITEX) to horses (the Arabian Horse Show). It has world class facilities – from hotels and restaurants to offices and residential buildings – to create a lifestyle for its many visitors to enjoy (this is something that the DIFC, understanding the importance of creating the right environment, has also done by developing the DIFC lifestyle concept).

This period also saw the first wave of major hotels to be built in Dubai, with demand stimulated by the rapidly growing economy and resulting influx of visitors.

Today, for many people, Dubai may be synonymous with luxury hotels, but this is a recent development. The first purpose-built hotel was opened in 1959 with just eight rooms, later expanded to 35. Before then, business travellers had few options apart from staying in private homes; even Sheikh Rashid had an apartment on his property converted for guests. Other smaller hotels were built in the late 1960s, but the InterContinental (since renamed the Radisson SAS Hotel) was the first major chain hotel to be built in the city.

Completed in 1975, the InterContinental was a haven for business travellers, and a shortage of alternative accommodation often led to people sleeping in the lobby or having to share double rooms. Other chains began building towards the end of the 1970s, but the InterContinental (now the Radisson SAS Hotel) retained a place in Dubai's modern history that illustrates the dynamism and hustle-bustle of that time. Since then there has been huge growth in the hotel sector. In 2004, there were 276 hotels with 26,155 rooms,[9] compared with 42 hotels with 4,601 rooms in 1985. Construction continues apace, with over dozens of hotels under construction or being built into the new developments. Some continue to question whether so much additional hotel capacity is needed, but the government believes that visitor numbers will continue to increase and that there will be sufficient demand. (see appendix 8)

Another important part of the government's strategy to attract visitors has been Emirates airline. It provided $10 million as an initial investment to get the airline off the ground in 1985. Emirates airline is owned by the government of Dubai, but, like other government-owned companies, it operates independently without support or subsidy and has been profitable every year apart from its second in operation, with annual growth of at least 20 per cent per annum since it started.

The airline is part of the Emirates Group, which also includes Dnata, a travel management services company, and other travel-related companies. Group executive vice chairman Maurice Flanagan (one of the quickest respondents to emails, notwithstanding where he is or when it is received!) is careful to point out that Emirates airline has succeeded on its own merits, without any help or protection from the government. It remained profitable despite the travel industry downturn following the events of 11 September 2001, and during the Dubai Airshow in November 2001 the airline announced its intention to proceed with its order for $15 billion-worth of Airbus aircraft. At a time when many large airlines were cancelling aircraft orders and struggling to remain in business, this demonstrated Dubai's confidence in its ability to succeed.

As of 2006, the airline served 83 destinations (which increased to 85 destinations in 2007 and to almost 120 destinations in 2008) in 57 countries, carrying 14.5 million passengers and one million tonnes of freight. By 2010, Emirates airline expects to have 156 aircraft carrying 26 million passengers per year to 101 destinations around the world (already achieved in 2008!). By 2013, the current projections of growth are to have 180 aircraft flying to 110 destinations. To support these ambitious goals, Emirates airline had $33 billion-worth of aircraft on order in 2006, with an expected delivery of one aircraft per month for the forthcoming eight years. Its first of 45 double-decker Airbus A380 super-jumbos flew its maiden flight to New York in the summer of 2008, (this order was increased to 55 in 2007). While rising fuel costs were squeezing the entire air travel industry, Emirates airline achieved its 18th consecutive profitable year in 2006, with a net profit of $674 million for the airline and $762 million for the group.[10] In the year ending March 2007 the group made a profit of $942 million, many believe they are shortly set to make a group profit of $1 billion – not a bad return for an airline started with a $10 million loan in 1985!

Dubai set about further developing its tourism sector in 1989 with the formation of the Commerce and Tourism Promotion Board, which has since become the Department of Tourism and Commerce

Marketing. Initially, there were few attractions to lure tourists apart from the climate and the beaches. Although operating on a shoestring budget, the Department of Tourism and Commerce Marketing has been able to build the tourism trade through its work with tour operators and clever marketing.

Tourism is now the fastest-growing sector of Dubai's economy, contributing about 19 per cent to the Dubai's GDP in 2005,[11] and 30 per cent as of late 2007. This is made possible by ever-increasing numbers of tourists. About 3.6 million tourists visited Dubai in 2001 and more than six million came in 2005.[12] As of 2007, Dubai's hotels received about 6.5 million visitors that contributed $3.5 billion to the local economy.

The development of luxury hotels and resorts has been crucial to the growth in tourism; the iconic Burj Al Arab, sometimes called the Eiffel Tower of the Middle East, has proved to be a major attraction in its own right (interestingly they are of a similar height).

Events and festivals have also been created to generate interest from abroad. Official sources estimate that the winter Dubai Shopping Festival attracted 1.6 million visitors in 1996, its first year, and 3.3 million visitors in 2005 who spent some $1.8 billion.[13] During the festival, hotels tend to approach full occupancy, with many rooms booked by visitors from neighbouring states.

The Dubai Summer Surprises festival was launched in 1998 to generate more tourism and shopping during the slow summer months, when temperatures can soar to the high 40s. This, too, has proven a major draw, with beaches filling up with intrepid European visitors. These festivals have also proven very popular with visitors from neighbouring countries. In 2005, this festival attracted about 1.5 million visitors, who spent around $500 million.[14]

Dubai has become a venue for many conferences and conventions, as well as for the Dubai Airshow and sporting events such as the Dubai World Cup horse race that draw visitors from around the world each year. These not only boost the local economy; they also provide valuable publicity, promoting Dubai's image around the world and throughout the region. Newer events in different cultural sectors such as the Dubai International Film Festival (DIFF) or Art Dubai are new events catering for both travellers to Dubai, but in addition creating a new type of tourist that like the other successful sporting and aviation events bring visitors to the events themselves.

The Jebel Ali Free Zone
Perhaps the most significant development of the 1980s was the Jebel Ali Free Zone, an industrial park that opened in 1985. The Jebel Ali Free Zone Authority, the regulatory agency for the area, offers attractive

incentives for investors to locate in the zone. These include 100 per cent foreign ownership, full repatriation of capital and profits, easy recruitment and sponsorship, and no currency restrictions. Outside the zone foreign businesses have to set up in partnership with a UAE national, who must own at least a 51 per cent share of the business.

Jebel Ali Free Zone Authority also provides infrastructure for companies, ranging from basic services to fully built facilities, as well as local representatives to handle any administrative needs. As it is a free zone, there are no import or export duties on goods or equipment within the zone. It is located next to Jebel Ali Port, so investors have access to the port's facilities; however, the zone has attracted a wide range of businesses, not just those dependent on shipping. Initially, only subsidiary companies were allowed to operate in the zone, but after 1992 independent companies could be incorporated there. By the early 1990s, there were around 300 companies inside the zone of some 49 square kilometres; by 2006, the number had grown to about 6,000 from over 119 countries and some 145 of the Fortune 500 companies operate there.[15]

Apart from its intrinsic value to the economy of Dubai, the Jebel Ali Free Zone also set the stage for future developments, such as Dubai Internet City and Dubai Media City, which would apply similar models tailored to their own industries and workers. The success of these 21st century developments would form a foothold for a variety of further free zones catering to financial services, healthcare, education, outsourcing, and biotechnology that were announced between 2002 and 2006.

Developing the knowledge economy
Sheikh Mohammed announced Dubai Internet City in October 1999 as a key part of his vision to attract the 'new economy' to Dubai. Taking advantage of the same type of free-zone status that had been so successful at Jebel Ali, the area was designed specifically to cater for the needs and desires of technology and media companies.

Research by Sheikh Mohammed's team (led by Mohammad Al Gergawi) had indicated that priorities for their target companies included full tax-free ownership, a solid technical infrastructure, and unfettered hiring and relocation of talent. Full ownership and no restrictions on hiring were easily included in the free-zone concept, but the infrastructure needed to be built, along with the buildings and landscaping. Sheikh Mohammed set a one-year deadline to complete the first phase of Dubai Internet City, which was to include not only designing and building the campus on what was then open desert, but also attracting and setting up businesses on the site.

Dubai Internet City was launched as planned in October of 2000 with full occupancy (85 companies) and a long waiting list. As well as the technical infrastructure, the zone's management provides a 'one-stop shop' for all visas, licences and other support needs; it also organizes roadshows and exhibitions for its companies focusing on specific market segments. This development was hailed by many as the beginning of a new page in Dubai's future chapters of accelerated growth.

By 2008, among the approximately 900 companies at Dubai Internet City were Microsoft, Oracle, Cisco, Hewlett-Packard, IBM, and many other high-profile names. The industry clustering certainly worked initially; one estimate suggested in 2001 that more business is conducted among Dubai Internet City companies themselves than with outside clients.

Dubai Media City was launched the following January using the same model, concentrating on the needs of local, regional and international media businesses such as CNN, Reuters and Bertelsmann. Dubai Media City also attracted the headquarters or operational centres of various Pan-Arab media groups because of its openness. By the end of 2006, Dubai Media City was home to over 1,200 companies.

DIC and DMC were funded by a government owned entity, now part of Dubai Holding, which was launched in 2004 by Sheikh Mohammed's Executive Office to lead and manage large-scale developments with commercial and social interest. Following on from the successes of DIC and DMC, several other focused free zones have been launched under the umbrella of Dubai Holding.

Over the five years that followed, a series of additional free zone developments geared towards further building Dubai's 'knowledge economy' were introduced.

Dubai Healthcare City was announced in 2002 with the intention of creating a medical centre that could serve the emirate and the region with top-quality care in addition to postgraduate education and research facilities. Dubai understands the need for credibility, brand recognition and the need for content and research leading to Harvard University setting up the Harvard Medical School Dubai Center (HMSDC).

Dubai Knowledge Village was launched in 2003 to serve as a base for universities and training organizations. The development proved so popular that it quickly reached capacity, and a sister zone was launched – Dubai Knowledge Universities.

Dubai International Media Production Zone was launched the same year, addressing the needs of media-related production, with a focus on printing, publishing, and packaging.

The following year, the Dubai Outsource Zone was announced. This free zone was intended to provide facilities and infrastructure for outsourcing companies which would be competitive with the likes of Bangalore. Also, the Dubai Biotechnology and Research Park

(DuBiotech) was announced in 2005 to serve the biotechnology, pharmaceutical, and life sciences sectors.

Each of these developments will fit right in with the existing buzz emanating from the originals – DIC and DMC. Together, they are set to attract world leaders across a wide breadth of knowledge-based industries. (Many of these free zones – including DIC, DMC, Knowledge Village, DuBiotech and other related initiatives are now known as TECOM – Dubai Technology, Electronic Commerce and Media Free Zone Authority).

Redrawing the map of Dubai

As recently as 2002 when the first edition of this book was being researched, there were just a handful of major residential developments being built, though they were major headline-grabbers. Construction of the Palm Jumeirah (a massive man-made development in the sea, enabled through land reclamation, in the shape of a giant palm tree with luxury properties) was underway, and the Palm Jebel Ali had just been announced, as had The World, another development of islands resembling a map of the world. At that time, there were also myriad other more traditional developments inland or along the waterfront seeking to capitalise on the increasing numbers of visitors and the recently-enacted legislation allowing non-UAE nationals to buy property.

Since 2002, one announcement after the next has emerged from Dubai describing increasingly ambitious developments. In 2004, the Palm Deira was announced, which, when complete, will dwarf both of its older siblings. The primarily residential Palm Jumeirah with 32 hotels and over 4,000 villas along 75 kilometres of beaches; the more entertainment-focused Palm Jebel Ali will be 50 per cent larger; and the Palm Deira is expected to be larger still, covering 80 square kilometres. Construction on this project was begun in 2004, with completion slated for 2015.[16]

Eventually, the Palm Jebel Ali will be partially surrounded by the Dubai Waterfront development, also from government-owned Nakheel Properties. This development will extend the coastline by 820 kilometres with 266 million square feet of man-made islands and waterfront property. Over 100 waterfront developments and over 150 distinct communities are planned for the project. A skyscraper called 'Al Burj' (The Tower) has been announced, which is planned to be taller still than the to-be-completed Burj Dubai tower.

Burj Dubai is the centrepiece of another large mixed-use development, Downtown Dubai. Estimated to cost $20 billion, Downtown Dubai will feature the 705 metre-tower (currently the world's tallest), the Dubai Mall (expected to be the world's largest), plus various themed housing, business facilities, entertainment, and leisure facilities. Developer Emaar Properties claims that the development will 'reconfirm Dubai's status as a global player.'[17]

Finally, Dubai Business Bay (a development by Dubai Properties, a member of Dubai Holding) is planned as a major business, commercial, and residential area adjacent to Downtown Dubai with its own creek extension. When complete in 2010, it will cover 64 million square feet and contain over 230 commercial and residential towers. Its most distinctive feature may be the Dubai Creek, which is being extended by almost 10 km for the project.[18]

If Dubai's plans seemed ambitious in 2002, they have now been taken to new heights six years later. But with construction of major hotels well underway on Palm Jumeirah crowned at the end of the Palm by the much trumpeted Atlantis hotel and entertainment complex with some 1,500 plus rooms and over 16 restaurants and cafes, bars and lounges (opened as this book came off the printing press in October 2008). Palm Jebel Ali not far behind, the sceptics may have reason to bite their tongues now. They may also take comfort in efforts to expand into less cyclical content driven areas such as finance, culture, education and high-tech.

Broadening the economic base

In addition to using free zones to build knowledge-based businesses, Dubai is also using the same concept to develop other industries.

The Dubai International Financial Centre is the highest profile development catering to the business and finance community in recent years. Initially developed on a 110-acre site (since increased) next to the Emirates Towers site, the DIFC is meant to be an international finance hub on par with its counterparts in New York and London, taking advantage of its location between the West and the East. While building work continues, the centre opened in 2004. It had a somewhat rocky start, when management and cultural issues effected its, yet to be formed, regulatory body; this was swiftly and efficiently dealt with by Dubai's leadership and by 2006, many of the world's most prominent financial institutions had established a presence. Indeed, by November 2007, the 200th company had been licensed in DIFC and by the end of 2008 this figure is set to near 300. What is now clear from this is that leadership is willing to step in and take whatever action may be required to provide stability and credibility, which is particularly important in areas such as financial services. They were able to quickly determine the need for two world class independent bodies – judiciary and regulatory. DIFC now has a globally recognized regulator in the Dubai Financial Services Authority (DFSA), with an international board of the highest calibre and an Executive team made up of some of the world's best regarded regulators. Interestingly, this is becoming an excellent training ground for UAE nationals (as part of the regulator's program known as Tomorrow's Regulatory Leaders), where the international executive team (largely from the US, UK and Australia) is raising standards in the finance industry by bringing with them international standards to Dubai and graduating UAE nationals every year who join the organization (DFSA). If they were to leave to join financial service firms or government institutions they will in turn take with them the high standards they have been trained to espouse. This is an excellent example of bringing the best from around the world to Dubai and importantly training the local work force to these high international standards, a "win-win" all around.

Further free zones have been developed to address other markets: the $1.3 billion Dubai Silicon Oasis will provide an environment for semiconductor design and manufacture (and related businesses); Dubai Textiles City will cater to the garment trade, which is already a major contributor to Dubai's GDP. Dubai Maritime City will establish shipbuilding industry in the emirate; and Dubai Aerospace Enterprise, a $15 billion aerospace, manufacturing, and services corporation.

With this continuing explosion of free zones, one question that the authors continually debated is why Dubai, itself, does not become one big free zone? It seems that it may not be long before many of the free zones expand and the physical infrastructures, such as the DIFC, will require more land and space. If we do not see all of Dubai becoming one big free zone, then will we possibly start to see the merger of related areas, such as say DIFC and the World Trade Centre with their geographic borders having expanded to almost border each other?

The area that separates them is the Emirates Towers complex. Indeed, in the case of DIFC, if its courts, regulators and practitioners were providing a truly world-class service, should this expertise and knowledge not be utilized beyond its existing boundaries? The same applies to many other sectors including education and medical, where truly global standards are emerging. We are conscious, of course, for the challenges that this would bring both for Dubai and the role Dubai would play in the wider federation of the UAE, but the idea is nevertheless an interesting extrapolation of current development activities in Dubai and beyond. As a point of reference, in the corporate world, it would be quite normal to expect mergers and acquisitions from growing and competitive firms – maybe Dubai will be a pioneer yet again in applying these ideas to its increasingly entrepreneurial public sector.

Key themes

Dubai has achieved a lot in the past 40 years or so. Its location has helped: the emirate is ideally located to serve the growing markets in the Middle East, India, Pakistan, Iran, East Africa and Asia. It is fair to say that a number of cities are as well located, so location, although important, is not the only factor. It is also easy and relatively inexpensive, thanks to the free zones and an array of agencies and policies, for organizations to set up in and do business from Dubai. It is becoming more expensive and continues to do so as it grows, although it will need to ensure that it is competitive and does not price itself out of what can be a fickle market. Indeed, for the short to medium term, inflationary pressures will probably continue and may become more exasperated as the currency is pegged against the US dollar, and monetary policy is not a tool it can use to try and manage such pressures. But there is much more to Dubai's success. Here is an overview of some of the key factors that have contributed to it.

Creating assets strategically
Dubai was forced to be smart from the start, building on its limited resources: a coastal location and a natural inlet. All infrastructural improvements and other developments had to be part of a vision that was grounded firmly in reality. Even when oil revenues began to flow into Dubai, the focus was on projects that would take it towards a diversified economy not dependent on oil.

Most of the emirate was desert. Building had been concentrated along the coast and around the Creek, stretching only a short way into the desert. But the government does not shrink from overcoming the apparent constraints on building; it is creating a new beachfront by building the Palm islands, extending the Creek, and cultivating vast oases of green living spaces in the middle of arid desert.

Dubai's 'never say never' attitude is not a recent phenomenon, but has been around since its early pre-oil days. As one of the early bankers in the region, the Earl of Home, now chairman of Coutts, the UK's leading private bank, echoes this point, adding that Dubai 'couldn't just sit back and watch the money roll in – they had to learn other skills'. Similarly, many in Dubai's leadership have observed that Dubai was 'blessed with a lack of resources'. In other words, people in Dubai were forced to think in new ways to create prosperity for themselves while their neighbours were cashing in on vast oil and gas reserves.

Vision and leadership is clearly important in deciding what should be done and ensuring that it gets done. Many in Dubai attribute much of the success of the emirate to the ruling Al Maktoum family. It's easy to see why, since they have been responsible for conceiving and driving major projects.

But it is not just about coming up with the projects and getting them done. It seems that every major project has a tale attached, describing how no one believed it could be done but the ruler knew better. Sheikh Rashid built and expanded the ports when few believed there was adequate demand. It was the same story with the World Trade Centre. More recently, Sheikh Mohammed indulged his passion for horses by setting up training stables in Dubai, defying established racing pundits in the US and the UK who claimed it couldn't be done. Godolphin Stables is now one of the largest and most successful stables in the world.

The government's willingness to accept risk is an important part of its ability to drive these projects. An early example of this is the modernization of the Creek, which essentially financed by mortgaging Dubai itself.

Businesses have often proved more risk-averse than the government. On a number of occasions the government has invested in a new sector to get it established, with the aim of encouraging private investors to enter the market. The development of the luxury hotel sector is a good example. When a government-owned company, Jumeirah (part of Dubai Holding), began to build some of the most distinctive and luxurious hotels in Dubai, it effectively raised standards and dared incumbents such as the InterContinental, Hyatt, Meridien, Hilton and Sheraton to try to keep up, attracting the attention of other leading hotel developers, almost all of which have since developed properties in Dubai.

Some examples of strategic asset creation include Port Rashid, the Jebel Ali Free Zone, Emirates airline, Dubai International Airport, Dubai International Financial Centre, Internet City, Media City, Dubailand and the Palm Islands. The government undertook each of these at a crucial point in the development of the emirate, often despite daunting risk. Each one has proved to be a valuable asset in the emirate's portfolio and, in parallel, has reinforced and added to the government's vision.

It remains to be seen how Dubai's latest ventures will pan out – with the earliest phases of Dubailand and most of Nakheel's island-building still years from completion, it will be some time yet before the world sees what will happen. Although, the first Palm Island is now partially occupied and early indications show that this Herculean feat has been implemented in record time. Indeed, one of the authors was taken for a drive (by a key member of Dubai's leadership) on the Palm in June 2007 with Kerzner group's Atlantis hotel being built and some of the houses in the Palm starting to get occupied, one cannot but be amazed at both the visionary nature and scale of these achievements. A year later in the summer of 2008, the author sat for a meal with the same person and his family and felt like he was relaxing on a holiday resort in the Maldives, except a three-minute drive away you are back in the hustle and bustle of Dubai.

It seems as though the government was emboldened by early successes and has now taken on greater challenges than ever. This time, however, it has invited the private sector along for the ride – each of these large developments relies on other companies to add their own touches in the form of hotels, residential, commercial, retail developments and attractions. But as before, the government through its holding companies like Nakheel and Dubai Holding, is setting a very high standard for its partners to live up to. It is interesting to note how different these two organizations are, both led by what Sheikh Mohammed referred to (in conversation with one of the authors) as his "Lions", Mohammad Al Gergawi, who leads Dubai Holding, the Executive Office and the Mohammed Bin Rashid Foundation, and Sultan Bin Sulayem, who leads DP World (which includes Nakheel) and the Corporate Office. Yet despite their differences they both continue to set new standards in their respective areas, and often spur each other on to greater accomplishments and higher standards – an interesting example of internal competition to accelerate learning in Dubai!

Accelerating growth

Growth in Dubai is not simply a matter of economic indicators; it is part of the culture. The notion of speed is pervasive, from racehorses to fast-track building construction. This is no coincidence. It is part of the Dubai model espoused by the rulers and another way that they lead by example. An often-repeated model in Dubai uses the example of a runner to explain how this works. It's important to keep running, and if you fall, you get right up again. But even if you do fall, because you're moving fast, you fall forward and get up ahead of where you were.

The acceleration effect has been created by bringing in the best from all over the world and putting them together: shipping companies in the ports and free zones; technology companies in Dubai Internet City; banks and financial services companies in DIFC, media companies in Dubai Media City; hoteliers in the red-hot tourism market; airlines at Dubai International Airport. While many developing countries have adopted a protectionist approach, Dubai has done the opposite, stripping out restrictions and regulation to invite all comers. To ensure the most positive RSVPs, in many cases the government has researched exactly what would be most attractive to potential foreign investors then put those things in place. During the development of Dubai Internet City, for example, senior managers of the world's leading technology firms were asked what it would take to bring them to Dubai, and their answers were written into Dubai Internet City's blueprint, one of whom called it the client's 'wish list'.

As a result, both the business environment and the population of the Emirate of Dubai are tremendously diverse, with representation from dozens of countries and virtually every industry imaginable. The acceleration of value created by this variety of people and businesses only increases as further relationships are established across and within discrete industries.

Leadership plays an important part, not just in creating free zones and courting foreign investment. Leaders in Dubai generally work within a framework of mutual trust, a legacy of its trading origins when a trader was taken at his word and there were no second chances. Trust between leaders and managers in both the public and private sectors often takes the place of formal rules or regulations, providing increased opportunity and freedom, and perhaps some temptation as well. Those who take advantage of this trust are dealt with severely, and unscrupulous traders get short shrift. As Dubai continues to grow, maintaining this environment will be a challenge.

Leveraging key assets

In an open economy, the ability of leaders to step back and let growth take place can be as important as knowing when to intervene. This appears to be another strength of Dubai's rulers. They have created an environment that encourages investment and growth without stifling regulations or trade barriers.

This leverage can readily be seen in the hotel industry. The government accelerated growth by stimulating tourism and building a handful of landmark properties; then competitors from around the world quickly emerged to add their contributions to the mix. The same sort of leverage can be seen in Dubai Internet City and Dubai Media City, where a hospitable environment was created and growth has continued ever since.

Further benefits of this leverage can be seen in the way that assets that have been created interact with and complement each other. The development of the airline, airport, hotels and tourist attractions is a good example of this.

Of course, this growth doesn't happen on its own. Although the government may step back to allow it to happen, it's part of a grand, articulated vision, the realization of which depends on trust. For example, Emirates airline is confident about investing in a seemingly never-ending stream of new jets because it trusts that tourist numbers will continue to rise, that the airport will have sufficient gates and hangars, and that there will be enough hotel beds for the tourists to sleep in. And this confidence is seemingly paying off, with the imminent opening of the new airport terminal (which is bigger than the much trumpeted Terminal 5 at London's Heathrow Airport) and the announcement of the new Al Maktoum International Airport (to give a sense of its scale, it will be as big as London's Heathrow and Chicago's O'Hare airports combined).

Managing the portfolio

Even though the government may step back and let growth happen, it takes care to remain in touch. Staying informed is crucial in managing growth and change.

Sheikh Mohammed is famously well-informed, as was his father, Sheikh Rashid. This was achieved through a combination of the *majlis* (the traditional forum in which leaders confer with their officials, hear grievances from the people and settle disputes) and personal involvement. Like his father, Sheikh Mohammed is a frequent visitor to the major projects he has instigated, checking progress and talking to managers and workers.

His senior officials, whom he meets regularly and at times daily, as well as frequently calling them from his mobile phone, play an important role in keeping him in touch. Most of them have both governmental and business roles, which help ensure cooperation, while shared values and trust help prevent conflicts of interest. Sheikh Mohammed also attends regular meetings with other leaders from Dubai's business community.

As an example of one of the many examples of Sheikh Mohammed's personal involvement and awareness – in late June 2007, one of the authors visited Sheikh Mohammed, and the meeting extended to a drive to the new airport terminal, which is adjacent to the existing airport. Sheikh Ahmed bin Saeed Al Maktoum, Chairman of Emirates airline and head of the Civil Aviation Authority (an interesting dual role that clearly works for Dubai, but can you imagine the Chairman of British Airways also being the head of the British Airport Authority!), was waiting for everyone, driving alone in his own car, with no officials. With great energy and enthusiasm, he took the small group led by Sheikh Mohammed, including Mohammad Al Gergawi and Sultan Bin Sulayem through the new terminal. They spent over one hour on a very warm Dubai afternoon walking through an electricity (and air conditioning) free building site. However, the warmth could not dampen their spirits during the visit. The excitement of this new project was shared by all, but particularly by Sheikh Mohammed, who was witnessing another new page of Dubai growth soon to be opened. Similarly, Sheikh Ahmed was particularly proud to point out how quickly luggage would arrive to one of the 25 conveyor belts delivering luggage to passengers. The goal of this massive logistics and engineering feat is to have passengers seamlessly married to their luggage as soon as they arrive at the baggage handling area (think about this as compared to your own favourite airport nightmare story!). The airport will be reorganized with the new terminal, which opened business in October 2008 (it was ready on time, but has been going through rigorous testing to avoid the embarrassment that faced other newly opened airports around the world). The newly expanded airport will be able to handle some 70 million passengers annually – more than double the airport's existing passenger numbers.

The accessibility of Dubai's rulers is strongly echoed in the management of government and business. The 'open-door' policy means that managers and even workers have the ear of someone who has the ear of Dubai Inc.'s CEO.

All this translates into a tight network of business and government leaders who work and communicate within a shared value structure towards common goals. This allows the government to judge when an asset needs investment to grow or to change in order to remain strategically useful, or when it is time to replace it with a different kind of asset that will contribute more to Dubai's economy.

Dubai has recently institutionalized various practices through the constitution of an Executive Council, which is chaired by Sheikh Mohammed's son and Dubai's Crown Prince, Sheikh Hamdan and run by its Secretary General Ahmad Bin Byat, Director General of Dubai Technology, Electronic Commerce and Media Free Zone, credited as a senior member of the team that put Dubai's Internet City project together in record time. Its members include heads of Dubai's government departments. This is meant to create greater cooperation between the departments resulting in a quicker and more efficient delivery process.

What next?

Many joke that there is no point in spending much time on business plans in Dubai because the actuals always overshoot the projections. This seems to have been the case from as far back as 1960, when the ruler repaid the Creek modernization loan much earlier than expected. But business planning is part and parcel of managing growth and Dubai has done its share.

In 2001 Sheikh Mohammed presented a comprehensive strategy for Dubai, setting out goals to achieve by 2010. These included becoming more integrated into the global economy; developing a knowledge economy; becoming known for innovation, dynamism and entrepreneurship; leveraging new and existing assets to create a powerful business network. A prominent part of the strategy involves making the most of Dubai's human resources by, for example, developing a new generation of young entrepreneurs; becoming a work environment of choice for talented knowledge workers; fully utilizing the female workforce; and taking advantage of the diversity of the population. Such desire for broad and rapid growth is a characteristic that Sheikh Mohammed has been able to infect Dubai with. For example, Dr Anwar Gargash (UAE cabinet minister and a leading

Dubai businessman) remembers one conversation with Sheikh Mohammed where he said his views on growth were, 'conquer, then conquer, then conquer'. This unending drive for change and success can be seen throughout Dubai today. This philosophy is succinctly represented by Sheikh Mohammed, who has been quoted as saying, 'Never miss an opportunity. Never leave a weakness unchecked.'

This philosophy is further echoed in Sheikh Mohammed's announcement of the UAE Government's Strategy in April 2007. This is a very interesting document to read, because on one hand you will find a sense of urgency to lift standards across government sectors, while on the other hand, balancing this change with the country's social needs. Although this book is about Dubai rather than the UAE, it is interesting to see how Sheikh Mohammed is taking his visionary leadership style across the UAE in wanting to ensure that his government is results based, often setting KPI's – something that must surely have come as a surprise to many public civil servants. His approach with its candid honesty and approachability, citing examples where governments have, not withstanding great expenditure, fallen in meeting the public aspiration. He often touches on themes of implementation, quality, best practice from around the world, strategy, training, innovation, performance management systems – all words that are at the heart of practice and thinking in the world's major and most advanced corporations.

Another recent development that the authors did not observe in the early days, was Sheikh Mohammed's growing interest in the environment and overall quality of life for Dubai's inhabitants – to be fair, possibly it has always been there, but the authors had not noticed it. In recent activities, Sheikh Mohammed is often asking for more green spaces and less density of development – an interesting shift in perspective in recognizing the need for balanced and sustained development. Again, a major challenge to those in charge of major development whose main task in the past was to optimize profitability – the set of goals is now more complex as Dubai worries not only about its economic impact, but also quality of life within the environment it is creating.

Clearly with all of these activities, stressing the importance of human resources and talent makes sense in light of the move towards a knowledge, and more globally intertwined, economy. It's also been an important factor in the growth of Silicon Valley and Singapore, with which comparisons are drawn in the following two chapters.

ENDNOTES

1   All current statistical figures quoted in this section taken from *Emirate of Dubai Socio-Economic Indicators 2005* and accompanying CD-ROM, published by the Government of Dubai Department of Economic Development

2   Wilson, G. 1999. *Father of Dubai*. Dubai, UAE: Media Prima

3   Goals for Dubai's Vision 2010 provided by The Executive Office

4   From Dubai International Airport website at www.dubaiairport.com

5   From Dubai International Airport website at www.dubaiairport.com

6   From *Emirate of Dubai Socio-Economic Indicators 2005* and accompanying CD-ROM

7   From DP World website at www.dpworld.com

8   From DUBAL website at www.dubal.ae

9   From *Emirate of Dubai Socio-Economic Indicators 2005* and accompanying CD-ROM

10 From Emirates Annual Report 2005–2006

11 Kassar, K. 2006. *1000 Numbers and Reasons Why Dubai*. Beirut: Beirut Information & Studies Centre, p. 119

12 Sherwood, S. 'The Sheikh of Dubai', *The New York Times*, 10 December 2006

13 Figures provided by The Executive Office

14 Figures provided by The Executive Office

15 From Jebel Ali Free Zone website, at www.jafza.co.ae

16 From the property website The Emirates Network at www.theemiratesnetwork.com

17 From Emaar Properties website at www.emaar.ae/Developments/Downtown/

18 From the property website The Emirates Network at www.theemiratesnetwork.com

CHAPTER 3

SILICON VALLEY

Silicon Valley has been a refugee camp for revolutionaries who couldn't get a hearing elsewhere.

Gary Hamel (from his book *Leading the Revolution*)

Silicon Valley is a region in northern California encompassing Santa Clara County and parts of several neighbouring counties with a population of more than two million. It is best known as the world's leading cluster of technology companies, including designers and manufacturers of the semiconductor, the chief ingredient of which gave the region its name. This chapter is included for three principal reasons.

First, Silicon Valley is a well-known model of organic growth. As such, it is useful to draw parallels and identify the organic elements in Dubai's growth model.

Second, there is general agreement about the 'ingredients' that led to the region's success. This set of ingredients can help us understand what has happened in Dubai. But it is not the ingredients alone that spell success. A great deal depends on the order in which they come together, how they are created if they don't already exist, and how they interact: in other words, the process.

Third, Silicon Valley is of interest in examining the success of Dubai because of its focus on technology and the value of intellectual capital. Dubai may be more easily compared to Singapore (see chapter 4) because of their outward similarities, but each has based part of their growth strategies on a Silicon Valley model. Each has created technology districts to attract high-tech companies; each is seeking to stimulate entrepreneurship and innovation; and each has explicitly articulated an intention to move towards a knowledge economy. By first understanding how the Silicon Valley growth model worked, we will be in a better position to understand how Singapore and Dubai have leveraged parts of it.

A brief history

The importance of Silicon Valley as a hotbed of technical innovation and creativity cannot be underestimated. There are few corners of the world not touched by the technologies that grew from seeds planted there, and companies large and small have adopted management techniques that first took root in the region.

William Hewlett and David Packard would have had no idea of what was to come when they started Hewlett-Packard in 1939. With the encouragement of Professor Frederick Terman, the two Stanford graduates started a small business based on an electronic device Hewlett had developed while completing his masters' thesis. Terman went so far as to lend them money personally as well as to help them get a loan from a local bank. The fledgling electronics firm operating from Packard's now-famous garage in Palo Alto had success with its early products, most famously with sales to Walt Disney, who used its oscillators during the production of *Fantasia*. But Hewlett-Packard's business really took off at the start of the Second World War, as the US government began ordering more and more of their electronic instruments.

There was more than enough government spending to go around at that time, and Sigurd and Russell Varian got their share. While also at Stanford, the two brothers developed a microwave receiver and transmitter called the klystron, which would prove to be an indispensable component of radar systems during the war. The Varians made a deal with the university that allowed them to use its physics lab and some materials in exchange for a 50 per cent share of any resulting patents.[1] Not a bad deal for Stanford, which received almost $2 million as a result over the next 30 years.[2]

Hewlett-Packard, Varian Associates and other Silicon Valley firms grew substantially during the Second World War as a result of defence contracts, and the local economy grew with them. The US Department of Defense has been called 'the original 'angel' of Silicon Valley'.[3] The largest employer in the region for years was Lockheed Missiles and Space (now Lockheed-Martin), at one point peaking at 28,000 workers in both manufacturing and R&D activities. Terman spent the war years on the faculty of Harvard, and when he returned to Stanford he had fresh insights. He had closely observed the symbiotic relationship between the north-eastern universities and neighbouring engineering firms, and he became committed to making the West Coast competitive, both commercially and intellectually.

Many of Terman's early initiatives are now considered prerequisites by would-be Silicon Valley imitators. He started by expanding the engineering department at Stanford with new faculty and programmes. To build relationships between students and local industry, the university organized field trips to businesses and events to inform managers about the latest research. Stanford established a research lab dedicated to practical applications. This was considered somewhat heretical at the time, but was important for forming links with businesses. An executive education programme was set up for local engineers, bringing them and their ideas into a stimulating, collaborative academic environment.

The Stanford Research Park was set up on nearby land owned by the university. Varian Associates moved their offices to the Research Park and others quickly followed, attracted largely by its close proximity to the campus. These programmes were crucial in the early development of the professional and social infrastructure of the area, providing great opportunities for those in industry and the university to mingle and cooperate.

An ambition to compete with the East Coast wasn't all Terman brought back from Harvard. He also brought a wealth of business and government contacts, which he quickly put to use, courting investment in research and industry in the Valley.

Although many contend that the genesis of Silicon Valley was the founding of Hewlett-Packard in 1939 (and some even believe it was much earlier), others believe that the formation of Shockley Transistor Corporation in 1954 was the critical event in the region's history. But whichever view you subscribe to, the real action started in 1956 when eight of Shockley Transistor's senior managers left to start a competing venture backed by New York's Fairchild Camera and Instrument Corporation.

Fairchild Semiconductor started well, selling its first 100 transistors to IBM for $150 each.[4] The patent was awarded in 1961, and two years later sales had reached $130 million, largely as a result of government contracts.

Myriad start-up companies were hatched by Fairchild alumni, including Advanced Micro Devices Inc., National Semiconductor Corporation, and Intel Corporation. Along with an entrepreneurial spirit and technical know-how, those who jumped ship from Fairchild brought with them a casual, laid-back management style that would come to typify Silicon Valley companies and would later spread to many other businesses in the US and other parts of the world.

Others left Fairchild (and other tech firms) to become venture capitalists, reinvesting their new-found fortunes in the growing technology industry in the area. Even Stanford got into the act, investing a portion of its endowment in new ventures in the region. The new venture capitalists brought with them more than bulging wallets; because many of them were highly experienced engineers with local business experience, they brought a bulging Rolodex with contacts and referrals, and they could also provide first-hand advice.

As the prosperity of the region grew, a new business and social culture grew around it. Companies were less formal and less hierarchical. People began to place more value on social and professional networks than on the organizations they were working for. Changing jobs frequently was accepted and even encouraged, reinforcing and accelerating the spread of the emerging value system. This led to information and ideas sharing among individuals within their networks, something that had rarely happened before.

The proliferation of start-ups wasn't limited to semiconductor companies. The need for supporting businesses and other links in the semiconductor value chain brought to the Valley a range of new businesses such as law firms, head-hunters and specialized testing and design operations.

The comfortable position of the Silicon Valley chipmakers came under threat in the 1980s from Japanese firms, which were producing higher-quality chips at lower cost. Many of the established players panicked and switched course in an attempt to beat the Japanese at their own game of mass production.

The large Silicon Valley firms struggled, and many of their best engineers left to create a new wave of start-ups, involved in the design and production of semi-custom and speciality chips. The result was that mass-manufacture of memory chips shifted to Asia, while research and development and more specialized, higher-margin manufacture remained in the Valley.[5]

The new ventures that emerged in the 1980s were able to build on the strengths of the existing network of suppliers and infrastructure and the pool of talent. With the backing of venture capitalists, they were able to build businesses that produced a broader mix of tech products.

Firms generally avoided vertical integration, preferring to specialize within the complex value web that was emerging. Established in 1982, Sun Microsystems is an example of the new generation of Silicon Valley start-ups which made an early decision to concentrate on their core competencies and relied on trusted suppliers for all else, while still managing the overall process. Because of this approach, firms like Sun Microsystems are able to respond to changing technologies, market conditions and customer demands quickly while still sharing risk with their partners.[6]

An organic recipe
The success of Silicon Valley is founded on several ingredients: universities and research institutes, a sophisticated service infrastructure, available knowledge workers, customers, lead users and early adopters.[7]

Universities and R&D

Before Hewlett, Packard or the Varian brothers arrived, there was Stanford University, which was founded in 1885. It seems clear that the initial seeds came from Stanford, and it was Frederick Terman who took the initiative to scatter them in the Valley. AnnaLee Saxenian describes him as a 'social and institutional innovator' and credits him with shaping 'the relationships among individuals, firms, and institutions in Silicon Valley, creating a community that has encouraged continuous experimentation and technological advance'.[8]
Terman saw the importance of exposing his researchers to the business world, as well as bringing the business world into the university to create the kind of synergistic, cooperative environment that he knew would spell success for the region.

But it wasn't just Stanford that educated the minds of those in the Valley. Programmes at the University of California, Berkeley, as well as local community colleges soon emerged to complement Stanford's contribution. As a result of the success of the co-operation between the academic and business worlds, there soon appeared R&D facilities of some of the most well-known technical innovators: Lockheed Aerospace, Westinghouse, ITT, IBM and Xerox's Palo Alto Research Center (PARC).

Of course, there's no way of knowing what might have happened in Silicon Valley without Terman's leadership and support. The region was already home to a number of radio technology companies[9] when Stanford started to spin out its first tech start-ups. But there is no doubt that the university was an early attraction for the skilled knowledge workers who started the growth of the network, and it seems likely that without the support of Terman, people like Hewlett, Packard and the Varian brothers would have ended up working for established companies in the east of the US.

Skilled knowledge workers

It's clear that the highly skilled engineers being educated by Stanford and University of California, Berkeley were a crucial part of the early successes of Silicon Valley. As the number of tech businesses grew and the Universities' programmes expanded, workers in the region became nodes in the network that was being created. As they moved between industry and academia, and from company to company, their personal contacts and the depth and breadth of their knowledge became more extensive.

This also helped to spread the emerging culture that would become typical of the region. Hewlett-Packard, one of the first and most enduring success stories, established a working culture distinct from the formal, hierarchical environment associated with most organizations at the time, particularly at engineering firms in the east. 'The HP Way' was the nickname for this way of working, and it quickly became characteristic of the rebellious attitude shared by Silicon Valley workers.[10] The frequency of job changes and managers leaving to start new ventures helped to spread this culture across the Valley, and the mobility of workers led to cross-pollination of ideas and knowledge from firm to firm.

In Silicon Valley, therefore, success was not solely due to the ready availability of knowledge workers; the role of the network and its primary nodes as carriers of a shared culture and technical knowledge added another important dimension.

Early adopters

None of the Silicon Valley start-ups would have got far without early adopters who were all too willing to buy new and unproven products. In Silicon Valley, the US military filled this role, and it continues to do so (though to a lesser extent) today. Walt Disney Studios may have been Hewlett-Packard's first major customer, but it was military contracts that fuelled much of HP's subsequent growth.

In an essay in *Understanding Silicon Valley*, Stewart W. Leslie, a John Hopkins University professor, points out that the role of defence spending is often overlooked in the analysis of Silicon Valley successes.[11] He reasons that failure to find a substitute for such early adopters can lead to the demise of would-be imitators. This rings true, particularly considering that this spending often went to initial orders for complex technical products while they were still on the drawing board, which amounts to an R&D grant combined with a substantial guaranteed production order.[12]

While companies such as Hewlett-Packard found markets in addition to defence and aerospace, others such as Varian Associates and Litton depended on large government contracts thanks to their expertise with microwave tubes, guidance systems and complementary technologies. Such contracts proved crucial for their growth and demonstrated great faith in the abilities of the Silicon Valley firms because, at that time, to make a substantial investment in small, young ventures was regarded as extremely risky.[13]

It seems clear that without its share of the military spending spurred by the Second World War, the Korean War, the Space Race and the Cold War, Silicon Valley would probably never have got off the ground as a technology cluster.

Service infrastructure

Another important element in the development of Silicon Valley was the robust service infrastructure. Martin Kenney, a professor at the

University of California, Davis, and Urs Von Burg, a PhD candidate at the University of St Gallen in Switzerland, call it 'Economy Two', the network of supporting service organizations that enable 'Economy One' to prosper. In their model, Economy One consists of the established tech firms and research institutions.

Just as front-office operations need the back-office to work, Economy Two allows Economy One to exist and, more importantly, to reproduce.[14] In this model, the service infrastructure consists of an interconnected network of firms such as law firms, investment banks, recruitment agencies, marketing agencies, accountancy firms and other highly specialized service providers.

Importantly, the firms that make up this group have the local industry experience and knowledge of the network and available resources that allow them to go beyond their normal role. Legal firms in particular serve a function beyond what their letterheads may indicate; they are frequently dealmakers and counsellors, or a combination of these, and may also undertake 'matchmaking' or help to arrange financing.[15]

A primary role of these firms is to serve start-ups. Although a top-tier branding agency might still work with well-known brands, firms within the network have the experience and tentacles in the network to enable them to advise and get the start-up company moving. The need for this local knowledge and network presence prompted many New York investment banks to set up local offices because they were unable to serve this market from the other side of the country.

Planners attempting to recreate the Silicon Valley model ignore the service infrastructure at their peril, because the unique needs of start-ups and, later on, focused industry clusters depend on the support that this infrastructure provides. Furthermore, Kenney and Von Burg point out that the strength of Economy Two in Silicon Valley was reinforced by the continual successes of industry feeding the growth and sophistication of the supporting businesses. This implies a high degree of codependence between start-up businesses and the service infrastructure, which becomes increasingly effective as growth continues. The risk for would-be Silicon Valley imitators is that supporting businesses cannot hope to be optimally effective without time to learn and develop based on the needs of the industry they hope to underpin.

Available venture capital

By 1974 there were more than 150 venture capital firms in Silicon Valley, and Stanford was also using part of its endowment to provide venture capital.[16] It is an interesting fact that much of the venture capital in the Valley was home-grown.

The success of Fairchild Semiconductor and its progeny created tremendous wealth for their founders and employees, and much of this wealth was reinvested in start-ups via venture capital funds. Because Valley venture capitalists, such as Eugene Kleiner and Floyd Kvamme of Kleiner Perkins, and Donald Valentine and Pierre Lamond of Sequoia Partners, were already integral players in the network with a wealth of technical knowledge, they were invariably able to provide advice and contacts as well as funding.

In their essay in *Understanding Silicon Valley*, Martin Kenney and Richard Florida make the important point that the venture capital system grew up along with the Valley as an integral part of the network, serving to fuel and attract new ventures while adding further robustness to the fabric of the business environment.[17] The codependent, mutually reinforcing nature of this relationship is similar to the one between the Economy One and Economy Two companies discussed earlier, further illustrating the complexity and robustness of the Silicon Valley ecosystem.

Complementary organizations

The final component that makes Silicon Valley work is the presence of complementary organizations, or 'production networks', as Saxenian calls them.[18] Not to be confused with the service infrastructure discussed above, these organizations work together to create a value-added product as links in a value chain or nodes in a value web.

Many of the new wave of tech start-ups that emerged in the Valley in the 1980s grasped this concept immediately. Sun Microsystems is a good example.[19] The computer workstation company specialized in designing, testing and prototyping hardware and software, but it left manufacture to a vast network of suppliers. This not only ensured that Sun's overheads were kept low, but it also enabled it to react faster, reduce risk and stay on top of the latest manufacturing technologies. Production networks like this, when managed well, also create lots of opportunities to share learning and accelerate innovation. It's important to note, however, that this model works best in fast-moving, volatile markets, when innovation is an important factor.

Lessons from the Valley

If assembling the ingredients discussed above was all there was to it, there would be Silicon Valleys springing up all over the world. But there have been enough attempts to recreate the phenomenon to confirm that it's not that simple. As David Rosenberg shows in *Cloning Silicon Valley*, even the top six would-be tech hubs – Cambridge (UK), Helsinki (Finland), Tel Aviv (Israel), Bangalore (India), Singapore and Hsinchu-Taipei (Taiwan) – all leave something to be desired.[20]

What are they doing wrong? In many cases, imitators fail to recognize that Silicon Valley was an organic process. Even if all the ingredients can be assembled for a new tech region, the personal and industrial networks in Silicon Valley developed a robustness over time that would be hard to replicate.

Looking back at the Silicon Valley story, we can see how the organic growth occurred and the path dependencies inherent in the process. The university and its research centre came first, and further research and skilled engineers soon followed. The initial tech firms grew quickly as a result of the spending of the military, a prominent early adopter. Then the service infrastructure grew to support the developing industry, often run by alumni of older, established firms.

Venture capital and complementary organizations also emerged, largely thanks to the wealth generated by existing firms and the demands of the diversifying range of interrelated industries. The networks created in the process enabled the industry to weather the shake-out of the 1980s, forming a new generation of tech firms; although the jury's still out on how the region will weather the downturn that has followed the bursting of the dotcom bubble. However, it seems that advancements and greater adoption of new technologies has allowed a new generation of companies to continue flourishing, with success stories such as Google, MySpace, YouTube and many others abounding.

It is interesting to consider, then, how rapid growth can be achieved without an organic process, or even all the elements looked at above. Is there a way to create the missing elements and make it work? The answer depends on contextual factors, such as culture, the business environment, prevailing public policy and any number of other variables. In Silicon Valley, these contextual factors combined in a way that helped it to be successful.

Corporate culture
The corporate culture that thrived in Silicon Valley was less formal, more collaborative and less hierarchical than was the norm in traditional firms outside the region. This culture grew out of a shared 'outsider' mentality that separated the region from its established competitors on the East Coast, and it was defined and communicated by managers at Hewlett-Packard and Fairchild.

On a higher level, this was happening within the broader American – or, more specifically, northern Californian – culture that values individual achievement and encourages entrepreneurs. This should be an important consideration for those applying this model elsewhere, especially within national cultures that tend to be risk-averse.

Business environment
The business environment is another important contextual factor. The growth of Silicon Valley began when demand for the technologies it was churning out was starting to explode. The Valley's industry has, on the whole, also been able to adapt its offerings to address changes in the market over the years.

The technology industry is characterized by rapid change and rampant innovation, and the network model works well precisely because it is able to accommodate the web of interrelated organizations and their partners and suppliers. As the large chipmakers discovered in the 1980s when the rug was pulled from under them, the Silicon Valley model supports specialization and discourages vertical integration.

Public policy
Public policymakers have a role to play as well. By determining the regulatory, tax, infrastructure and zoning policies, officials can make the difference between a stifling, inhospitable place to do business and an easy, welcoming one.

Silicon Valley benefited directly from favourable tax treatment and indirectly through the relaxation of laws governing venture capital.[21] Public policy can also help take some of the sting out of the negative side of growing prosperity in a region, including traffic congestion, housing price inflation and pollution.[22]

What next?
The economic downturn and fallout from the dot-com bubble burst cast a long shadow over Silicon Valley at the start of the 21st century. At the end of 2002, Deloitte & Touche's Silicon Valley Venture Capital Confidence Survey was full of gloomy predictions.

But by 2004, things were looking brighter. It was the most profitable year ever for Silicon Valley's largest companies, largely driven by consumers and strong retail sales. And the online companies like Yahoo and eBay that had weathered the storm successfully did better than ever due to growth in online advertising. One economist described the climate in 2004 as 'the internet economy without the hype'. Google also made headlines that year with its IPO, drawing attention worldwide to Silicon Valley and recalling headier days. However, the recovery was still not complete, with stocks of the Valley's largest companies down slightly on the previous year and much lower than five years before.[23]

In 2006, the optimism seems to have grown. A survey in early 2006 by venture capital firm Leapfrog Ventures shows that Silicon Valley entrepreneurs were more optimistic about their prospects than the year before.[24] Consumer confidence in the Valley was also much improved by the end of 2006, owing in large part to the results of the November elections. This confidence may be well-founded; the *Wall Street Journal* found in 2006 that of the half of the nation's most inventive towns were in Silicon Valley.[25]

The roller coaster ride that is Silicon Valley over the past decade doesn't seem to have discouraged any of its would-be imitators – Dubai in particular has continued full steam ahead. While Dubai's ambition to become a leader in semiconductor production may still lie years in the future, it is making progress in assembling the ingredients of the knowledge economy that Sheikh Mohammed envisioned in the 1990s, and which continue to sow the seeds of Silicon Valley's success.

ENDNOTES

1   Saxenian, A. 1994. *Regional Advantage: Culture and Competition in Silicon Valley and Route 128*. Cambridge, Massachusetts: Harvard University Press
2   Saxenian's footnote 26 on p. 21, referring to a paper by Edward Ginzton in *IEEE Spectrum*, February 1975
3   Leslie, S.W. 2000. 'The Biggest "Angel" of Them All: The Military and the Making of Silicon Valley' in *Understanding Silicon Valley*, ed. M. Kenney. Stanford California: Stanford University Press
4   From Public Broadcasting Service
5   Preceding history based on Saxenian, pp. 84-95
6   Saxenian, A. 'Origins and Dynamics of Networks' in *Understanding Silicon Valley*
7   Bahrami, H. and Evans, S. 'Flexible Recycling and High-Technology Entrepreneurship' in *Understanding Silicon Valley*
8   Saxenian, A. 1995. 'Creating a Twentieth Century Technical Community: Frederick Terman's Silicon Valley'. Paper presented for inaugural symposium on 'The Investor and the Innovative Society', The Lemelson Center for the Study of Invention and Innovation, National Museum of American History, Smithsonian Institution, 10–11 November 1995
9   Sturgeon, T.J. 'How Silicon Valley Came To Be' in *Understanding Silicon Valley*
10   Saxenian, *Regional Advantage*, cited by Leslie in *Understanding Silicon Valley*
11   Leslie in *Understanding Silicon Valley*, p. 49
12   Leslie in *Understanding Silicon Valley*, p. 50
13   Leslie in *Understanding Silicon Valley*, p. 50
14   Kenney, M. & Von Burg, U. in *Understanding Silicon Valley*
15   Suchman, M.C. 'Dealmakers and Counsellors: Law Firms as Intermediaries in the Development of Silicon Valley' in *Understanding Silicon Valley*
16   *Understanding Silicon Valley*, p. 211
17   Kenney, M. and Florida, R. 'Venture Capital in Silicon Valley: Fueling New Firm Formation' in *Understanding Silicon Valley*
18   Saxenian, *Regional Advantage*, pp. 145–6

19   Saxenian, *Regional Advantage*, p. 141
20   Rosenberg, D. 2002. *Cloning Silicon Valley*. London: Pearson Education
21   Kenney and Florida in *Understanding Silicon Valley*
22   Saxenian, *Regional Advantage*, pp. 167–8
23   Boudreau, J. and Davis, J., 'Valley rakes in record profit', SiliconValley.com, 8 April 2005
24   Survey of Silicon Valley entrepreneurs conducted by Leapfrog Ventures, 21 March 2006, available from www.leapfrogventures.com
25   Albergotti, R., 'The Most Inventive Towns in America,' *Wall Street Journal*, 22–23 July 2006

CHAPTER 4

SINGAPORE

For a country to rise from the threshold of subsistence to one of the highest living standards in the world in 30 years is no common achievement.

Jacques Chirac, commenting on Singapore

If Silicon Valley has achieved its growth organically, bottom up, Singapore has grown in the opposite way: top down. Silicon Valley was left to market forces, whereas the leaders of Singapore since its independence have calculatedly driven the country forward to achieve its remarkable growth.

A brief history
Newly independent in 1965 after a brief two years as part of The Malaya Federation and over 100 years under British rule, Singapore's government had its work cut out. The country had to gain international recognition, secure its borders and build an economy. With no natural resources, a minuscule domestic market, reluctant neighbouring trading partners and high unemployment, Lee Kuan Yew, the country's prime minister (he held this position for 31 years and the post is currently held by his son), made a commitment to transform Singapore into a dynamic, prosperous independent country. It was an ambitious goal for a largely undeveloped country of two million people (today's population is approximately 4.4 million) squeezed on to an island of only 250 square miles. Lee and his staff sought advice wherever they could find it, on industrial development, defence and tourism.

Early efforts to kick-start the economy included promoting tourism abroad and encouraging new factories and small businesses. But despite such moves unemployment continued to rise. It was the loss of the British military presence in 1971 (the same year the British pulled out of Dubai) that provided the spur for Singapore's transformation to begin. The British military had accounted for 20 per cent of

Singapore's GDP, occupied 11 per cent of the total landmass and employed 30,000 people. An aggressive development programme meant that by the end of 1971 all the real estate that the British had used had been reallocated, much of it for use by foreign investors, transport or leisure facilities.

Lee Kuan Yew's government decided that the key to Singapore's growth would be multinational companies. The Economic Development Board set about attracting them to the country by providing better trading conditions than its neighbours and raising its standards to those of the West. The government paved the way by building solid infrastructure and transport systems, providing fiscal incentives, promoting exports and building industrial parks. By the mid-1970s, Texas Instruments, National Semiconductor, Hewlett-Packard and General Electric had all set up in Singapore.

At first the local workforce was enthusiastic but lacked skills, so public and private training schemes were put in place. Courses for factory workers were set up in conjunction with investors and local government. These produced skilled technicians and unemployment was soon reduced to a tiny percentage of the workforce.

As well as becoming a home away from home for foreign multinationals, Singapore set out to become a financial centre. The first steps were taken in the late 1960s, when one of Lee Kuan Yew's advisers noted that Singapore could fit neatly in the gap between markets closing in San Francisco and opening in Zurich. The government attracted foreign financial institutions by removing taxes on interest earned by non-residents. By starting slowly and creating an international reputation for integrity in financial markets, Singapore had developed into a leading banking centre by the 1990s.

Singapore was already an important port by the time it became independent. In 1819 Sir Thomas Stamford Raffles, an Englishman, had signed a treaty with the sultan of neighbouring Jahore, establishing Singapore as a trading station for the East India Company. Shortly thereafter, it was declared a free port. As a major stopover point on the route between the Indian Ocean and the South China Sea, the port flourished and developed during the 19th and 20th centuries. Today, Singapore is one of the busiest ports in the world.

As part of the quest to raise standards in Singapore, Lee Kuan Yew set in motion a huge range of improvement projects. Strict 'clean and green' measures were adopted, ranging from comprehensive landscaping and planting programmes to prohibition of the sale of chewing gum, smoking and spitting in public. Strict anti-pollution and traffic-calming measures were also put into place.

When Changi Airport was redeveloped and reopened in 1981, it was the largest airport in Asia. Together with Singapore Airlines, it has made Singapore even more accessible, as well as boosting its international reputation. By developing their ports, airports and airlines, both Dubai and Singapore were able to build on their existing strengths as entrepôts and their strategic locations to accelerate their development as international business centres.

English is the working language in Singapore and one of four official languages in schools. This policy was contentious when it was introduced – many faculty members spoke no English at the time – but it has borne fruit. Widespread fluency in English has helped create a hospitable environment for foreign companies locating in Singapore. It has also provided a common secondary language for Malay, Mandarin and Tamil speakers and helped Singaporeans learn to find their way around the internet efficiently.

Lee Kuan Yew's paternalistic policies created stability, prosperity and order for his people, although sometimes at the expense of individual freedoms, particularly among the media and political dissenters. He stepped down in 1990, appointing his trusted deputy to take his place, but Lee Kuan Yew remains a 'senior minister' and is an active force in the government.

When Lee Kuan Yew took office in 1959, GDP per head was $400. When he stepped down, it was $12,200. By 2007 it had reached $35,163, ranking Singapore as one of the richest countries in the world.[1]

But Singapore may have become a victim of its own success. After decades of prosperity, the government began to doubt that growth could continue based on its core industries (petroleum refining, petrochemicals, electronics assembly, and trade-related and financial services).[2] So in 1997 the government began working towards a transition to a knowledge-based economy, creating programmes designed to foster entrepreneurship and innovation, putting in place a range of supporting services. This appears to be presenting a substantial challenge. The Global Entrepreneurship Monitor study, which evaluated the entrepreneurial activity of more than 40 countries in 2006, ranked Singapore near the bottom. The study found that less than five per cent of adults aged 18–64 were engaged in early entrepreneurial activity; in the US, the corresponding figure was found to be just over 10 per cent. Singapore fares no better in terms of adults 18–64 engaged in running established businesses, also ranking in 9th place.[3] There does seem to be reason for some optimism, however; in 2000, the study found that only 2.1 per cent of Singapore adults aged 18–64 were currently setting up or running a new business.

Putting it together
The challenge for Singapore was quite different from that faced by

Silicon Valley. For Singapore it was a matter of survival, not just competitiveness, and Lee Kuan Yew concluded that:

An island city-state in South-east Asia could not be ordinary if it was to survive. We had to make extraordinary efforts to become a tightly knit, rugged, and adaptable people who could do things better and cheaper than our neighbours, because they wanted to bypass us and render obsolete our role as entrepôt and middleman for the trade of the region. We had to be different.[4]

Creating the ingredients

The previous chapter outlined the principal components or ingredients that contributed to the success of Silicon Valley. Since Singapore had none of these in place when Lee Kuan Yew took office, they had to be created. If the country was to attract US multinationals, it would have to provide both the infrastructure and the levels of service these investors would demand.

The Economic Development Board (EDB) was established in 1961 before independence to help put the economy on a stronger footing in anticipation of the British withdrawal, and specifically to woo foreign investment primarily in four industries: ship breaking and repair, metal engineering, chemicals, and electrical equipment and appliances.[5] As a statutory board, it had a degree of independence while remaining ultimately under government control. Its role was to do whatever might be necessary to get foreign investors to close the deal. This included finding land and facilities, hiring and training staff, providing any required infrastructure, providing attractive fiscal incentives and tax relief (or direct investment in some cases) and generally helping to overcome any difficulties.[6]

Like Silicon Valley, Singapore needed the key ingredients of higher education and R&D, skilled knowledge workers, early adopters, supporting industry and services, venture capital and complementary organizations. But its starting point necessitated a completely different approach. Thus the EDB began courting foreign investment at the same time as building infrastructure to suit investors' current and future needs.

An often-told example from the 1970s shows how the EDB worked. Singapore was chosen from a shortlist of four countries for a manufacturing plant for Hewlett-Packard. Representatives of the EDB impressed HP with their enthusiasm, willingness, energy and ability to articulate what HP could expect. In essence, the EDB provided a 'one-stop shop' for HP throughout the process. The degree to which the EDB would extend itself was illustrated once the deal was done and William Packard planned to make a site visit. The electrical systems needed to power the elevator to the sixth-floor facility were not in place by the date of his visit. So a representative of the Jurong Town Corporation (a spin-off of the EDB that managed land development and buildings) decided to power the new HP facility's lights and elevator with an immense cable strung from a nearby building.[7]

The EDB was selective about the types of industry it would court. It was interested only in attracting multinationals that would bring long-term investment and growth, technologies that would complement Singapore's growing portfolio of industries and opportunities for skilled employment. HP fitted the bill, and the firm enthusiastically entered into a cooperative relationship with Singapore.

In parallel to the EDB's activities in encouraging foreign investment, a wide variety of infrastructure projects have been undertaken since the early 1960s. One of the earliest, and largest, was the Jurong industrial estate. It was considered a risky venture at the time, being built speculatively on reclaimed swampland on the western side of the island. Spun out of the EDB in the late 1960s, the Jurong Town Corporation develops and manages properties including industrial estates, business parks, science parks and other specialized industrial zones, many developed speculatively.

Further important infrastructure improvements included continuing development of the seaport, building the new airport and improvement of the road network. More recent projects have been geared towards building the information technology infrastructure. Singapore ONE is a government programme encompassing the development of a high-bandwidth infrastructure that will make broadband internet access available to all Singaporeans and the development of applications and services that take advantage of this network. Infocomm 21 is Singapore's strategic plan for developing its 'infocomm' industry and allowing all aspects of the public and private sectors to make the most of these technologies.

Skilled knowledge workers

When Singapore became independent, it was often said that its only resource was its people. Although initially divided by language, culture and religion, Singaporeans were hard working and willing to learn.

Increasing the supply of talent proved a challenge. Beginning in the early 1970s, the government granted scholarships to outstanding cadets in the military in exchange for an eight-year commitment to the service. A similar programme was put in place to groom top scholars. Many of them went on to attend graduate school at a leading Western university before returning to Singapore to take a post in the civil service, on a statutory board, or in a government-linked company. This scheme demonstrated the willingness of the government to learn from outside sources. Programmes with a wider scope were established in the early 1980s to address the loss of highly skilled Singaporeans who were emigrating. Adopting a model similar to the EDB's, outposts were set up in various countries to recruit well-educated people.[8]

On a larger scale, incoming multinationals and government training schemes have created a rich pool of talent that helps attract foreign investors. In the early days, the EDB often conducted week-long training sessions to teach inexperienced workers the basics of factory work, including the importance of discipline and turning up on time.[9] More advanced technical training was made available as demands on the labour market increased. In many cases, incoming multinationals provided training programmes as well, frequently in conjunction with the EDB, as part of an incentive package. And some foreign governments set up and financed training centres in Singapore to provide technical skills for local workers.[10]

In 1979, the government launched the Skills Development Fund to help employers provide training for their least-skilled workers. The scheme imposed a levy on employers with low-paid workers, then used the funds to share the cost of training with participants. The catch is that eligible training programmes must be 'relevant to the economic development of Singapore'. This is a good example of how the Singapore government has been able to share with the private sector the costs and responsibility of broadening and deepening the indigenous skills base. The scheme seems to have been a success, having supported millions of training places since its inception.

As on-the-job learning increased, the collective experience of the workforce in areas such as electronics had become a major asset for Singapore. It was one of the main reasons firms such as Seagate were attracted to the country, thus laying the foundations for a hard disc drive technology cluster in Singapore.[11]

In the past decade or so, more programmes have been put in place to attract foreign talent and entrepreneurs to Singapore. In keeping with the government's stated objectives of moving the country away from manufacturing to knowledge-based industry, the education system has been/is being revamped to encourage more creativity and entrepreneurship. This is what is required, according to the Global Entrepreneurship Monitor study, which indicates that schools had not focused enough on encouraging such qualities. This may be because the ingrained collective culture had not encouraged individualism or risk, and because the government has tended to encourage brighter students to pursue engineering and technical studies exclusively, instead of the humanities and arts, which it now realizes are important to stimulate the creative thinking it is seeking to foster. The study also shows that the most popular career choices are with large, established companies, not start-ups. Another finding indicates that people under 35 and those with higher education (especially at the tertiary level) are most likely to engage in entrepreneurial activities.

Universities and R&D

Singapore's universities have traditionally been good at churning out graduates with specific skills, but not so good at encouraging innovation and creativity. Curricula at universities and polytechnics have and continue to be overhauled to stimulate creative thinking, and interdisciplinary programmes are being offered involving interaction between Singaporean and overseas students.

The largest and oldest university is the public National University of Singapore with some 32,000 plus students followed by the newer, but just as large (by number of students) Nanyang Technological University. Then followed a spate of openings of specialist well known academic institutions from 1998 onwards, either by or in association with global institutions, such as the University of London, The John Hopkins University, MIT, Wharton, INSEAD, University of Chicago, Stanford and others.

The Ministry of Education allocated funds in 2002 to create a new polytechnic and maybe another university, and the addition of programmes in 'creative reasoning and other skills essential for the knowledge-based economy'.

The government began a campaign to develop more research and development activity in Singapore in 1991 with the formation of the National Science and Technology Board, which became the Agency for Science, Technology and Research (A*STAR) in 2002. A*STAR is an umbrella organization for councils focusing on biomedical research and science and engineering. It also has an agency that manages intellectual property and a division that helps with administrative support. At the end of 2000, the state accounted for 37 per cent of R&D spending in Singapore, and efforts are under way to encourage more private-sector spending. Since the late 1990s, the EDB has been responsible for providing R&D assistance to the private sector and has various grants and incentives at its disposal.

The Singapore Science Parks were established in 1980 to serve as a focal point for R&D in the region. By 2000, over 300 businesses were established on the site, almost half focusing on information technology. One North is a new development that will contains space for offices and business services, biomedical research facilities, an entertainment and media complex, hospitality and conference facilities, and an incubator for 'technopreneurs'. The initial phase was opened in early 2001, and by the end of the following year, about 50 tenants had been attracted to its incubator, Phase Z.Ro. While the development is slated to continue for 15–20 years, the site continues to grow, with new zones being introduced at regular intervals. As of 2006, One North included Phase Z.Ro; Fusionolpolis & Media Hub for information and communications technology businesses; Vista Xchange with hospitality and conference facilities; and Biopolis, with a mix of public research institutes and private companies in biotechnology.[12]

These initiatives are geared towards increasing local R&D; multinationals account for much of the current private-sector R&D investment. In a 1999 paper by Hang Chang Chieh, the author suggests that in order to create a sustainable indigenous R&D culture in Singapore the role of a research engineer must represent a respectable career and the path to commercialization of innovations must be well-marked.[13] If this is the case, it follows that the future success of R&D in Singapore will depend on the success of the efforts to create a culture that nurtures entrepreneurs and innovators.

Available venture capital

Prominent international venture capitalists operate in Singapore, but the government also has a major role in providing venture capital to budding entrepreneurs. Cumulatively, the venture capital industry in Singapore had raised $11.5 billion by 2000, of which around $8.5 billion had been committed to 2,200 projects around the world.

Chief among the government's venture capital contribution is the $1 billion Technopreneurship Fund. Established in early 1999, the fund consists of three main sub-funds with the aims of supporting Singapore start-ups, developing the indigenous venture capital industry by attracting top-tier venture capital firms and establishing a worldwide network of firms investing in Singapore.

Many other options exist for funding new ventures, and there is a wealth of information for entrepreneurs available through the government's websites and offices.

By 2006, the venture capital scene in Singapore had progressed, thanks to government initiatives and the involvement of venture capitalists themselves. Before 2000 when the government began its push to increase technology entrepreneurship, about 2,600 high-tech businesses were registered in Singapore each year, and by 2004, more than 3,500 were registered. 670 foreign high-tech start-ups were established in Singapore in 2004 as well. And in 2006, around 160 VC firms were active in Singapore, managing some $16 billion in funds. And a number of business angels have also emerged, with 3.5 per cent of Singaporeans investing in non-listed businesses started by others.[14]

Early adopters

Singapore's early adopters were its government-linked companies. Set up by Lee Kuan Yew's government to drive the economy forward, these have played a significant role in the development of the country since they were established in the 1960s, although their precise contribution is difficult to gauge because of the complex web of ownership and control in many cases.

Lee Kuan Yew described the government-linked companies as 'new industries', providing opportunities to make entrepreneurs of some of Singapore's scholars by putting them at the helm of these behemoths. According to him, the government-linked companies spawned other companies, and the most successful were made into 'separate entities, free from ministerial control'.[15] It is worth noting, though, that the government in many cases retained ownership through a holding company.[16]

The government-linked companies provided a stable base for the growing economy, but it was the multinationals that acted as lead users and testing grounds for technology-driven products. As Hang suggests, the multinationals have the technology, expertise, global market and financial resources required to test and refine new tech products.[17]

Hard disc drive manufacturer Conner Peripherals, and later Seagate, put a different spin on the idea of a lead market. Until the early 1990s, leading hard disc drive makers would test new products in small volumes in their US markets, refine and debug the design, and then send the specifications to Singapore for mass production. The need for shortened development cycles made Conner Peripherals eliminate the home-market testing phase, shifting the process to its Singapore facility for initial testing, refinement and production, before mass production in China or Malaysia. This was an important development because it signalled that the quality of the Singapore facilities' capabilities was now comparable to that of Silicon Valley.[18]

Complementary organizations

Complementary organizations in Singapore can have as many dimensions as there are industries. In the case of the hard disc drive industry, well-documented by David McKendrick, Richard Doner and Stephan Hagard,[19] manufacturers such as Seagate, Conner Peripherals, Maxtor and MiniScrib, when they first set up in Singapore, had to bring all their own equipment and train local workers up to their standards. Seagate's managers sought to lower costs by outsourcing the production of some metal parts.

With the assistance of the Economic Development Board, several entrepreneurs were identified who were up to the task. Many of these had become established with the demise in 1981 of Rollei, a German firm that set up a Singapore manufacturing facility in 1970 and conducted extensive training before going into receivership. Seagate and Conner each had programmes in place to help suppliers develop.

By the 1990s, the hard disc drive industry in Singapore had evolved into a production network, with a range of specialized suppliers and expertise recognized around the world.[20]

Service infrastructure
The previous chapter described how a network of local Economy Two firms sprang up organically with the specialized knowledge to support the Economy One players. The Economy Two firms comprise the network of support services with the specialized knowledge and skills to enable the growth and development of the start-ups that form the backbone of the cluster. Although these firms almost certainly had their counterparts in Singapore to support multinationals, it can be argued that the EDB fills this role as an intermediary, ensuring that incoming and established companies in Singapore have everything they need, including a range of support services. Like law firms in Silicon Valley, the EDB also acts as a dealmaker, providing introductions and guidance, and helps with funding.

In at least one case, these elements have been provided by design. At the Singapore Science Park, management has installed a suite of service providers including a venture capital firm, a financial services firm, a law firm, a PR agency and a management consulting firm. These services should prove welcome to local entrepreneurs since a robust professional service infrastructure for start-ups has impeded the development of Singapore's entrepreneurial ventures in recent years, according to the Global Entrepreneurship Monitor study. While this is a step in the right direction, this service infrastructure will need to expand and develop synergies with technology firms and other start-ups in order to approach the effectiveness of these businesses in Silicon Valley.

Other factors

The growth of Singapore has been achieved primarily through top-down management and direction by the government, particularly through the EDB. As a result, the path dependencies are less clear than they are in Silicon Valley. In most cases, the major initiatives were planned, executed, monitored and corrected by the state's numerous statutory boards, which seem to have been created for every conceivable purpose.

The EDB has an important role as ambassador, promoter, facilitator and supporter. Comments by company chairmen highlight its 'dedication to Singapore and its growth; optimism and self confidence; commitment to learning, adapting and innovating; strategic pragmatism and a commitment to partnering; marketing and sales philosophy built on technical competence; and a global outlook based on a sense of vulnerability as a small city state'.[21] This illustrates the success of EDB in attracting investment and cultivating growth.

Cultural considerations have also had to be taken into account. The traditional Confucian or collectivist culture is at odds with the innovative spirit that drives the entrepreneurs of Silicon Valley. Through its educational reforms and the creation of technology parks, the government is trying to encourage would-be entrepreneurs to 'think outside of the box'. But overturning deep-rooted ways of thinking may take longer than expected.

Another important element is trust, which is essential in a growth model like Singapore's that is led from the top. By following through on commitments, tackling issues fairly, demonstrating honesty and not tolerating corruption, the government gained the trust and confidence of both Singaporeans and foreign investors, who find a business-friendly and stable environment particularly attractive.

One of the things that impressed the authors was the openness of everyone they talked to, including the challenges that lie ahead and in terms of transparency they were fascinated by the easy availability of data and statistics on Singapore and the approachability of some of the most senior public figures.

What next?

The Ministry of Trade and Industry declares:

> *Our vision is for Singapore to become an advanced and globally competitive knowledge economy within the next decade, with manufacturing and services as its twin engines of growth.*[22]

As with so many of its ventures, the government is putting substantial resources into achieving this objective. It is planning to encourage innovation (with the new National Innovation Council intended to 'help Singaporeans look for new ideas and new ways of doing things'); increase entrepreneurship to supplement the body of multinationals with home-grown businesses; expand the talent pool through the creation of three junior colleges, a fourth polytechnic and potentially a fifth university; continue to recruit foreign talent.

The Infocomm Development Authority is a new statutory board dedicated to providing the infrastructure needed for the transition to a knowledge-based economy. The Infocomm 21 programme includes initiatives geared towards putting everyone in Singapore online and making the country a 'premier infocomm hub' and an 'infocomm talent hub', while providing a 'conducive business and policy environment'.

Common themes, different methods

Many of the strategies and initiatives in Singapore are familiar, and it has borrowed many of them, building on and modifying them as appropriate. But it is the differences in the methods used that are more telling.

Getting noticed by the world

The driving force behind the growth of both Singapore and Dubai seems to have been gaining importance at the international level. Become indispensable and you can't be ignored. The best way to do that, as we've seen in both of these examples, is to become better than your competitors, especially your regional competitors.

Both Dubai and Singapore had to work their way out of relative obscurity, and the similarities between their starting points are striking. Both flourished as entrepôts. Lacking any substantial natural resources, each recognized the importance of developing trade and, in particular, luring foreign investment from multinational corporations with the promise of liberal trade policies and generous incentives. Foreign investors were brought into each area with careful hand-holding, and only companies that would contribute high-value-added industry were invited.

Each was made more attractive to foreign investment with the development of high-quality infrastructure. In both, companies owned wholly or partly by the government have been the stimulus for developing indigenous industries. Both have set out to become major financial centres. Singapore has succeeded; Dubai has recently started, seemingly inspired by Singapore's example. Education has been a challenge for both, and Singapore's system is substantially more mature than that of Dubai. Both Singapore and Dubai seek to encourage entrepreneurship and knowledge-based enterprises.

Each government also seeks to lead its people and businesses by example: the development of two of the world's top e-government programmes is a good illustration of this. According to a 2005 study of 191 e-government programmes conducted by the UN, both the United Arab Emirates and Singapore rated well, with indices of 0.5718 (ranked 42nd) and 0.8503 (ranked 7th) respectively, compared with a global index of 0.4276.[23]

Both Singapore and Dubai are strongly led. Their leaders have clear visions and ambitious plans, which the supporting government structures allow to be put into effect without delay. But it is where the two governments' methods diverge that it becomes interesting.

Top-down versus middle-out

Since his People's Action Party took power in the 1960s, Lee Kuan Yew has advocated a paternalistic, detail-oriented government, which leaves little room for ambiguity. Politically, economically and even culturally, the government of Singapore is careful to prescribe what's allowed and what isn't, down to the level of personal behaviour (no chewing gum or spitting) and restricted freedom of the press. Political dissent is carefully controlled and sometimes suppressed. Government-linked companies still make a large contribution to the country's GDP. The government has invested in large-scale public housing and has introduced a mandatory savings scheme. It's a government that likes to be in control.

Lee Kuan Yew and his successors are unapologetic about their government's no-nonsense, no-compromise policies, which, despite recent economic difficulties, have created a prosperous, well-ordered country. The combination of father-knows-best government and traditional Asian education has created a nation of followers, not leaders, worker-bees, not innovators (as much of the feedback appears to reinforce). Hence the Singapore government's recognition that it needs to stimulate innovation and entrepreneurship.

Whatever similarities there are between Dubai and Singapore, many in Dubai attribute much of the emirate's success to the long tradition of trading and entrepreneurship. This is apparent at its most basic level in the Creek, where goods still flow in and out by dhow, and in the Gold Souk, with its hundreds of tiny shops. But it is also clear on a much grander scale, when the names of the prominent trading families begin appearing on all kinds of business ventures. Names like Al Futtaim, Al Ghurair, Juma Al Majid: family businesses that have built up substantial fortunes over just a few generations based on the rapid growth of trade in the area.

The government of Dubai focuses on growing the economy by creating an environment that encourages business without being too overtly controlling. The free zones operate free from almost any type of restriction. Industries such as tourism may have been stimulated by government investment, but now market forces operate free from government intervention. As a case in point, recently, some of the biggest shopping and multi-purpose developments have been initiated by some of the historical trading families previously mentioned. For example, the Mall of the Emirates, the world's largest shopping mall outside of North America, boasts over 450 retailers, cinemas, restaurants, a five star hotel (400-room Kempinski Hotel), and an indoor ski resort was developed by the Al Futtaim family. Another project, with a similarly grand vision, which is coincidentally also developed by the Al Futtaim family, is Dubai Festival City, which includes a Four Seasons, InterContinental and Crowne Plaza hotels – with some 2,500 rooms in total – to cater for this enormous shopping, leisure and entertainment waterfront area development. These are but a few of the many examples to illustrate that the government is no longer the only major risk taker or major developer. However, as the size of the projects continue to grow (such as the various Palm Island developments), the government continues to play a vital role in initiating and developing these projects.

In creating the stimulus for entrepreneurial growth, it can be argued that Dubai takes a 'middle-out' approach, as opposed to top-down (as in Singapore) or bottom-up (as in Silicon Valley). By undertaking projects that would be too risky for any one company in order to stimulate an industry, then stepping back as private investment begins to roll in, the government of Dubai has adopted a model that seems to be mid-way between those of our other two examples. However, it should be noted that both Singapore and Dubai have been incredibly successful in the last few decades – transforming themselves from obscure places to vibrant parts of the global economy. The above analysis is not to say that one method of transformation was better than the other – but rather that each country had to develop a strategy based on its resources, capabilities, immediate competitors, and desired future position within their region and the global economy. This advice should be carefully noted by anyone trying to imitate the success of Dubai or Singapore – the challenge is to adapt their successful transformation strategies, not blindly adopt them within their country or institution.

ENDNOTES

1   From Singapore government website at www.singstat.gov.sg/keystats/hist/gdp.html

2   Rosenberg, D. 2002. *Cloning Silicon Valley*, p. 149. London: Pearson Education

3   2006 GEM study available from www.gemconsortium.org

4   Lee Kuan Yew. 2000. *From Third World to First*. New York: HarperCollins, p. 7

5   Lee Kuan Yew, p. 59

6   Schein, E.H. 1996. *Strategic Pragmatism: The Culture of Singapore's Economic Development Board*. Cambridge, Massachusetts: MIT Press, p. 42

7   Schein, p. 22

8   Lee Kuan Yew, Chapter 10

9   Schein, p. 22

10 Lee Kuan Yew, p. 12

11 McKendrick, D.G., Doner, R.F. and Haggard, S. 2000. *From Silicon Valley to Singapore*. Stanford, California: Stanford University Press, p. 160

12 From One North website at www.one-north.com

13 Hang, C.C. 1999. 'What It Takes to Sustain Research and Development in a Small, Developed Nation in the 21st Century' in S*ingapore – Towards a Developed Status*, ed. Low, L. Oxford: Oxford University Press, p. 35

14 Keynote address by Mr Teo Ming Kian, Chairman, Singapore Economic Development Board, at the NUS Global Entrepreneurship Summit 2006 Opening Ceremony

15 Lee Kuan Yew, p. 67

16 'Whither Singapore Inc.?', *The Economist*, 30 November 2002

17 Hang, p. 28

18 McKendrick *et al.*, pp. 165–6

19 McKendrick *et al.*

20 McKendrick *et al.*, pp. 165–6

21 Schein, pp. 96–7

22 www.mti.gov.sg

23 2006 GEM study available from www.gemconsortium.org

CHAPTER 5

ASSET CREATION

Companies failed to create the future not because they fail to predict it but because they fail to imagine it.

Gary Hamel (from his book *Leading the Revolution*)

Dubai started its development with a clean slate and few resources. As such it faced immense challenges, but at least it was free to develop exactly as it chose, and in time borrowing from the experiences of others, such as Silicon Valley and Singapore. The Silicon Valley model is a bottom-up organic one. Singapore's model is led from the top. Dubai falls into a middle ground between the two, with some intervention by the leadership, as well as some organic growth.

Introduction to the models
Dubai's experience is a lesson in how to create something where there was nothing. Dubai could still be a small, obscure emirate of little international importance. Instead, it has become a vibrant, cosmopolitan powerhouse of tourism, tolerance and commerce which

Strategic trajectory

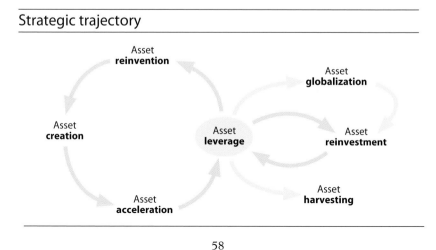

Asset
reinvention

Asset
globalization

Asset
creation

Asset
leverage

Asset
reinvestment

Asset
acceleration

Asset
harvesting

has gained recognition worldwide. In the past four decades, the emirate has built up a range of valuable assets and it continues to do so.

This momentum driving the development of Dubai is an important underlying factor in what we call its strategic trajectory: a calculated, strategic thrust in a specific direction, with focused goals.

The Dubai model we outline borrows from systems theories that have emerged since the middle of the 20th century. Recursive and iterative, it requires multiple actors working together to create the exponential value increases that produce large-scale rapid growth. The diagram above is a graphic representation of the model.

The starting point of the model is asset creation, in which resources are put in place and assets – be they technology systems, intellectual property, physical infrastructure and so on – are created. In essence, something new. Of course, this kind of thing happens all the time, but on its own it doesn't explain the rapid growth of a company or economy. It's only when we place this phase into the context of the model that its strategic value begins to emerge.

Once an asset has been created, its value may go up or down depending on its output and a multitude of external factors. It's only through asset acceleration that we can realize greater value from its outputs than would ordinarily be dictated by market forces. The pent-up demand may be achieved by anything from infrastructural development to the accumulation of know-how or experience. These in turn will make further asset creation even easier.

Closely tied to asset acceleration is asset leverage, the next phase in the model. This is where pent-up demand for and the unreleased value of the asset are realized. Expertise and knowledge developed the first time round can be leveraged, and network economies begin to exhibit rapid value creation. In many cases this stage is not reached, and any potential value is dissipated either because of management failings or because of market conditions. This underlines the importance of astute management and reliable, real-time data gathering.

In many ways, this stage of the model is where the real action is. It is where a successful concept achieves great visibility in the market and really takes off. The asset leverage stage is also as important because it is a decision point – what happens here dictates where the asset goes next. At this stage of the model, there are four possibilities – asset reinvestment, asset reinvention, asset globalization, and asset harvesting.

If the asset is continuing to achieve optimal returns and the market continues to respond positively, asset reinvestment will still be necessary to keep it fresh and maintain its position.

However, if market changes or internal management issues leads the asset astray, asset reinvention may be necessary – this could involve a simple facelift, management change, or any intervention that reinvents the asset and sends it back in the right direction. In the model, this leads back to the asset creation stage since the asset is effectively new again and must continue through acceleration and leverage to reach its full potential.

A third possibility, asset globalization, has really only become prevalent in Dubai in the past four years as successes within the emirate have been taken abroad. When the value has been maximized (or close to it) in a domestic market and the business model, operations, and management are robust and confident enough, the asset can be expanded to a global market. As the graphic view of the model shows, this creates an expanded cycle that requires continued asset reinvestment and leverage on a whole new level to keep up with the myriad challenges of globalization.

Finally, if the asset has been exhausted and little potential for increasing value remains, it can be retired. While the need for asset harvesting can be difficult to recognize when this step is appropriate, it is all the more important to approach this pragmatically in a constantly changing environment like Dubai since experienced senior managers are scarce and it is crucial to make good use of them.

Strategic vortex

Create   Accelarate   Leverage

Once the cycle has been completed and started again, the effect of multiple iteration and ever-increasing speed and momentum creates a strategic vortex (see diagram above).

The combined effects of the strategic vortex result in large-scale rapid growth. As additional assets are added to the portfolio and existing assets are iterated, several things happen. Momentum increases, allowing speed to be maintained and minimizing any slowing effects from external factors. The solidity of base assets increases as they are reinvested. The scope of the portfolio of assets increases, and risk is reduced as the portfolio is expanded and diversified.

But it is a process that depends for its success on quick and effective decision-making and the ability of leaders to step back when appropriate. Executives (or government officials, as the case may be) must choose which assets to introduce, monitor their development through the acceleration and leverage stages, and then decide whether to reinvest, reinvent, globalize, or harvest. Equally important is knowing when to step back and let market forces take over; this is the only way to maximize the benefits of the leverage stage. To enable all of this to happen, two things are necessary: good, real-time data for decision-makers, and a governance structure that allows for fast and effective decisions to be made.

Going, going, gone

Many dotcoms failed because their business plans and management approach were not grounded in common sense. One dotcom that has been extraordinarily successfully is eBay. In only 12 years, the company developed an online commerce community with users around the globe, and by its own estimates it is the most popular shopping site on the internet. It went online as AuctionWeb in 1995 with one broken laser printer for sale, and in 2006 it had 13,000 employees running websites localized for many countries with millions of items for sale on any given day. eBay has also made some canny investments, acquiring PayPal (online payments), Skype (internet telephony), Rent.com (real estate), and other companies.

By the end of 2006, eBay had some 200 million registered users, who traded $50 billion in gross merchandising volume during that year. This resulted in net revenues of almost $6 billion, and net income exceeded $1.1 billion.[1]

The company was floated on NASDAQ in 1998 at a stock price of $0.75 per share (split adjusted). By the start of 2007, eBay's stock was trading at around $30.[2] eBay is successfully bucking market trends, just like the Emirate of Dubai, whose airline – by way of example – is growing fast and investing billions in new aircraft despite a worldwide downturn.

The genius of eBay was that it provided a more efficient means of online auctioning than the existing methods, which were based on newsgroups and email lists that, although functional, had none of the transparency and visibility of traditional auctions. This illustrates the importance of the asset creation phase. If eBay had not developed the auction software and put the technical infrastructure in place, it would not have got off the ground.

Asset acceleration followed quickly as the network of users on the growing auction site expanded by 'word of mouse': buyers would find other items of interest via searches and links from items they bought, and many were enticed to become sellers themselves. By 1997, the year that the popular Antiques Road Show first aired in the US, there were some 150 competing auction sites, thus demonstrating the pent-up demand for auctions.

The asset leverage phase resulted in fourth-quarter 1997 revenues of $55 million, and the company was already profitable. By that time, more than five million auctions had been completed on the site, and there were more than 400,000 registered users.[3] This created opportunities for learning within the company and within the extended network of traders that used the site. The synergies between buyers and sellers grew and grew.

The company's founder, Pierre Omidyar, had been involved with every detail of the company's growth and development. He was also smart enough to realize in late 1997 that he needed to bring in a more experienced management team. This kind of realization or insight often proves to make or break a growing enterprise. The business model remained solid but further investment was needed to enable further growth. Omidyar handed over to Meg Whitman, who became CEO in March 1998. This helped transform the company from a fabulously successful internet start-up led by a young techie to a fast-growing market leader run by a highly experienced management team. The company would subsequently reinvest and reinvent itself many times as the market developed, seeing off many competitors in the process. There would be asset harvesting as well, such as eBay's decision to pull out of the Japanese market in 2002.

Of course, by the time of the management change, there had already been substantial investments in new technologies, employees and other resources. This reflects the strategic vortex that began back in 1995 with the creation of the original asset, AuctionWeb. The combination of many strategic trajectory cycles has enabled eBay to become a seemingly unstoppable network of trading services, for buyers and sellers large and small.

A new way to think about strategy

Several clear points emerge from the eBay story. Management has created an environment where radical growth can take place, but the growth has occurred because of expansion within the stakeholder network. Tools and services have been developed through listening to stakeholders and watching what third parties come up with. These tools are usually much more complex ones than most individual eBay members could develop on their own. Later investments and developments have involved less risk because of the already thriving business base.

All this plays a critical part in the strategic trajectory model. What counts in the end is the ability of leadership over the long term to listen to and learn from all the stakeholders – customers, suppliers, competitors and the collective voice of the market ecosystem – and to make decisions fast and effectively.

The asset creation phase

The asset creation phase is a starting point. During a first iteration of the strategic trajectory model, it is where an idea is combined with resources to create an asset. During subsequent iterations, it may be that a new asset is created from an existing one, or something new is spun out, leaving the parent intact.

Just about any new venture or initiative could reasonably fall into this part of the model, but there are specific characteristics that you should expect to see if the assets created are to form the basis for rapid growth.

It is important to be bold, not tentative, eschewing recognized limitations to create something of real value to the growing ecosystem or strategic vortex. It is also crucial to create assets selectively and strategically, taking care to choose the ones that can grow and change over time to form a solid base for a developing portfolio of assets. To accomplish this, there must be strong leadership. Leadership underpins everything, and during the asset creation phase, vision, acceptance of risk and decisiveness are the crucial factors.

Starting with a bang

It is important to be bold, not tentative. This doesn't necessarily mean bursting out of the starting gates like horses at the Kentucky Derby; it may mean taking risks or being seen as an industrial heretic, or just setting off with a new idea like eBay did in 1995. This marks a distinct difference between this model and the organic model that emerged in Silicon Valley over decades. If you want rapid growth it is crucial to start with a bang, because there isn't time to wait and see what develops. This is particularly true when coming from behind, when there are established competitors to contend with. In these cases, there is the potential to leapfrog the incumbents, so it's even more important to make a strong start.

It's equally important not to be deterred by potential constraints but to acknowledge and overcome them. Dubai Internet City was conceived, planned, built and launched in a year, a fraction of the time it would have taken in many parts of the world. It is now a key component in Dubai's portfolio of assets, attracting foreign investment and workers, facilitating knowledge transfer and contributing to Dubai's international standing as an emerging technology hub. The DIC model, is another such example, it has been tested and is now being frequently replicated.

The Palm projects were born from the need to overcome a limitation: a shortage of coastline. The Palm have already entered the world's consciousness indications of the innovative spirit of Dubai. This builds upon the foundation established by the Burj Al Arab hotel, which was the first globally-recognized symbol of Dubai along these lines. With the announcement of each new initiative like The Palm Deira, The World, DIFC, Dubailand, and the new mega-airport, Dubai redefines for the world what it means to 'think big.' Although the vast amount of planning and study that went into each of these examples shouldn't be minimized, they are typical of the bold strokes being made on the canvas of Dubai by its leaders.

In the words of a Dubai leading businessman: 'When you believe in something, go for it. Don't hesitate. When you're flying a plane, put the full thrust into take-off. Burn half the fuel tank. Once you're airborne, then you're fine.'

Choosing key assets

The initial assets created underpin everything else that comes after; so, just as it's crucial for skyscrapers to be built on solid foundations, the initial assets must be the right ones. They must be able to develop and they must contribute to the vision behind the drive for growth. The choice of new assets to be developed must not be whimsical or random or merely to take advantage of a short-term opportunity. Decisions motivated by such forces simply divert resources and management attention from where they are most usefully employed.

Timing is also crucial. In Dubai, for example, there is a long history of creating assets as part of the process of anticipating or even creating demand. Most of the large investments made by the government since the 1960s were attacked by critics who said there was no demand for them. But they have since proved successful: the demand emerged or was stimulated. The DIFC seems to be an example of good timing. Certainly, there seems to have been a gap in the international financial market stemming from the time difference between the established Eastern and Western markets, and competition in the region seemed less than formidable. Despite early growing pains as the Dubai International Financial Centre was getting off the ground, it has proven to be an excellent fit for Dubai, and the presence of the world's leading financial institutions has validated the concept. Still, as it grows and develops, this will be an interesting project to juxtapose the financial market's need for control and regulation against the free-market, anti-bureaucracy approach of Dubai.

Sheikh Ahmed, Emirates Group chairman, makes the following point about the combination of vision and timing:

We believe that you have to put supply before demand. If you wait until demand exists, you may be too late. Go wherever your vision leads you, and the business will come through good business practices.

By remaining focused and developing the right assets at the right time, the business ecosystem can sustain itself through periods of rapid growth and it can remain intact in times of difficulty. One of Dubai's leading business women from a prominent, diversified family-owned business in the emirate says:

Dubai is like the water of a river. Sometimes, a big stone will fall into the river, but the water will go around the stone. Dubai is like that. Even with all the regional problems in the 1990s, Dubai was at its peak. Dubai is well-established, with good foundations, and the government knows exactly where it's going.

Communicating a vision
Unlike many so-called corporate visions that amount to little more than a motto or slogan, the vision of the leadership in Dubai seems to be widely understood. Generally, it is about transforming the emirate into a magnet for tourists, workers and corporations from around the world based on high-quality facilities, infrastructure and way of life. There have been various explicit vision statements, including those expressed in Dubai 2010,[4] which sets out the following targets for 2010:

• Dubai will have become the symbol of what a knowledge economy can achieve.
• Dubai will have become emblematic of a mindset of innovation, dynamism and entrepreneurship. It will be synonymous with high added-value creation, high-tech and a spirit of excellence and integrity.
• Dubai will be the benchmark showing how a well-implemented strategy focused on the optimum use of existing and new assets, on well-defined positioning and on the impact of 'networking power' can create successful new businesses both large and small.

In 2006 it seems clear that Dubai is largely on track to achieve this and more. Dr Anwar Gargash (UAE Minister) says:

You can see the vision of Dubai going back many years. You see it reinforced by Sheikh Mohammed, but the rulers have always been visionary and very focused. Sheikh Rashid was very focused on trade and re-export. His sons have focused on different areas as times have changed.

Talking about Sheikh Mohammed, people often mention his enthusiasm and energy, and the following was said by many in Dubai: 'A lot of people cannot understand the relationship we have with His Highness. Knowing him or not knowing him is not the point. He gives you a lot of energy just by being around.'

As he articulates them, Sheikh Mohammed's goals for Dubai are visionary yet explained simply, some would say even in a humbling manner, but they provide an indication of his leadership style. When asked by the authors how he would like to see Dubai perceived around the world, he replied that he would like people to have heard of it. He then added that he would like Dubai to be a place where people are happy, where they enjoy their work, their lives and their families. And as simple as it seems, it is clear that the emirate is being managed with precisely these goals in mind. For this reason, it is little wonder that this vision is so widely known.

Accepting risk

Another important part of effective asset creation is accepting the risk that goes with it. Seeming to fly in the face of a level of risk that would deter others has been inspirational in Dubai; and every time the risk has paid off, there has been a strengthening of confidence in the leadership and its vision. As mentioned above, the high-risk projects undertaken in Dubai before an obvious business case may have helped to solidify both the Dubai vision and confidence in its leadership.

Indeed, risk-taking appears to be a crucial part of the government's role, as family-owned businesses in Dubai are famously risk-averse. Sultan Bin Sulayem relates one example: Sheikh Mohammed approached a group of ten family-owned businesses, offering them the opportunity to develop a large swathe of land into a theme park. After protracted discussions among themselves, the families were sceptical about the potential of the investment. So they returned to Sheikh Mohammed and asked if they could develop the area with 75 per cent in property and the remaining 25 per cent as a theme park. They were given the go-ahead but failed to agree on how to proceed. The area is now being developed by Emaar Properties as Dubai Marina, at a cost of around $200 million. When complete, it will house around 120 thousand people in Venetian-style luxury accommodations, along with a range of restaurants and facilities.

Sultan Bin Sulayem is circumspect about the government's role as a risk-taker in Dubai:

If the government waits for someone to build the Dubai Marina, it will never happen. If Sheikh Mohammed waits for someone to build the Palm, they will look at it and keep thinking: 'Should I do it? Is this a good investment?' But now that the government has taken the risk, all the traders are investing because it is already becoming successful.

A leading Dubai business woman echoes this point from the merchant's perspective, saying that they 'can't stay in a tent and watch the tall skyscrapers being built all around'. The results show that the government's strategy is working. By investing first it reduces the risk for others, who then invest when they find conditions sufficiently attractive. Despite the risks taken by the government and a long history of entrepreneurship in many forms, Dubai may find its growth hampered if some of the stigma associated with failure is not alleviated. As in Singapore, but markedly different from Silicon Valley and much of the West, failure in business inevitably entails a 'loss of face', the prospect of which may prevent some from starting new ventures. As new sources of capital emerge, this reluctance to fail may begin to wane as entrepreneurs become less reliant on funds from their families and friends, and failure leads to less personal consequences.

But rapid growth need not always involve living on the edge. As a portfolio of assets grows, the risk profile of the portfolio stabilizes, and new assets can be created with substantially reduced risk. An example is the second Palm Island, where all the feasibility had already been completed and demand was proven. Of course, it still involved risk, but it was much less than for the first Palm Island. Moving a step further, this also means that new assets can be introduced with a much higher degree of risk because their failure would not be catastrophic to the business ecosystem. This pattern has been echoed with the commencement of The World, the third Palm, and the Dubai Waterfront islands that will surround the Palm Jebel Ali.

The Earl of Home – chairman of Coutts Bank in the UK, has been involved with Dubai since the 1960s while at merchant bank Morgan Grenfell, when he helped engineer the financing for building Port Rashid, the first hospital and many other projects. According to The Earl of Home, early projects were so large, relative to the resources available to the government at that time, that the failure of any one of them might have bankrupted the country. But he also stresses that many projects today, although large and important, present less risk (in relative terms) to the emirate than early major projects.

This has less to do with the importance of the financial centre than with the solidity and diversification of the asset base that has been developed in Dubai, which is such that the failure of one project, even of this magnitude, could be absorbed by the ecosystem. Indeed, the ability of the DIFC to move past its initial missteps shows that this is the case. Of course, such risk can never be completely eliminated, particularly in the context of very large projects like this or, say, Burj Dubai, announced in May 2003 and planned to be the world's tallest building. Burj Dubai is set back from Sheikh Zayed Road as part of the massive Downtown Dubai complex. At 705 metres tall, the building is taller than Taiwan's Taipei 101 (509 metres), and the yet-unfinished Incheon Tower 1 & 2 in South Korea (640 metres).[5] As if containing the world's tallest building is not enough, the myriad attractions of Downtown Dubai include the world's largest shopping centre.

As Dubai extends into the sea (with the Palm Island developments and others), into the desert and into the sky, it seems to be embracing risks that would prove unacceptable to many, fully expecting that these projects will ultimately prove technically feasible and commercially viable. Mohammed Ali Alabbar explains the reasons behind the tower:

> *Dubai is keen on being on the world map. There's a lot of competition around creating the tallest buildings, so that is another opportunity for Dubai. At first, Dubai was competing regionally, now we compete globally.*

Which, of course, means that the risks increase, but Dubai appears eager to meet these risks head-on. This all stems from the confidence required to create supply in advance of demand. Dubai's leaders have demonstrated this again and again, and perhaps no recent example shows it more effectively than the new airport, which will increase the capacity of passengers by 120 million per year when added to the existing airport. Al Maktoum International Airport is not being developed in isolation, of course; it will be feeding tourists into the expanding beaches and attractions and business travellers into the DIFC and other free zone centres. And its world-class logistics hub will also help ensure that the Dubai machine has the fuel it needs to keep running.

Being decisive

Vision and being unafraid of risk are of little use if the decision-making process is cumbersome and slow. You must be able to identify and implement new projects and roll them out quickly, because if you wait too long you may be too late to benefit from the opportunity. In Dubai, Sheikh Rashid's government went ahead with large infrastructure projects despite scepticism. His son, Sheikh Mohammed, has done the same.

The key players involved in these projects recall what happened when Sheikh Mohammed gave them the go-ahead. A solid business case was presented, after which he simply told them to begin. In the case of Palm Island, Sultan Bin Sulayem was given the green light while driving one evening with Sheikh Mohammed. He could scarcely believe it and asked for clarification. The reply came: 'I told you to go ahead with Palm Island. Let's start.' The project team has remained as lean as it was at the start, with just Sheikh Mohammed, Sultan Bin Sulayem and a couple of finance people and engineers as the only decision-makers.

Gerald Lawless, Executive Chairman of the Jumeriah Hotel Group, reinforces how important this straightforward approach is:

> *It's the leadership that makes things work here, and its simplicity. The simplicity of the connection from somebody saying 'do it' to somebody who will start and get the job done. Dubai has the ability to get things done very quickly because the lines of command are very clear and straightforward.*

Asset creation in Dubai

There are many examples of strategic asset creation in Dubai. In most cases, they differ from projects elsewhere in the region in that they are indeed strategic, each taking its place in the formation of Dubai's strategic vortex and helping to strengthen the asset base. Neighbouring countries have begun staging conferences, developing property and organizing sporting and other events, and these are frequently very successful on their own. But they invariably appear to be one-offs that neither work towards a cohesive vision nor consistently strengthen the country's or organization's brand name internationally. By contrast, Dubai's strategic management of its assets and their cohesive marketing domestically and internationally make each initiative appear to be part of the emirate's grand plan.

Port Rashid

Dubai's origins as a port and trading centre are the cornerstone of its success. After the modernization of the Creek showed the potential for Dubai as a shipping hub, Sheikh Rashid began planning for a new man-made port near the centre of Dubai. Following a series of studies between 1965 and 1967, plans went ahead to build a deep-water free port with four berths near the mouth of the Creek. Many of the design features of the proposed port, including the free port model, were based on benchmarks, notably the highly successful free ports in Singapore and the Netherlands. When the project was well under way, Sheikh Rashid and his advisers became anxious. They wanted more berths because the booming trade in the area indicated that four berths might not have been enough. So Sheikh Rashid told the engineers to increase the capacity of the new port to 16 berths. This is a good illustration of the decisiveness that is so important in the asset acceleration phase.

However, the change in plans came at a price; the cost of the 16-berth port was estimated at about $32 million (equivalent to about $142 million today). Despite the recent discovery of oil, Sheikh Rashid sought to cut costs wherever possible. The engineers had planned to construct the two large breakwaters from imported stone, but Sheikh Rashid suspected that there was a local source. He had heard that nomadic people had experienced difficulty in digging wells in remote areas of Dubai, so he commissioned a study to determine whether any potentially useful material existed there. Sure enough, a deposit of limestone was found that would provide enough material for the breakwaters and several other future projects as well. Using local stone shaved almost one-third off the original cost estimate. When the project began to fall behind schedule because of delays in trucking the limestone to the site, the ruler is said to have demanded 24-hour deliveries, routing the clamorous trucks past his palace to save time.

The port was officially opened in 1971, and its 16 berths were immediately put to use. Sea trade in the area had grown massively since the project began, so Dubai's new port was a welcome and valued addition. Of course, this was not the end of the story. Further indications of growth led to expansion of the port to its current capacity of 35 berths and the creation of the much larger Jebel Ali port.[6]

Port Rashid was the first of several large projects to be put in place by Sheikh Rashid and his successors. As such, it is a good example of asset creation for the strategic trajectory model. It built on an existing competency in the region and involved committing huge resources in anticipation of future demand. The strategic value of the port was substantial. It opened just as demand in the region was at an all-time high and neighbouring ports were oversubscribed. This not only brought a lot of business to Dubai, it also helped to raise Dubai's profile and reputation among shippers, traders and other countries in the region.

It was the largest project ever undertaken in Dubai. If the initial design had seemed risky based on two years' worth of studies, the revised plan with four times the capacity must have seemed like madness to some.

Despite the unprecedented size of the project, it was completed quickly. This was made possible by the ruler's decisiveness and facilitated by a system that allowed decisions to be implemented immediately. All this was helped by the ruler's frequent presence on the site, enabling him to keep in touch with progress and deal with any problems that arose.

Sultan Bin Sulayem describes Dubai's philosophy toward development and the role of the ports within it:

> *The philosophy the government has for Dubai is to provide facilities before the business opportunity comes. It is very critical to Dubai's expansion. We are pioneers. And if we target our business, we don't say 'I'm going to provide these facilities but you have to sign this document that you are going to use it'. This is what would happen in many countries. Not in Dubai – we take a chance. We say, if we provide facilities, opportunities will come.*

Jebel Ali Free Zone

Sheikh Rashid is regarded with reverence and admiration throughout Dubai, and his leadership set the stage for the emirate's development. An indication of the fondness Dubaians still have for Sheikh Rashid is the proliferation of anecdotes about him that are heard almost anywhere. One concerns how he identified the site where Jebel Ali Port and Jebel Ali Free Zone would be built. Apparently, he was walking on the beach and stuck his staff into the sand, declaring that spot the ideal site for the huge development. When surveyors and engineers turned up later to complete the feasibility studies they confirmed his view, and that is where the port and free zone were built. The accuracy of this story is less significant than its popularity, reinforcing the commonly held affection for him and placing the development of the Jebel Ali area in the context of Sheikh Rashid's vision for Dubai.

Jebel Ali Free Zone was established in 1985 on a site adjacent to the Jebel Ali Port. The object was to attract international investment by companies that would benefit from proximity to the port and the ability to operate independently of the UAE's employment and company ownership regulations. Freedom and ease of doing business formed the basis of the value proposition at Jebel Ali Free Zone from its earliest days. Freedom to hire whoever you like, to manage your finances and assets as you like and to set up almost any sort of enterprise you like.

Establishing a business in the zone is eased considerably by a kind of corporate concierge service, which helps investors with all aspects of setting up and operations, including obtaining permits and licences and even building premises.

The project got off to a shaky start with only 35 companies investing over the first couple of years, but the zone is now home to around 5,000 companies. According to one senior manager involved from the start, 'we evolved an industry by building an infrastructure for industry'. This infrastructure has been a big selling point for many of the investors in Jebel Ali and other free zones.

Because of UAE regulations, though, companies cannot set up shop inside the free zone to sell directly to the domestic market. A partnership with an exclusive local 'agency' is still required for that. So, for example, although Sony has a large warehouse in the free zone, it supplies a company in the Emirate of Dubai that has the exclusive local distributorship.

The import and re-export business has been a mainstay for the free zone, but the infrastructure has allowed manufacturing, services and other industries to prosper since the zone was established. Furthermore, the thousands of workers (over 90 per cent foreign, by one estimate) employed there contribute to the local economy by renting housing, using services, consuming utilities and buying from local businesses.

The free zone is another important strategic asset. It fits with the vision of transforming Dubai into a world-class commerce hub. The goods were flowing in and out of the port, and it was a natural next step to allow companies to operate freely in the same area. Since the free zone was created only after Jebel Ali port was thriving, risk was lessened, as would be expected as further assets are created over time within the scope of the expanding strategic vortex.

The free zone concept has since been used in a variety of contexts in different industry concentrations in Dubai. Some examples of this are examined later.

The Jebel Ali Free Zone is a good example of how Dubai creates assets despite apparent constraints. It also helped communicate and reinforce Sheikh Rashid's vision, focusing on making it easier for foreign companies to invest and do business in Dubai.

Emirates airline

Emirates is a young airline, established in 1985. Again, it is a strategic addition to Dubai's portfolio of assets, making a similar contribution as Singapore Airlines has made to its home country. By the mid-1980s, the ports were booming, international companies were setting up in the free zone and the economy was in good shape. The airport had been operational for a quarter of a century and was used by the regions' then-dominant airline, Gulf Air, and other international carriers.

But even though the UAE had no national airline until then, there was already airline experience in Dubai thanks to Dnata, a travel services company originally established in 1959 to provide ground handling and ticketing services. With a virtual monopoly on cargo management and ticketing, Dnata was known as an airline without any planes. Today, it is part of the government-owned Emirates Group along with the airline. Employing over 6,200 people, Dnata still manages many of the operations at Dubai International Airport and has a successful IT spin-off, Mercator.

When the government resolved to start its own airline, the management team at Dnata already had the skills to do the job. Dnata's head, Maurice Flanagan, who was on secondment from British Airways, was approached by Sheikh Mohammed and asked to start a new airline with an initial investment from the government of $10 million. It was not a lot of money with which to start an airline, particularly one which was meant to be self-sufficient and not to come back for more handouts, and which would have to compete under the airport's open-skies policy, which exposed Emirates airlines to competition from larger established airlines. However, Emirates airline has done extremely well in a very turbulent industry – for the financial year ending March 2007, the Emirates Group made a profit of US$ 942 million on group revenue of US$18.5 billion, and profits in 2008 are expected to exceed $1 billion.

In addition to the experienced management team from Dnata, Sheikh Rashid's young half-brother, Sheikh Ahmed, was appointed chairman at the age of 25. He took up the role with enthusiasm after completing his education in the West. Maurice Flanagan recalls giving him a series of tutorials on the airline industry:

> *And increasingly those tutorials turned into an equal dialogue . . .*
> *several times a week; the sort of dialogue you would expect between*
> *a very switched on, active, involved chairman and his chief*
> *executive.*

Maurice Flanagan and Sheikh Ahmed meet every week. Maurice, in a recent discussion with one of the authors, attributes the success of the airline to its Chairman, Sheikh Ahmed, diverting praise to the one who deserves it, as he puts it.

Emirates airline started with a small fleet of leased planes, and its first routes connected Dubai, Mumbai, Karachi and Delhi. Now the airline is the world's fourth most profitable non-US airline and the 21st largest in the world. Maurice Flanagan attributes much of this success to the necessity of surviving without subsidy. At the start of 2007, Emirates airline flew to 90 destinations in 59 countries. It had 103 aircraft and another 130 on order. This includes 45 super-jumbo A380s, the first of which were delivered in 2008. Even though Dubai operates under an "open skies" policy, currently more than 50 per cent of all flight movements in and out of Dubai International Airport are Emirates airline aircraft. By 2010, that figure is expected to increase to 70 per cent.

The airline's growth plans are coordinated with the government's plans to increase visitor traffic to Dubai, ensuring that as visitor numbers grow, there will be sufficient hotel rooms, seats on Emirates airline's planes and capacity at the airport. According to company communications, the demand for the increased capacity already exists: 'We don't need to create customers – they already exist, waiting for a chance to use our services. It's up to us to get the capacity and the reach in place to serve them. With its large scale investments in tourism and leisure projects in Dubai, the government is anticipating that by the year 2010 the city will play host to some 15 million visitors annually. We need to be in a position to service this gigantic growth.'[7]

When it was hatched in the mid-1980s, Emirates airline was a necessary piece of the puzzle that would help underpin Dubai's growing importance as a business centre. Over time, it has become a key component in providing access to the city as part of the larger strategy that includes the development of the tourism and business industries. (Similarly, it is worth noting the earlier establishment of Singapore Airlines and its role in helping to establish Singapore as a business and tourist hub.) Additional economic benefits are the jobs it provides and the contribution it makes to the local economy.

The airline also serves an important function as an ambassador for Dubai. Its levels of service are among the best in the world, and its approach reflects a high degree of professionalism. Emirates airline is a strategic asset that has been developed as an increasingly important component of Dubai's portfolio of assets. The ability of its managers to work together and make decisions fast has been crucial, but a large part of its success is due to the fact that it has to be profitable and competitive and does not have the umbrella of subsidy and protection that some national airlines enjoy.

Emirates airline had the advantage of starting with a blank slate. Mike Simon, Senior Vice President Corporate Communications, believes that this was a major reason for the airline's success. In building the airline from scratch, those in the initial management team (most of whom are still with Emirates airline) were able to draw on their experience and avoid mistakes they'd seen made in the past.

The experience available to Emirates airline was not limited to its management expertise. The history of immigration and trade with the Indian subcontinent made routes connecting with Pakistan and India obvious early choices for Emirates airline, with every chance of the airline being able to run those services at close to full capacity. So the risk involved in creating the airline was reduced by building on the existing platform of collective industry experience and a strong knowledge of the initial markets. Similar logic has more recently played out as Emirates airline has recently begun flying to Houston to take advantage of traffic related to the oil and gas industry. Yet another example of how Emirates airline continuously seeks ways to lower the risk of expansion.

Palm Jumeirah, Palm Jebel Ali, Palm Deira, The World and the Waterfront

There is no better illustration of asset creation today than the Palms: three palm-tree-shaped islands being built up from the sea bed off the coast of Dubai. The project reflects all the hallmarks of strategic asset creation: thorough planning, rapid execution, groundbreaking scope, flexible parameters and hands-on leadership. It's part of the government's plan to lure increasing numbers of tourists.

Visible from space, the landmasses and the crescent-shaped breakwaters that protect them are taking shape in the Gulf as the world's largest dredgers help construct the islands from rock and sand. When complete, the Palm Jebel Ali and Palm Jumeirah will have thousands of full-time residents, around 80 hotels by top hotel chains, sports, leisure and shopping areas, and over 12,000 palm trees. The cost of land reclamation, infrastructure and landscaping is estimated to be around $3 billion for both islands (not including private or commercial building development).

The project grew out of a need for more beaches for the increasing numbers of sun-seeking tourists. Among the ideas for adding to the coastline was extending the landmass into a series of islands. As this concept evolved, it began to take on the shape of a palm tree. These Palms will lengthen the coastline from 72 kilometres to 192 kilometres, an increase of 166 per cent. The Jumeirah Palm will measure about five kilometres in length and width, and the Jebel Ali Palm will extend about two kilometres further along each dimension. Each also a crescent breakwater providing shelter from the open sea and more space for development. The Jumeirah Palm's breakwater measures about 11 kilometres in length and Jebel Ali Palm's measures about 15 kilometres.

A land reclamation project of this magnitude had never been attempted before, and the government of Dubai wasn't about to take any chances. So 50 separate studies were completed by 42 different consulting firms to investigate the feasibility of the project and the implications for the environment and economy of the region. Once the results were in after four years of planning and study, Sheikh Mohammed announced the project in May 2001. Construction of Palm Jumeirah began the following month.

Sultan Bin Sulayem led the conception and development of the first Palm project, and he is now Chairman of Dubai World, the government-owned holding company that manages the Palm developments and other mega-projects. He explains how they approached the inherent risk in a project of this magnitude:

> *We prepared all the ingredients for success before we started. But speed is very important. Because opportunities are true only if you catch them at the right time. Otherwise, you might be ready, but people will not be interested. So we took risks. But we believe there are always bigger opportunities when you take risks. And if there's no risk at all, everybody is doing it.*

Sultan Bin Sulayem is talking about the Palms, but also, more generally, about Dubai's approach to risk. With his responsibilities extending across all of Dubai's ports, free zones and customs operations as well as the development of the Palms, he might be expected to sit behind a desk and rarely make an appearance in the field. But this couldn't be further from the truth. He is a frequent visitor to the Palm sites to check progress, and he even learned to scuba dive in order to be able to inspect the progress of the geotextiles that make up the new landmasses. On a late-night excursion to one of the sites, on his own in a small boat, he found that the landfill had progressed further than he'd expected. The boat became stuck and he only narrowly escaped being blasted by one of the computer-controlled nozzles that shoot sand into place using satellite guidance.

Sultan Bin Sulayem's close involvement with the project has allowed it to evolve and change as it goes along. The first release of 2,000 residences on Palm Jumeirah sold out within three weeks while the designs were still on the drawing board. When the initial designs were completed they were criticized, so, despite the engineers' protests, he had them changed.

The initial plans did not include building all the residences; plots were to be sold and buyers would be responsible for building their own homes. Sultan Bin Sulayem began to have second thoughts about this while staying in a development in California. The undeveloped plots were unsightly, and the noise of one-off building projects here and there was a nuisance. Based on this experience, he recommended to Sheikh Mohammed that an additional phase be put in place in which all the residences would be built.

The ability to be connected to the day-to-day progress of the project and make decisions fast is a crucial element of success for Sultan Bin Sulayem, and one reason the time required to execute large projects like this can be compressed:

> *When you collect all the information on a project, then you have some control on your destiny. You have some control on timing. You have some control on success. And that is what we do on every project.*

And how are the decisions made? Easily, according to Sultan Bin Sulayem:

We are not bureaucratic on the Palm Island project. We only need a few people to make any decision. With any tender, I do the analysis with a finance person and my engineers, then we take the recommendation to Sheikh Mohammed. It takes me ten minutes. I tell him, 'This is the project, these are the costs, this is the timing and this is our recommendation.' And he says, 'Go ahead.' His go-ahead is verbal. Then we do it, and we do it fast. If we have to make a change, we do it. I have total authority – if everything has to come to somebody, we'll never finish.

This method seems to be effective. The first keys were handed over to Palm Jumeirah villa owners at the end of 2006, and 'certificates of completion' for all 4,000 villas and apartments on the development have been handed over by mid-2007.

The creation of the Palms has strategic value for Dubai as a tourist attraction in itself, in addition to the individual hotels, restaurants, shops and leisure facilities that will be built on the islands. It will also provide thousands of beach-front residences for the growing population of Dubai residents, now including expatriates, who until recently were not allowed to own property.

The government is funding the project, along with the UAE and international banks, assuming substantial risk, not only financial, to develop an asset from which many sectors of the economy will benefit. In one go, the project more than doubles Dubai's beach area, adds housing, entertainment, leisure, sports and retail facilities, and, most importantly, adds another superlative asset to Dubai's existing portfolio.

The project management and decision-making processes are similar to those that have been used in other large-scale projects. Management is involved at all levels and is able to make decisions immediately, thus avoiding the chance of any problems that arise getting out of control or delaying progress.

When the Palm Jebel Ali was announced, it might have seemed over-the-top, coming as it did right on the heels of the Palm Jumeirah. But Dubai was not about to stop there. These two developments will be joined by The World, the Palm Deira, and Dubai Waterfront – each of these developments more impressive than the last. Each of these developments is by Nakheel Properties, which is owned by the Dubai government.

The World is a series of 300 man-made islands in the shape of the world's continents situated off the coast of Dubai, near the Palm Jumeirah. The development will create an additional 232 kilometres of coastline. Land reclamation is due to be complete in 2008, after which time construction can begin. Some islands will be available for private development; others are being developed as exclusive resorts, and some will have 'community' amenities. The islands will only be accessible via marine or air transport.

One early investor in the project is developing Oqyana across the 19 islands that represent Australia and New Zealand. Due to be complete in 2012, the development is expected to cost upwards of $3.5 billion and will accommodate 10–12 thousand people in a variety of building types. Two hotels and a spa are also planned.

The third and largest of Palm developments is the Palm Deira, announced in 2004. When complete in 2015, it is expected to have 8,000 residential villas, plus retail, sports facilities, clubs, and various public services and amenities.[8] The development will cover 80 square miles with its trunk, 41 fronds, and surrounding breakwater.[9]

Nakheel Properties has also set its sights on the neighbouring mainland and plans to extend the land mass out past the Palm Jebel Ali – but it also plans to bring water inland. The Dubai Waterfront development will create a series of six new islands that extend from the mainland out and partially around the Palm Jebel Ali. Much of the development, though, centred around the 70-kilometre Arabian Canal which is being built in the desert adjacent to the coastline.

This project will extend the Dubai coastline a further 820 kilometres and will cover over 81 million square metres. As planned, the project will purportedly represent the world's largest man-made development. The project has been divided into ten distinct zones, each of which will feature a variety of developments. The prime beachfront area called Madinat Al Arab will also feature the Al Burj, tower which, at 750 metres, will be taller still than the Burj Dubai.[10]

Just as we thought the four major Nakheel land reclamation projects were huge, then comes the fifth and largest of their projects, the Waterfront, which dwarfs all of the other projects put together. It is projected to be three to four times the size of Hong Kong and projects a community of over one million inhabitants!

In the context of other developments in Dubai over recent years, the Palms seem to fit in naturally. But imagine if those running your organization were able to cast aside any perceived limitations (like a limited coastline, or the daunting prospect of manufacturing a small city on mounds of sand in the ocean). What breakthroughs might result?

New free zones

One of the earliest of these is Dubai Knowledge Village, which was set up to provide a base for universities and training organizations. Since its launch in 2003, the site has been filled almost to capacity, with 15 international universities and over 150 other companies specializing in training, development, and related disciplines. In 2005, some of the universities running programmes at Dubai Knowledge Village included Middlesex University, European University College Brussels, and Mahatma Gandhi University. The amenities within Dubai Knowledge Village seem to be tailor-made to serve a student population, including KFC (fried chicken), Subway (sandwiches), and Starbucks. The popularity of Dubai Knowledge Village led to the announcement in 2005 of Dubai Knowledge Universities, which is slated to house 30 international universities and over 40,000 students on a 24.8 million square foot campus.[11]

Dubai Healthcare City was launched as 'the world's first health care free zone' to provide facilities for disease treatment, prevention, and wellness. The first phase focuses on disease treatment and prevention. This phase will encompass 4.1 million square feet, and healthcare organizations from around the world are expected to be attracted. The anchor of this development is the Harvard Medical School Dubai Center, which is 'part of the Government of Dubai's mission to develop DHCC into a center of excellence for health care delivery, medical education, and research', providing state-of-the art facilities. One of the authors was fortunate enough to be driven through the area on a very hot August evening and saw first hand how this ecosystem actually works.

Dubai Outsource Zone is yet another initiative to fall under the Dubai Holding umbrella. Opened in 2004, it was established to take advantage of the rapidly-developing knowledge economy in the emirate. And while initial sceptics questioned the competitiveness of Dubai as an outsourcing hub relative to Bangalore, the experiment seems to be a success in 2007, with 72 companies operating in the zone.

The Dubai International Media Production Zone was established to serve as a traditional media counterpart to the DMC, focusing on the 'three Ps' – publishing, printing, and packaging on a 43 million square feet site. The first phase of the development was slated to open in 2007.[12]

Another initiative was launched in 2005: DuBiotech, the world's first free zone dedicated to the Life Science industry. It applies the free zone model to biotechnology, with facilities for private companies and a government-funded R&D facility.[13]

The DIFC addresses the need for a stable, well-regulated financial centre in the region, bridging the gap between western hubs in New York and London and eastern hubs in Tokyo and Hong Kong. This unique position allows the DIFC to serve the Middle East region, North Africa, the Caspian States, and the Indian subcontinent –

representing a third of the world's population with a GDP of $1.5 trillion. Moreover, Dubai and DIFC are continuing to expand their ambitions by focusing on broader parts of Asia, in particular China, with its own enormous growth potential. In 2002, construction began on the 110-acre (44.6-hectare) site adjacent to the Emirates Towers complex just behind the gleaming high-rise office buildings lining Sheikh Zayed Road. The centre opened for business in 2004, and in 2008, financial institutions based at the DIFC included Merrill Lynch, Lloyds TSB, Credit Suisse, Morgan Stanley, HSBC, Standard Chartered, Goldman Sachs and Deutsche Bank to name but a few of the over 300 licensed entities (expected by the end of 2008).

The financial centre model is based on the core values of 'integrity, transparency and simplicity', with the aim of creating a dynamic hub for institutional finance and a nexus for capital investment in the region. An important ingredient of the Dubai International Financial Centre is its regulatory framework. Recognizing this, the Dubai Financial Services Authority (DFSA) was established to enforce laws and regulations based on best practices worldwide such as the UK's Financial Services and Markets Act of 2000.

These systems were put to the test early, with issues in 2004 that resulted in the high-profile departure of two senior regulators. Many have put it down to a cultural misunderstanding, but the DIFC proceeded full steam ahead since then and has overcome this initial early setback. Dubai's leadership stepped in as it quickly recognized the importance of an independent regulator and judiciary. The DFSA was strengthened with senior representations from around the world which reflects the international customer base. It proceeded further with hiring a world class executive team and in turn a world class institution has been built, giving confidence to existing and potential customers. The independent judiciary started operations in early 2007 with the DIFC court hearing its first case with a Singaporean judge and the court headed by a senior UK legal figure. The centre is overseen by its Governor, Dr Omar bin Sulaiman, who acts as Sheikh Mohammed's representative, Sheikh Mohammed being the DIFC's President.

The first phase of development included The Gate, which houses the DIFC's headquarters, the DFSA, and offices flagship financial institutions. Subsequent phases include leisure, education, residential and even art and cultural facilities. The entire area will be linked with pedestrian walkways lined by parks, public spaces and retail arcades.[14] As you enter the impressive very high ceilings of the Gate, one is struck by how modern and international this operation must be. The walls are adorned with contemporary modern art from around the world, as well as many regional works of art. In addition, buzzing coffee shops surround the reception area and you can start to see what lies ahead once it is fully developed.

A possible insight into the future of DIFC was garnered from a conversation one of the authors was having in October 2007 with Mohammad Al Gergawi (seen as the person that Sheikh Mohammed entrusted in 2004 to take charge of making the DIFC the success that it is today) about the evolution of Dubai. It should be noted that the growth of DIFC follows our model of government stepping in to put the pieces of the puzzle in place and then stepping back and letting things develop. As Mohammad looked out of his Emirates Towers office window at Sheikh Mohammed's Executive Office and saw DIFC's Gate building, he suggested walking over for a coffee and having the meeting there, rather than at his office. It was early evening, and as they crossed into the open terraces connecting some of DIFC's buildings, they passed the following people in a span of less than 100 metres: the Executive Chairman of Dubai Group (part of Dubai Holding) having coffee with members of his team, the head of a leading multinational consulting group, the chairman of a large US investment bank, and then a group of London Business School Executive MBA participants on their way out of class.

Along the way, shops passed included Borders (large US bookstore), Starbucks, Boots (the UK chemist/pharmacy), a large gym full to capacity opposite the DIFC Courts, restaurants full to capacity and an art exhibition, but to name a few; a few minutes later, on the walk back to the office they were joined for a coffee by DIFC's Governor. After seeing all of this, Mohammad Al Gergawi said, "this is why DIFC cannot be replicated anywhere else in the region and this is why Dubai is distinguishably Dubai." This is a very poignant point – replicating Dubai's success is not just creating new buildings – it is also replicating the intellectual assets and relationships that exist inside these buildings and throughout Dubai!

Dubai Silicon Oasis (DSO) was announced in the autumn of 2002, with construction planned to begin in 2003. The development will cover 7.2 million square metres in the Nad Al Sheba district. The zone's ambitious goal is to become 'the world's foremost centre of Silicon Intellectual Property creation and knowledge through high technology initiatives'. At a cost approaching $1.3 billion,[15] it is the world's first purpose-built industrial park dedicated to the semiconductor industry. It is planned to house businesses from all parts of the semiconductor value chain and related industries, including semiconductor foundries, integrated device manufacturers, design and testing facilities, and research institutes. Hundreds of residential units are also within the complex.

While adding a high-value manufacturing industry to Dubai's

portfolio, this project is also expected to provide educational opportunities for hundreds of UAE nationals over the first ten years through a combination of work experience and programmes at affiliated universities.

The DSO's development is staged over about 20 years, but it is off to a running start: during the first quarter of 2006, the DSO had issued licenses to around 20 companies, and upwards of 30 were expected by year end.[16] When complete, the DSO is expected to contribute around 10 per cent to Dubai's GDP.[17]

In addition, the government of Dubai is developing further free zones to grow existing industries. The textile industry, already a major contributor to Dubai's GDP, will be modernized through Dubai Textiles City, a $60 million initiative being developed in conjunction with an industry body based in the emirate. This free zone will provide space for 250 units for companies involved in all aspects of the textile and garment trade.

Dubai Maritime City is another free zone initiative intended to develop a major shipbuilding industry in the emirate building on Dubai's rich history as a shipping centre and its current powerhouse status as a port. Dredging for the 25 million square foot peninsula that will house the zone began in 2003.

And finally, the Dubai Aerospace Enterprise (DAE) was established in 2006. While still in its early stages of development, this $15 billion initiative has created subsidiaries to address a wide range of needs in the aerospace industry: DAE Capital will focus on aircraft leasing; DAE Manufacturing will conduct R&D, manufacturing, and assembly; DAE Airports will provide airport development and operations expertise; DAE Engineering will provide aviation maintenance services; and DAE Services will provide related consulting services. Additionally, DAE University will create an aviation school for all levels of education, attracting students from around the world.[18] This initiative in particular seems to be a good fit with Dubai's established capabilities in developing and running airports, and with biennial Dubai Airshow. During the most recent Dubai Airshow in late 2007, DAE stunned the world with the size of its first order for over $27 billion for 200 aircraft – 100 aircraft each from Airbus and Boeing.

Mixed use developments

The 700-metre-plus Burj Dubai is part of Emaar Properties' Downtown Dubai development. In addition to the skyscraper, which includes an Armani hotel, the Downtown Dubai complex has nine further towers containing luxury freehold apartments, several smaller residential buildings designed in a 'traditional' architectural style in the 'Old Town' zone, and a series of residential 'lofts'. Additionally, the

Burj Dubai Mall will contain various retail and leisure facilities in what is expected to be the world's largest shopping mall, covering nine million square feet in total.

Perhaps the most ambitious development is the government-owned Dubailand, which will include tourist destinations, hotels, residential properties, entertainment venues, leisure facilities, and retail on a site covering three billion square feet. The first of four building phases will be complete in 2010, and the final phase is scheduled for completion in 2020. The development is separated into five distinct 'worlds'[19]:

• Attractions and Experience World (including Falcon City of Wonders, which reproduces ancient and current major world landmarks; an indoor ski area, and other attractions)
• Sports and Outdoor World (with an 'autodrome', various sporting venues, a golf course, and an 'extreme sports world')
• Eco-Tourism World (with three announced developments – Dubai Heritage Vision, Pet Land, and Sand Dune Hotel – but few other available details)
• Themed Leisure and Vacation World (with themed destinations including Andalusian Resort and Spa, LEMNOS (Women's World), and Thai Express Resort)
• Downtown, Retail, and Entertainment World (including various themed retail developments and a further development called Teen World)

In addition, Dubailand will feature the Mall of Arabia, which is expected to be larger still than the Dubai Mall.

Creating the key ingredients
A number of elements emerged in Silicon Valley that many believe were essential to its growth. They were introduced in chapter 3 and revisited in the context of Singapore in chapter 4.

A supply of workers
As in Singapore, Dubai had little to work with at the start, apart from a trading culture, a willing population and strong leadership. These three components remain important. One of the principal selling points of Dubai's free zones has been the freedom to bring in workers without complex immigration regulations. But although the free zones offer benefits, such as 100 per cent ownership for foreign firms, which are not allowed outside the zones, it appears to be reasonably easy to get a work visa with the promise of employment for most foreigners. The difference inside the free zone is that the 'concierge' service helps with and fast-tracks this process. Inside the zone or outside, foreigners are

not welcome in Dubai if they are not working or making a positive contribution to Dubai's economy.

Nevertheless, most companies setting up in Dubai must bring in skilled workers from abroad, simply because the indigenous pool of talent is too limited. One of the value-added services provided by Dubai Internet City is assistance in recruiting. Recognizing the importance of bringing in outsiders to fill posts, the government of Dubai actively promotes the cosmopolitan, liveable qualities of the area – as well as the tax benefits – to entice skilled workers to move there.

Dubai has also been able to draw on a pool of labour that many neighbouring areas can not, will not, or have been slow to use: women. Female UAE nationals and foreigners alike are welcomed into the workforce with a degree of freedom virtually unheard of elsewhere in the region. Apart from the cultural and historical reasons that were discussed earlier, the government actively encourages women to take part in the economy. Indeed, women are assuming increasingly important roles in the public and private sectors, in ever greater numbers. In addition to proactive government initiatives geared towards creating opportunities for women, prominent businesswomen such as Anita Mehra Homayoun, Raja Easa Al Gurg and Sheikha Lubna Al Qasimi make a point of acting as role models. They are now joined by a new cache of women playing their part in Dubai's success story. This trend is also evident in the public sector; in the latest cabinet reshuffle, four women were named to the cabinet – a clear message of the importance of engaging women. The authors believe that the leadership of Dubai in their support of and energetic encouragement of women as part of Dubai's growth is a key component in the success of the Dubai model, which will become even more apparent in the fullness of time.

One of the authors, who frequently visits Dubai and was privileged to attend some high level strategy meetings, observed the increasing number of young, educated, hard working and aspiring UAE females in the work force, at all levels. These women at times formed half of the participants, and had an understandable edge over non-nationals concerning insights on cultural matters, getting their points across in an effective, inclusive invariably discreet manner. This cultural almost "shyness" should not be confused with the determination to get things "done". "Done" being a word that's becoming synonymous with the Emirate of Dubai's spirit of getting things activated and achieved. When asking someone to do something, the swift "done" answer can be both disarming and effective, of course as long as things do get done! A visible change since the first edition of this book when written in 2002 is the increase in the number of women in the work place at all levels.

The Silicon Valley model assumes that attracting sufficient intellectual capital is the challenge that must be overcome; Dubai seems to be doing just fine in this category for now, it is clear that it must continue to draw and attract talent in order to achieve all that it wants to do in the coming years. Instead, Dubai has had to struggle with the problem of its unskilled workers. Numbering in the many thousands, these workers remain largely invisible to many in Dubai from day to day. Then around a thousand of them stepped out of the shadows to protest not being paid by a contractor to one of the Palm developments. The protest on a main thoroughfare in Dubai tied up traffic for miles and at once created the rare public-relations challenge for Dubai. Dubai recognizing the importance of this growing pain, dealt immediately with the issue by establishing minimum standards for labourers and sending out a clear message that it expects these standards to be followed.

Early adopters and lead users
Another essential ingredient is the presence of early adopters and lead users in the economic ecosystem. The US military filled this role in Silicon Valley, and large government-linked companies in Singapore did so in that country. This is not dissimilar from the approach in Dubai, with the large projects undertaken by the government. The big difference is that the government of Dubai sets out to break records and explore uncharted territory. Then it invites competitors from around the world to get on with the work.

By setting high standards and assuming risk too great for any private enterprise, the government drives innovation and attracts the best of the best to figure out how to meet its ambitious goals. The Palms development is an obvious example. The scale and timeframe of the project are unprecedented, so the engineers and designers have had to stretch their existing capabilities and develop new ones to get the job done. These new capabilities will remain in Dubai after the project is completed, augmenting the experience of local contractors who work with the foreign firms enlisted to do the work.

Service infrastructure and complementary organizations
These elements lead naturally to the creation of two more key ingredients: a service infrastructure and a network of complementary organizations. A business network has been in place and growing for over half a century in Dubai because of its strength as a natural port and its pro-trade policies. The stimulus the government has provided for the creation of new industries has also resulted in entirely new networks.

In the construction industry, architectural and engineering firms are often brought in from abroad to design and manage large projects, but the rest of the capabilities required seem to come from a growing pool of local providers.[20] The equestrian industry also shows how a sophisticated web of supporting and complementary providers can emerge in response to a developing market.

Within the free zones, a network of businesses has formed to support the variety of industries within them. In the Jebel Ali Free Zone, for example, there are all manner of logistics and shipping equipment supplies and services, providing businesses with a wide choice of suppliers for virtually anything they require. Services inside the zone include a chamber of commerce, international banks, insurance companies, consultancies and real estate firms. Essentially, everything an investor might need lies within the gates of the free zone. The ease of setting up business in the free zone and market requirements have clearly contributed to the creation of this robust business ecosystem, but the Jebel Ali Free Zone Authority also makes a point of helping its investors, satisfying any need that might arise. In many ways its role within the free zone is similar to that of Singapore's Economic Development Board.

Networks like these are also developing rapidly within the newer free zones. In Dubai Internet City, for example, more business seems to be conducted among the companies inside the zone than with outside customers and suppliers. Companies such as Microsoft and IBM, in particular, work hard to develop suppliers and partners inside Dubai Internet City.[21] Tejari.com, a home-grown business-to-business exchange kicked off by a government initiative, is based in Dubai Media City. The company works with many suppliers inside Dubai Media City and Dubai Internet City (both part of the same free zone area). Sheikha Lubna, the company's initial CEO, attributes much of the success of the business network to the free zone's management, which actively tries to get companies together to develop business.

Venture capital, local universities and R&D
The remaining two ingredients, a dynamic venture capital environment and world class local universities and R&D, have been slower to emerge in Dubai. But government initiatives starting from around 2000 onwards have been under way to overcome these shortcomings.

The heretofore relatively unsophisticated financial markets in the UAE have produced little venture capital to fuel entrepreneurial growth. Although the entrepreneurial tradition in the region dates back to the earliest days of traders along the Creek, ventures have been financed by organic growth and the reinvestment of profits. Thus trading families that became wealthy during the middle of the 20th century have become involved in new industries and in the last few years have been joined by new entrants, some of whom became wealthy out of being in Dubai over the years, from all nationalities although those from the region (including the important Indian sub-continent) dominate, and more recently newcomers from all parts of the world. Nevertheless, trade remains a mainstay for many of them. There has also been little incentive to enter the venture capital market because of the absence of the straightforward exit route, something that most venture capitalists would expect.

Recognizing these difficulties, the government established a $190 million fund as part of the Mohammed Bin Rashid Establishment for Young Business Leaders to help young entrepreneurs get businesses off the ground. The programme offered incubator-like services, including advice, connectivity, premises, training and a network of recommended suppliers. This was only a drop in the ocean, of course, but it was most likely the precursor to the substantially greater, highly visible and influential Mohammed Bin Rashid Foundation, with its massive US$10 billion capital base, which was launched in 2007. Although the DIFC is focusing on attracting institutional investors, the resulting emergence of Dubai as an international financial centre can also be expected to pave the way for the growth of a local dynamic venture capital industry, as awareness, sophistication and comfort levels grow. The question that remains is whether there is room in Dubai for the true grass-roots entrepreneur when it seems that a project must be a Guinness record contender to attract attention.

Lastly, the government of Dubai has recognized the importance of creating local top-class universities and centres for research and development. And towards this end, Dubai Knowledge Village and Dubai Knowledge Universities have been developed, with dozens of international universities and industry-focused training organizations taking up residence. But advanced learning opportunities will not be limited to these programmes; Dubai Healthcare City, Dubai Aerospace Enterprise, Dubai International Financial Centre, and Dubai Silicon Oasis are all integrating educational programmes into their business models. An example of this is London Business School (LBS), one of the world's top graduate business schools, launched in 2007 at the DIFC (an oversubscribed) Executive MBA program in Dubai, with participants from 32 nationalities and almost 20 per cent women. This is a great example of one of the world's top MBA programmes bringing their own world class faculty to teach some of the brightest rising stars in the region and beyond, importantly, doing so in both Dubai and London. In its early days, the program seems like a strong win for both sides, a "win-win" as Dubai would say. It is these types of partnerships that will allow Dubai and the partners they choose to continue to flourish together in delivering on their respective global education aspirations. However, it should be noted that to create such successful ventures, both partners must have a similar approach to risk-taking, but even more importantly similar aspirations for all the dimensions of success for the joint undertaking. At the same time, both partners must realize their comparative advantages to make these partnerships truly work – Dubai providing the environment for growth and exposure to new opportunities, and the partner bringing world class skills to a new market with real commitment to the ventures' sustainable success.

Despite these innovative educational ventures, one of the most significant transfers of knowledge to the local population takes place in the workplace. Attracting the world's most innovative companies, and individuals, to Dubai allows UAE nationals to work alongside and learn from skilled workers from abroad.

In all these cases, the government has developed the principal components for growth and then allowed them to develop naturally. When more capital is made available for entrepreneurs and appropriate facilities for higher education and research and development are created in Dubai, the emirate's portfolio of assets will be complete and will be able to fuel further the momentum of the strategic vortex.

It should be noted that the actions of Dubai further enhance the strategic vortex at two levels. At the more macro level, Dubai creates these bold strategic partnerships with world class institutions that will bring in new skills, such as London Business School (in DIFC) or Harvard Medical School (in Healthcare City) or The Harvard Kennedy School of Government (presently located at Dubai World Trade Centre). Dubai launches these ventures with their partners ensuring that their leadership, which often includes Sheikh Mohammed, which obviously attracts much media attention, is present at the main launch event. This has three important implications. First, it signals to the new partner how seriously Dubai takes the relationship; second, it signals to the local market that Dubai's leadership is very much behind the initiative and third it signals to the world that Dubai is "open for business" and actively growing in this area.

At the more micro level, Dubai's actions also further enhance the strategic vortex. For example, by creating a partnership with, by way of example, London Business School to offer an Executive MBA, participants have come from throughout the region and beyond (from North America, Asia, Africa and Europe) to enrol in the program. These participants will enrich the local economy through spending money in hotels, restaurants and when time allows, shopping too! In addition, in the process of obtaining the degree, people from throughout the region may be further exposed to the dynamic business cultures and opportunities within Dubai and choose to do business with Dubai or in some cases relocate there at some point or go back to their home countries and spread the word about Dubai. Thus, these strategic partnerships are important at multiple levels and timeframes, and are an important element of Dubai in growing the strategic vortex.

ENDNOTES

1   eBay 2006 annual report
2   www.ebay.com
3   'Auctioneers ready for prime time?', *Inter@ctive Week*, 9 February 1998, Vol. 5, Issue 5, p. 53
4   Goals for Dubai's Vision 2010 provided by The Executive Office
5   Di Justo, D. 'Manhattan Projects', *Wired*, December 2006, pp. 52–53
6   Description of the creation of Port Rashid summarized from Wilson, G., *Father of Dubai*
7   From Emirates website at mediacentre.ekgroup.com/home.asp?TYPE=FAQS
8   From Al Nakheel website at www.nakheel.ae/Developments/The_Palm/The_Palm_ Deira/
9   From the property website The Emirates Network at www.theemiratesnetwork.com
10 From the property website The Emirates Network at www.theemiratesnetwork.com
11 From Dubai Knowledge Village website at www.kv.ae
12 From IMPZ website at www.impz.ae/about-impz/about-impz.html
13 From DuBiotech website at www.dubiotech.ae
14 From DIFC website at www.difc.ae
15 Russell, E., 'Dubai Silicon Oasis Moves Step Further to Completion,' The Competitiveness Institute, 19 June 2005, from www.competitiveness.org/article/ view/595/1/9
16 'Dubai Silicon Oasis aims for 30 firms by year-end' in *Emirates Today*, 13 March 2006
17 Smallay, B., 'Dubai Silicon Oasis', *Al Shindagah*, Jan–Feb 2004
18 From Dubai Aerospace Enterprise website at www.dubaiaerospace.com/ca5.html
19 From the property website The Emirates Network at www.theemiratesnetwork.com
20 From an interview with Charles Neil, Dubai International Financial Centre
21 From an interview with Ahmad Bin Byat

Dubai Creek in the 1970s.

Dubai Creek now.

Jumeirah Beach in the 1960s: an oil storage construction facility at the time.

Jumeirah Beach now: the Jumeirah Beach Hotel and the taller Burj Al Arab.

Dubai World Trade Centre in the 1970s.

Dubai World Trade Centre now.

Dubai International Airport in the 1970s.

Dubai International Airport now.

Dubai and the Creek in the 1960s.

Al Maktoum International Airport, the main part of Dubai World Central, showing the six parallel runways.

CHAPTER 6

ASSET ACCELERATION

We must use time as a tool, not as a couch.

John F. Kennedy

The next phase in the strategic trajectory model is asset acceleration. Less tangible and less obvious perhaps than the other components of the model, this phase might be compared to elastic potential energy in the study of physics. It can be described as the coiling of a spring, which creates increasing amounts of potential energy as it is compressed. The energy is realized when the spring is released.

Assets can create the potential for a huge burst of commercial activity when conditions reach the right point. This acceleration can happen in many ways and at many levels. The announcement of a new product can create demand that results in the product selling out on its launch.

On a larger scale, tourism in Dubai has grown hugely over the past decade through a combination of many assets: hotels, attractions, Emirates airline and Dubai International Airport, as well as clever marketing and great service. In either example, it is important to recognize the management role. The product might have sold out without the pre-launch marketing, and Dubai's tourism industry might have grown on its own, without careful coordination and marketing. But to achieve dramatic asset acceleration, a catalyst must be introduced and managed.

In the context of the strategic vortex, it is important to remember that the acceleration of one asset will depend on the state of the business ecosystem at the time it is introduced, so a new asset will benefit from the base assets and the synergies that already exist. The greater the size of the assets in play, the greater is the risk; but risk can be mitigated as the strategic vortex develops. Some risk might also be avoided by relying instead on a slower and less predictable organic route to growth.

This concept becomes clearer when regarded as a precursor to the next phase – asset leverage – where explosive growth is realized. In Dubai, there has been one prominent factor and three aspects of strong leadership that have enabled such explosive growth. Persuading people and companies from all over the world to come to Dubai has had a natural acceleration effect on its own, stimulating competition, learning and collaboration. The leadership has created an environment that allows acceleration to happen by instilling confidence at every level, replacing regulation wherever possible with mutual trust and balancing control with freedom of action.

Aspects of asset acceleration

Welcoming the world

Inviting outsiders into Dubai, which has few natural resources, makes sense. In a region where many view foreigners with a degree of suspicion, Dubai has long taken a contrary view, believing the presence of outsiders helps trade thrive. This is reflected in the population of the emirate, where fewer than one in five are UAE citizens.

By welcoming the involvement of foreigners, Dubai's economy has benefited in many ways. High-profile projects have attracted a wide range of skills to the area, and Dubai is now a recognized source for highly skilled workers and managers in specific areas of expertise such as construction. Their skills may have been developed abroad, but they have been honed on cutting-edge, fast-track commercial and residential building projects. These projects involved top-class companies from around the world, which competed keenly for the chance to participate. An example is the pioneering Palm Jumeirah development, as Sultan Bin Sulayem explains: 'It's unique. Everybody wants to be involved in something historic.' The dredgers needed for the massive earth works, for example, were brought from the Netherlands.

Historic or not, the accumulation of skills combines with best practices from around the world to benefit further development. UP Tower, a 54-storey residential building on Sheikh Zayed Road, was completed in less than 18 months despite numerous technical challenges and was fully occupied by the time of its opening. A fast-track process was used for construction, allowing a floor to be completed every three days during the most productive periods. As well as the extremely tight completion deadline, further difficulties were introduced by the small 30 x 30 metre footprint allowed for the structure, making it one of the slimmest skyscrapers in the UAE. To overcome these constraints, contractors used fast-track building techniques that were introduced to Dubai during the building of the neighbouring Emirates Towers complex. Elements of the structure were redesigned and many were pre-made offsite. The importance of cooperation and coordination among the multitude of contractors on a project of this size meant that hundreds of skilled engineers, construction workers and other specialists were able to learn new techniques, which they could then use on future projects.[1]

The high proportion of expatriates helps create and reinforce high standards, as Ahmad Bin Byat, (Director General of Dubai Technology, Electronic Commerce and Media Free Zone and Secretary General of Dubai Executive Council), explains:

> *You come here for access to talent. This is one of our key successes. It's a melting pot of good and very skilled people. Even if he's a cleaner, he's going to be the very best because he wouldn't be here otherwise.*

A glance across the senior management teams of Dubai's leading corporations shows how extensively these organizations rely on international managers; but this can be a double-edged sword. The two senior regulators who departed from the DIFC in 2004 were both British, and one had recently retired from the Bank of England. While the CVs of incoming executives may seem to fit the bill precisely, those doing the hiring will need to remember that success and experience in one culture may not necessarily imply the same sense of discipline and, or of doing business in another.

Because of the high mobility of the immigrant workforce, it's very competitive, and unemployed people cannot remain in Dubai unless they are contributing to the economy in other recognized ways. This may seem harsh, but it acts as another force in raising and maintaining standards. Dubai's agency laws were designed to help bring outside expertise and investment to the emirate. By requiring foreign investors to take on a local partner owning at least 51 per cent of the business, the regulations appear to have accomplished their initial goals.

Local traders have learned much from their partners, and many have grown wealthy in the process. Raja Easa Al Gurg's family business based its early success on working with foreign investors in this way, but now she finds opportunities elsewhere, particularly in the free zones, which are attracting a new breed of wholly owned multinational competitors:

> *We are learning from the free zone enterprises because they're new, and whenever anything new comes, you have to consider what the impact on your business will be. We can't just depend on the companies for whom we are agents.*

The accelerating effects of opening Dubai to the world are readily apparent in the free zones. In Dubai Internet City and Dubai Media City, over 1,000 companies were licensed in their first two years, and this figure more than doubled five years later as the zones neared capacity. The creation of these early knowledge-based free zones had an accelerating effect more generally as they paved the way for more zones based on the same model focusing on myriad other sectors – including academics, biotech, electronics, print media, and others.

The open-skies policy has helped to attract airlines from all over the world and encouraged the growth of the existing airport, the spawning of the new mega-airport, and expansion of Emirates airline.

In the hotel industry, the growing trade in tourism and conferences has attracted investment from the world's leading chains. This has led to new hotels popping up all over Dubai, many of the most outstanding examples are being developed within the major projects like the Palms, Dubai Marina, and Dubailand.

Instilling confidence at every level

Throughout the strategic trajectory model, leadership plays an important part. For asset acceleration, one component of leadership is instilling confidence. This works on several levels: the individual, the organization and the business ecosystem.

Seemingly impossible deadlines are invariably met because the ruler gives those in charge of projects the confidence to do it. Now Dubai's UAE Minister of Foreign Trade, Sheikha Lubna describes her experience of the e-government project and the Tejari.com exchange earlier in her career:

> When Sheikh Mohammed gave us 18 months to launch the
> e-government portal and two months to launch the exchange, I was
> so scared I couldn't tell him. It was a public announcement. But I
> had a great confidence boost because of him. He developed that in
> me. He pushed me beyond my boundaries.

Sheikh Mohammed confirms his strategy, stressing the importance of remaining at arm's length:

> I give people the confidence to complete a project, but they can't
> succeed if I'm standing right on top of them. Leadership is giving
> people the courage to succeed themselves.

How can Dubai's leadership instil this confidence? The key seems to be that people must have genuine confidence in the leaders. When Emirates Group's Maurice Flanagan explains the fast growth of the airline and airport, he reinforces this point:

> *Because of Sheikh Mohammed and Sheikh Ahmed, it all happens
> at a pace you would not find anywhere else in the world. It needs
> that push, and probably more than anything else, absolute confidence
> in the authorities behind it to make it work. This is exceptional, and
> I don't think you'll find it anywhere else in the world.*

Confidence is also important in a much broader sense. Tourists must
be confident that Dubai will be a good, fun, safe holiday spot that offers
value for money. Investors need confidence that the government and
the economy are stable. This has never been more important than with
the advent of the Dubai International Financial Centre, where success
will hinge on the world's confidence in its new regulatory framework
and the quality and independence of the regulatory organization
through its board and executive management. The government's record
of investment in Dubai, it seems, has gone a long way towards creating
much of the confidence that investors want to have.

The regulatory organization that was put in place was in many ways
a unique experience (at the time) for Dubai's leadership. They showed
courage in selecting a truly world-class international board to cater
for DIFC's international aspirations. These actions further instilled a
sense of confidence and a sense of responsibility in the DFSA's board,
as it was entrusted with running the organization independent of
Dubai's government. To date, the success of DIFC has proven Dubai's
leadership correct in their bold actions. Other financial centres around
the world might argue that just a few short years is not enough time to
truly evaluate the success of a new financial centre.

However, Dubai's early success has not gone unnoticed by other
financial centres. For example, London is undertaking a study to be
conducted by one of the world's leading consulting groups to evaluate
the potential impact of Dubai and other financial centres emerging
around the world. The confidence of these new financial centres has
clearly woken up established financial centres, such as New York and
London to realize that future success is not automatically guaranteed,
but must be earned.

Confidence in itself can create potential value. When people believe
that they can make breakthroughs, they are more likely to do so. And
when customers or investors become confident in an opportunity,
their money will soon begin to flow. The reverse may also be true –
therefore, instilling and maintaining this sense of confidence is very
important, and even more so in new and emerging markets.

Replacing regulation with trust

The need for good and strong regulation in the Dubai International Financial Centre to gain the confidence of the international financial community appears to be at odds with the apparent relaxation of regulation that has brought so many investors to Dubai. The trading community has thrived on trust. But what has been good enough for traders has not been enough to encourage growth in the region's capital markets. Strict regulation in the financial centre will be needed to help create the same level of trust and confidence in the system. Creating this sense of trust, using regulation where appropriate, is another important aspect of leadership for the asset acceleration phase of the model.

While the business dealings of the regulated companies at the DIFC are governed by the independent Dubai Financial Services Authority (DFSA), the free zone is unique in that it is subject not to UAE or Dubai laws (except for criminal matters which are not heard by DIFC's courts), but to its own DIFC law (based largely on British common law). It's presided over, not by a UAE sitting judge, but by a British Chief Justice Sir Anthony Evans and has other judges (from various jurisdictions, including the Deputy Chief Justice, Michael Hwang from Singapore) who hear and determine cases. The DIFC courts, like the DFSA are also independent. This is another measure to increase confidence among the international community, who would likely have little tolerance for the slow pace at which local courts operate.[2] And while this may seem a departure from the traditional atmosphere of trust between business people that has such a long history in Dubai, it is an important measure that will in the end increase trust between foreign workers in the zone as they will be more at ease, knowing what to expect from the system.

For Dubai and its leadership to have understood, early on in 2004, the importance of and need for these two independent parts of the DIFC is seen today by many as the cornerstones for DIFC's success. It also shows Dubai's ability to respond quickly to market needs and to do things that may not be what it is usually accustomed to doing. Its leadership seems to have been well advised, but importantly they took the courageous decision to allow this degree of independence to be established – akin perhaps to the UK Chancellor, giving away decision on monetary policy in determining interest rates to the newly formed Monetary Policy Committee.

Keeping regulations, restrictions and red tape to a minimum, yet maintaining very high standards, helps maximize opportunities for interaction among the players in the system to create value. (Think of the restrictions imposed by the agency laws to see the opposite effect.) It also allows things to happen more freely and quickly, since there are fewer impediments to change or growth.

As with so much of the ingrained culture in Dubai, this comes back to the generations-old traditional trading culture. With little enforceable regulation, early traders were only as good as their word and their last transaction. Any swindlers would be shunned and unable to trade in the Creek. 'Trick me once, shame on you; trick me twice, shame on me', says an old Arab proverb. Unscrupulous traders generally never got the chance to trick twice.

Things are not so different today, as Shehab Gargash, founder and director of Daman Securities, explains:

> *When you have a trading port, you have a trading code. It's probably unwritten. When you have a trading code, everyone knows his rights and obligations. You've got your honesty; you've got your commitment to deals and your word. Today, that's supported by documentation and letters.*

Anis Al Jallaf of Union Properties learned this as a teenager, watching how business was done in his brother's shop in the 1970s.

> *My brother used to import silverware. I used to tell him how funny some of it looked to me, but he would tell me that it was made for a specific area in Iran. So one day, an Iranian man came in and liked the silverware so much, he asked to buy every piece my brother had. That was two containers. But the man didn't have money with him. He asked if he could take the two containers, then bring back the cash when they were sold. My brother said, 'no problem'.*

> *'No problem?' I asked. I couldn't believe it. My brother told me that he knew the man's father, and he was honest, so his son should be honest. My brother believed he would come back, maybe in two months, maybe in four months, maximum six months. It had a lot to do with simplicity. My brother said, 'I look at his eyes, and I read him, and he doesn't look funny.' A lot of business happened that way.*

If letters of credit and official documentation had been required to do this deal, it would have never been completed. This example shows the continuing importance of trust and reputation in the trading community. Many passionately argue against letting the dishonest few dictate regulations for everyone:

> *We cannot have a law that cripples the honest 99 per cent just because one per cent have done wrong. We have to work on how to detect that one per cent and punish them.*

Trust between the rulers and their lieutenants is clearly important. It's no coincidence that the same names appear repeatedly at the heads of high-profile projects. The rulers trust certain people to get the job done, and then they're rewarded with more responsibility. It's also clear that the business community trusts the government. Of course, this is closely tied to the sense of confidence that the government creates. It also creates trust through its fair treatment and follow-through on commitments. Khalid Bin Sulayem, Director General of the Department of Tourism and Commerce Marketing, points out:

> *Even in the worst of times, Dubai has done well. That's why people have full trust in Dubai: because of the history.*

As Dubai grows, civil servants advocate more regulation, which the merchant community argues against. There have even been incidents in which new regulations have been put in place then retracted by the government after an outcry from the business community. But high-profile examples, such as the loss of over $200 million by Dubai Islamic Bank in 1998 resulting from the actions of dishonest employees, make it clear that there are always some people prepared to take advantage of the trust which underpins the business environment.

So the challenge is to create an environment where inherent trust exists but is buttressed by sufficient regulation to keep the business and financial sectors upright. Charles Neil, secretary to the board of the Dubai International Financial Centre, talks of the objective to create 'a 21st century economy, with little but good regulation, minimal bureaucracy, visionary leadership and a drive in people to succeed'. This is consistent with Sheikh Mohammed's often-articulated desire to prevent over-regulation from stifling Dubai's growth and development. The DFSA's pragmatic approach perhaps best articulates this.

Maintaining control

In the asset acceleration phase, leaders must set the right balance between control and freedom of action. In many societies, controls and regulations have increased, sometimes stifling business growth or individual creativity. Even Singapore has accepted that it needs its people to be more creative, and the challenge will be achieving this in the shadow of long-established customs and government policies.

Dubai's method of control is through informal networks, based on trust and ethical norms; it is not regulation-based, as in most developed countries. It works in Dubai because companies are closely held and the network of leadership is tight; those who stray from accepted practices soon find they have no future in the emirate. This ad hoc method of control has proved flexible and able to cope with the rapid change Dubai has experienced. Creation of the free zones shows how an intelligently controlled operation can increase available freedoms instead of restricting them. Within the free zones, the management issues trading licences, provides services and acts as a one-stop local government for the companies within them. In the highly specific legal structure of investors' tenancy agreements and the infrastructural and managerial powers retained by each zone's management, a substantial amount of control exists. But the companies inside the zones actually benefit from much greater freedom than they would elsewhere in the UAE.

An intelligent management approach that exercises control while allowing considerable freedom of action will increase the rate of asset acceleration by providing the ability to tweak and adjust as necessary without stifling growth. In sailing terms, which seem appropriate for a country that owes a lot to the skills of its dhow traders, it is the equivalent to a light but firm hand on the tiller to ensure that everyone moves in the right direction as quickly as possible.

Asset acceleration in Dubai
In each of the examples examined below, an existing asset has been accelerated through intervention of some sort, and then grown through asset leverage. It is important to remember that acceleration occurs on many levels. Even without 'catalysts', a degree of pent-up value would almost certainly be created, through either organic growth or the influence of other assets in the system.

Open skies and the airport
Only a few decades ago, Dubai's airport was not much more than a local airfield, virtually indistinguishable from other regional airports. In 1969, nine airlines served 20 destinations from Dubai. The airport has since been transformed. In 2006 it handled 28.79 million passengers, 16.17 per cent more than in the previous year. Over 113 airlines operate out of Dubai, serving 194 destinations. The airport is now the main hub for air travel in the Middle East and a major stopover point for passengers continuing from Europe to the Indian sub-continent, the Far East, South Pacific and Australasia, even to South Africa as well as travelling the other way around. The airport in 2008 is expected to see in excess of 35 million passengers; you can now fly directly from Dubai to many of the major US cities including New York, Houston, Chicago and Los Angeles. From the UK alone Emirates airline flies to Dubai from more airports than the national airline British Airways.

The open-skies policy, originally put into place by Sheikh Rashid when the airport was first opened in 1960, has been a major driver in attracting so many airlines from around the world. Even in the 1950s, when air travel was only for the privileged few, Sheikh Rashid had ambitions to make Dubai a major air hub. To kick-start this plan, the open-skies policy ensured that any airline could begin flying to Dubai without the need for international treaties or bilateral agreements.[3] At the airport's inception, Sheikh Rashid was so confident about its prospects that he had a 500-space car park built next to the single air strip and small terminal, telling Dubai and those willing to listen that great things lay ahead.

By eschewing the protectionism that has held back air travel in many parts of the world, Dubai has seen its passenger traffic grow over fourfold and its cargo traffic twelvefold since 1980. This growth has occurred hand in hand with increasing the capacity of the airport itself. With passenger numbers expected to reach 60 million by 2010, expansion and improvement are continuous. The expansion program of over US $4 billion was completed in 2008, designed to increase the airport's capacity to 70 million passengers per year. A new terminal exclusively for Emirates airline was completed and will be open for business by the end of 2008. In addition, the programme will provide gates for the super-jumbo Airbus A380 jets and increase the cargo handling capability significantly.

The open-skies policy created massive asset acceleration for the airport. The more airlines allowed in, the more planes will come; and the more planes there are, the more cargo and passengers there will be. It's as simple as that. While the open-skies policy on its own has no direct economic effect, it serves as an accelerator for increasing imports by air, business travel, stopover traffic and tourism. The policy is analogous to Dubai's free trade and relaxed immigration policies. It all comes back to the ruling family's oft-expressed credo: 'What's good for business is good for Dubai.'

Anita Mehra Homayoun, director of marketing and corporate communications at the Department of Civil Aviation, calls the airport the 'window to Dubai'. She goes on to describe how passenger traffic fuelled further growth:

Most of our passengers in the 1980s were transit passengers, and they began to notice the great duty-free facilities in the airport. Our intention during that time has been to 'wow' people with the quality of the shops compared with the ones at other airports in the region.

If the Dubai International Airport is indeed the window to Dubai, then the planned Al Maktoum International Airport will be a much larger window at almost ten times the size of its predecessor. The new airport will have a capacity of over 120 million passengers per year, six 4.5 km runways, and a 92 metre control tower, which will, of course, be the tallest in the region. The airport will have three terminals, one for Emirates airline exclusively, one for other international and regional airlines, and third for low-cost airlines. Separate facilities will be available for private jets. The airport will also have a range of hotels, dining, and shopping centres. It will be linked to Dubai International via a dedicated rail link. It will also be served by the forthcoming Dubai Light Rail Network, also known as the Dubai Metro.

But this will ultimately become much more than just an airport – it will be what urban planner John Kasarda has called an 'aerotropolis', or airport city.[4] When complete, the Dubai World Central will have a permanent population of 750 thousand people and all the facilities they will need – including a golf course maintained by the Four Seasons. The zone will also contain Dubai Logistics City, which will have three times more capacity than the FedEx hub in Memphis, and a Commercial City with employment for 130,000 people. While it is easy to regard this development as a single aerotropolis, all of Dubai in modern times might be considered a grander version of this model, with so much of its growth and commerce being fuelled by the airport.

The expansion of Dubai's airports shows how, over time, increased demand has been created through word of mouth and return visitors, building a competitive advantage for Dubai.

The open-skies policy also stimulated innovation and competitiveness, as is often the case in the asset acceleration phase of the model. Emirates airline might have been the first one to cry 'unfair' when it was established in 1985 and was expected to compete with much bigger established airlines already flying out of Dubai. In fact, it was the requirement to compete and be self-sufficient, the need to learn and improve, that made Emirates airline succeed; and it has been profitable in nearly every year of its existence.

When Dubai began to be used by long-range aircraft, a new emphasis was put on the range and quality of its services, facilities and duty-free shopping. The Dubai Airport Cares programme was put in place to coordinate the way the airport authority, airlines, customs, security, duty-free concessions, shops and other organizations and their employees dealt with customers. According to Sheikh Ahmed, the message is:

You may belong to someone else's department or have a different boss, but you must believe that this is your airport, and forget about who your boss is. Ignore all of that, and remember that we are as one.

The education programme designed around this initiative is meant to instil a confidence and professionalism in all airport workers that passengers will notice.

The airport and its duty-free facilities have received several government service awards, government officials believe they help create confidence among shoppers:

> *You see government awards in the airport for excellent service, and you will trust them and you will trust that you are buying good products and that you'll get good after-sales service.*

In maintaining the open-skies policy at Dubai International Airport, the government preferred to rely on trust rather than regulation in turning the airport into a dynamic transport hub. Sheikh Ahmed explains:

> *We found that the more you are flexible with the airlines, the more likely they are to want to come here and fly to other points. And as they become a user of the airport and the traffic goes up, others will also try to connect because you are creating that competition. Then airlines will feel more confident going to a busy airport than to an empty one.*

The confidence that continues to attract air traffic to Dubai is the essence of asset acceleration.

With regard to Dubai's recent airport expansion, many would have waited until the new international airport was built, but not Dubai, in order to ensure that they stay up to date and cope with unexpected demand. Instead, Dubai went ahead with what they have described as an "interim" solution by building one of the world's largest airports (i.e. the extension of the existing airport, which now creates an airport with an annual capacity of over 70 million passengers).

Had Dubai not done this extension and started building ahead of demand, the existing airport would not have coped, and importantly they would have had to wait years until the new 120 million passenger capacity airport is built. This would have slowed down the asset acceleration phase – an outcome which is unacceptable to Dubai's leadership. For them, the speed and momentum of asset acceleration must be maintained by anticipating whatever may slow it down and reacting to it in advance.

Tourism and hotels

Tourism has acted as a major accelerator for the hotel industry in Dubai since the early 1990s. Growth in tourist numbers is related to the growth of Emirates airline and the increasing capacity of the airport. Each of these assets develops within its own strategic trajectory while gathering momentum and feeding off the growth of the others.

The number of hotels increased from 70 in 1990 to 272 in 2002, and over 300 in 2008 with dozens more being planned or being built. Between 1990 and 2001, the number of visitors to Dubai for business or pleasure increased from 1.7 million to three million, and occupancy rates averaged 57.2 per cent (with lows in the early 1990s because of the Gulf War).[5] By 2004, around five million tourists were visiting Dubai,[6] and occupancy rates reached 81 per cent.[7] By 2010, more than 15 million tourists are expected per year.[8]

One prominent hotelier describes the implicit agreement between entrepreneurs and the government. The government encourages investors to build new hotels, even when hotels seem to be springing up everywhere, with a promise that tourists will arrive to occupy them. To keep its promise, the government ensures that Dubai tourism is adequately marketed and that the airline and the airport are equipped to handle the traffic. Then, as more visitors arrive, they spread the word about Dubai, leading to further increases in visitor numbers. A leading business person describes how the government invests to raise the profile of Dubai:

They don't think just one or two years ahead. When they built the Burj Al Arab hotel, they didn't think they'd get their money back in two years. They thought of how many times the Burj Al Arab would be seen around the world, and how many people would come to Dubai to see it.

Indeed, Jumeirah's properties often appear to be much more than hotels. The Burj Al Arab and the Madinat Jumeirah resort are all landmarks that present formidable challenges to incoming competitors. The Burj Al Arab was the first iconic building to appear in Dubai, rising up over the coastline in the image of a sailing ship. The newer Madinat Jumeirah is a complex of luxury hotels and spas built in a modern take on traditional Arabian architecture. The complex includes 40 hectares of outdoor landscaping with 3.7 kilometres of working waterways; a one kilometre private beach that connects to the Burj Al Arab, and Jumeirah Beach Hotel; a 4,550-seat multi-purpose venue; a theatre; and other facilities for recreation and conferences, as well as its own Arabian souk complex.

The hotelier mentioned earlier described his experience of opening a 600-room luxury hotel in early December 1997 and his surprise at seeing it become fully booked that Christmas. It was an indication of the pent-up demand being created. He recalled going to Europe and finding that almost no one knew much about Dubai; he realized what potential for tourism there could be if the travel logistics, infrastructure and accommodation were first class.

Some of the high-profile hotels have been built by the government rather than by private investors. Their success has encouraged other hotel chains to enter the market. The resulting competition and the innovation spurred by the need for the new assets to stand out from the crowd are typical of the effects of the asset acceleration phase of the model. Such government investments help make new investors sufficiently confident to enter the market, and Dubai now has one of the fastest-growing portfolios of luxury hotels in the world. Virtually every major chain is represented, with each new entrant striving to outdo the last.

Events and conferences are also important in creating the asset acceleration effect. The Dubai Airshow and other major events, as well as international conferences, help fill the hotels and make other contributions to the local economy. Trade shows have accelerated development of corporate apartments, hotels and the new Dubai International Convention Centre.

The acceleration effect extends beyond Dubai's borders. Sharjah, a neighbouring emirate, may have become more conservative over the past decade, arguably as a response to the influx of Western tourists to Dubai. In Sharjah, women must dress traditionally and alcohol is no longer served. Oil-rich Abu Dhabi, the capital of the UAE, remains conservative but is changing very fast and some would say this is due to the positive effect that Dubai has had. Qatar appears to be seeking to emulate Dubai's successes by developing shopping centres, hotels, an airline and a new airport complex, creating festivals and events to lure tourists, promoting sporting events and setting up its own financial centre. It is too early to understand each country's strategy in the region. However, it is clear that the impact of Dubai is felt far outside its borders. Some countries may emulate Dubai's model, while others seek to differentiate and segment themselves to a different audience, but almost no one is idly setting by. Many feel the energizing effect of Dubai, and the only question is how to best take advantage of these new opportunities in the region.

Knowledge-based free zones

Each of the knowledge-based free zones is a good example of Dubai's approach to asset acceleration. A more detailed examination of the originals – Dubai Internet City and Dubai Media City – should reveal some insights about how this concept works across the full range. Located within the same free zone area known as the Dubai Technology, Electronic Commerce and Media Free Zone (TECOM), Dubai Internet City and Dubai Media City are highly valuable assets developed in line with the government's strategy to diversify its portfolio and become a knowledge-based economy. They are also good examples of how asset acceleration has taken place as a result of the synergies between the companies within the zones. In this case, the 'corporate concierge' services provided by the management of the zones have been a strong catalyst in creating this acceleration.

The origins of the two developments are typical of large-scale projects in Dubai. The idea started with Sheikh Mohammed, who became interested in immersing Dubai in the so-called new economy in the late 1990s, when the dotcom boom was roaring ahead. Studies commissioned by his office revealed that the two most attractive industry clusters to promote were information technology and media. At that time (and, indeed, today), the Middle East represented one of the fastest-growing markets for IT, so that was an obvious choice. Media's appeal owes a lot to the freedom of expression enjoyed in Dubai relative to some other states in the region.

The Jebel Ali Free Zone had shown that Dubai was an attractive location for multinationals. To determine exactly what would lure technology and media companies to the area, government representatives surveyed a number of large companies. The results were not surprising: the top priorities included freedom of ownership and financial management, no restrictions on hiring from abroad, and a solid technical and communications infrastructure.

Once the studies had been completed, Sheikh Mohammed set aside an area 35 kilometres from the city and imposed a one-year deadline for completing the first phase of Dubai Internet City, including finding tenants to occupy it, entrusting this task to one of his rising stars (Mohammad Al Gergawi). To the amazement of many, Dubai Internet City was opened on schedule in October 2000 – one day early, in fact – with 85 companies in residence and a long waiting list. Dubai Media City was launched three months later.

By early 2008, Dubai Internet City had over 1,000 companies operating within its confines (112 established in 2007 alone) and Dubai Media City had over 1,200.[9]

Within the combined zone where the two cities are located, firms can enjoy full foreign ownership, no restrictions on repatriation of capital, no currency restrictions, tax-free status for 50 years and freedom to hire who they like. There are also stringent intellectual property and so-called cyber regulations in force. In short, as with the Dubai International Financial Centre, there is regulation and unique laws where they are needed – in this case to protect intellectual assets – but otherwise firms are given a pretty free hand. This is why so many companies have set up in the free zone. Outside it they would be subject to UAE agency laws, requiring any foreign company to take on a local partner with a controlling interest in the business of at least 51 per cent, which is not an attractive proposition in comparison.

From the perspective of visitors, the distinction between Dubai Internet City and Dubai Media City isn't readily apparent. The most obvious clue that you're in Dubai Internet City is the giant @ signs on every building and much of the signage. Many buildings also bear the names of large companies such as IBM, Cisco, Reuters and CNN; which camps these fall into is clear. But there are other examples that are not so easy to place, such as MasterCard and other financial services companies. There are also dotcoms such as Tejari.com, a business-to-business exchange, in Dubai Media City. Because it's all part of the same free zone, the same regulations and benefits govern companies in both areas.

The stated mission for Dubai Internet City is:

To create an infrastructure, environment and attitude that will enable Information and Communications Technology (ICT) enterprises to operate locally, regionally and globally from Dubai, with significant competitive advantage.

Providing the infrastructure is the easier part. Creating a business-friendly environment is more difficult, and it's where many would-be Silicon Valleys around the world have fallen short, often ending up as little more than office parks. This is where asset acceleration comes in, enabled in large part by the 'corporate concierge' service provided by the management of both Dubai Internet City and Dubai Media City.

Part of this service focuses on relieving companies of administrative tasks such as incorporation, real estate management, visas and licences, and voice, data and satellite communications. The management of both cities will do whatever it takes to allow their partners (as they call their tenant companies) to concentrate on doing business. Other services provided by the management are geared towards enabling partners to work with one another and helping them get new business, which helps to generate the asset acceleration effect.

To create synergies inside and get business from outside, Dubai Internet City groups companies by industry focus and then invites major buyers from those sectors to workshops, where contacts can be made and potential opportunities explored. It also arranges for company representatives to attend relevant trade shows in promising locations.

The services provided for these companies bolster their confidence through association with, and the support of, the management of the two cities. The support encourages firms to make marketing efforts, such as visiting a trade show that they might not otherwise have contemplated. As part of the Dubai Internet City community, they have more visibility and legitimacy. And not just in terms of outward appearance or marketing spin: the network effect enhances what the companies in the community have to offer.

In her role as CEO of Tejari.com, Sheikha Lubna was enthusiastic about many aspects of her company's position in Dubai Media City, where the company is still based with its new leadership. Her employees enjoyed working in a safe, well-maintained, attractively landscaped office park among technology and media people. But she is also quick to put the role of technology in its place when she says that Dubai Internet City exists:

> *to drive transition and transformation for people . . . in business. It's not the techies who are important here. It's what these techies are going to do for the rest of the community.*

This idea is reinforced by Abdullatif Al Mulla, once General Manager of Microsoft's regional office in Dubai Internet City, now TECOM CEO:

> *The whole concept of Internet City is when you need something, you know where to go. Internet City is a hub, where anybody looking for something to do with IT knows where to head . . . If I'm looking for partners, I don't have to email anyone or look for negotiators. I just meet, and we finish on the spot. So the proximity helps us a lot, and increases the flow of communication.*

As one of the first companies to sign up to Dubai Internet City and a relatively large operation, Microsoft works actively to cultivate suppliers and partners. Abdullatif Al Mulla describes the benefits for companies large and small within the city as completely reciprocal, with large companies needing the smaller ones as much as the small ones need big ones like Microsoft. He also describes the difficulty in finding good people to work at Microsoft, but this isn't a problem unique to his regional office, it's one experienced throughout the company. Like most companies in Dubai Internet City and Dubai Media City, Microsoft recruits from around the world through agencies and websites, thus adding to the extremely diverse population of the free zone. Since the majority of companies and their employees are foreign, the diversity of the group creates its own synergies as people from vastly different backgrounds come together to compete and collaborate with one another. They are open to the world's companies and its workers.

In the common areas of the two cities it is clear that the developments are much more than an office park. Like the lobby of the Emirates Towers hotel, they are constantly buzzing and crowded with business people having meetings or waiting for appointments. The main area of Dubai Internet City is alive with visitors chatting while sitting in comfy armchairs or at the espresso bar with a view of the man-made lake, with the management's busy staff visible through a glass wall in their open plan office. The asset acceleration inside the zone is evident in several ways: the fast take-up of office space and the waiting list for it, the demand for housing, leisure, and retail facilities within the site, and the amount of business done among partners within the zone. This effect has also brought Dubai closer to the larger value proposition of becoming a knowledge economy.

When the idea for Dubai Internet City was first conceived, Sheikh Mohammed compared it with the business environment of the Creek, but it's already become much more than that. Through the initiative of the management of the two cities, companies of all sizes have become part of a thriving network of businesses and extended their marketing reach far beyond the borders of the UAE. Abdulhamid Juma sums up the accelerating effect of Dubai Internet City and Dubai Media City and their management services:

> To be very honest, we did not expect such demand. Maybe it's because we have talked to the companies. We did not know what to offer, so we ran workshops to find out what the companies want. They wanted infrastructure as number one. They wanted Starbucks as number two, for some reason. Then breaking down red tape and making things work. The one stop shop: I do everything for you here. I call it the package.

And at this basic level 'the package' is exactly what has been provided to each of the free zones that have followed in the footsteps of DIC and DMC. They all offer the same benefits of existing in a free zone (operation free of corporate and personal tax, 100 per cent foreign ownership, 100 per cent repatriation of funds, etc.), and each one offers its own version of the corporate concierge to help speed companies through the set-up process.

In addition, the proliferation of free zones provides much more opportunity for cross-pollination and synergy between companies inside the zones. For example, the traditional publishing companies that set up initially inside DMC may find advantages in relocating to Dubai International Media Production Zone. Dubai's free zones are rapidly creating a place for virtually any sort of business, whether in the garment trade, microprocessors, academia, ship building, or airplane design. And with the advent of Dubai Business Bay and other corporate facilities in other free zones, the question now becomes who would actively choose to operate outside of a free zone.

Conclusion

There are many different facets to the asset acceleration phase, but they all contribute to the creation of greater value that can be

released later on. The early adoption of an open-skies policy at Dubai International Airport allowed airlines from all over the world to come to Dubai which created the foundation for the airport's growth.
The building of a massive number of hotels has been fuelled by an acceleration effect from the growth in visitor arrivals. And the bundle of services provided by the Dubai Technology, Electronic Commerce and Media Free Zone has caused demand for real estate in Dubai Internet City and Dubai Media City to grow beyond all expectations – necessitating the creation of a range of free zones with complementary industry focus.

In each of these cases, innovation and competition were spurred by the interactions between companies and individuals from all over the world. The speed of both change and growth has been fostered by an underpinning of confidence and trust between customers and suppliers. Controls and regulations have been put in place to enable further value creation rather than stunting it.

The acceleration effects of these and other players in Dubai's strategic vortex over time are described by Dr Anwar Gargash:

> *You can't go into fourth gear unless you've already shifted through first, second and third. This is how Dubai constantly raises the threshold. Other regions that try to compete with Dubai have to build up infrastructure and quality of life. A cumulative process is essential to accomplish this; it's taken Dubai many years to reach this stage.*

Next, we'll see how the value generated in the asset acceleration phase is released, often with dramatic effect, in the asset leverage stage.

ENDNOTES

1   Gulf Construction Online, April 2002, Vol. XXIII, No. 4, www. gulfconstructionworldwide.com
2   Rozenberg, J. 'British law is oasis of reassurance in Dubai', *The Telegraph*, 2 February 2006
3   Wilson, *Father of Dubai*
4   Lindsay, G. 'The Rise of the Aerotropolis', *Fast Company*, July 2006, p. 76
5   Department of Economic Development, *Development Statistics of Dubai 2002*
6   From AME Info website at www.ameinfo.com/38860.html
7   From *Emirate of Dubai Socio-Economic Indicators 2005* and accompanying CD-ROM
8   From AME Info website at www.ameinfo.com/38860.html
9   Figures provided by The Executive Office

The Palm Jumeirah in 2008.

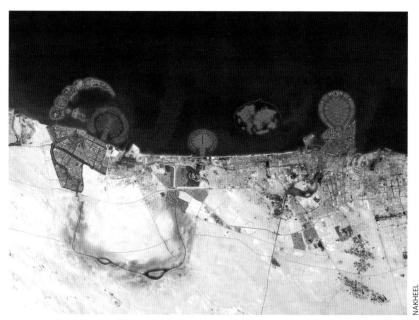

The new developments lining Dubai's coastline (note the three Palm Island developments, The World and expansion of the Creek).

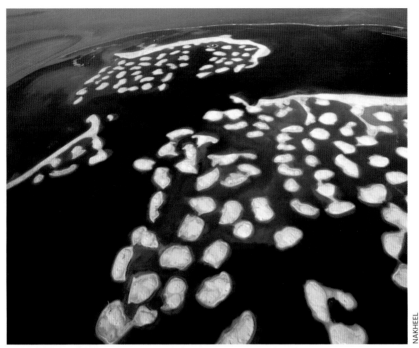

The World, an archipelago of 300 man-made islands in 2008.

The Gate at DIFC, featuring a groundbreaking Modern Art exhibition – a blend of finance and culture.

MOHAMMAD ARFAN ASIF

Burj Dubai, a part of the new development, Downtown Dubai is the tallest structure in the world, scheduled to be completed by 2009.

An aerial view of Jumeirah Beach Residence, showing the Palm Jumeirah in the distance.

Ski Dubai in Mall of the Emirates.

DAVID STEELE

Dubai Media City.

GULFPICS/ KAREL KITA

Dubai Internet City.

CHAPTER 7

ASSET LEVERAGE

Just as there can be but one Singapore; Dubai must be distinctive in what it wants to be, and there will be but one Dubai.

Professor John Quelch (2002)

Asset leverage picks up where asset acceleration leaves off. In this stage, radical growth results from the acceleration effects of the previous stage. To return to the analogy from physics, it is when potential energy becomes kinetic or actual energy. Knowledge is used to create something fantastic, synergies become productive, competition creates innovation. This is where the real growth happens in an asset which, when combined with the growth of other assets within the strategic vortex, leads to the kind of results achieved in Dubai.

Asset leverage is about using the interactions among an existing portfolio of assets to create – through innovation, competition and collaboration – radical growth and development.

Compared with the top-down growth model in Singapore, where the government keeps a tight rein on many aspects of life and work, and the bottom-up organic growth model of Silicon Valley, the Dubai model is middle-out. The leadership guides the business ecosystem, intervening and stimulating here and there, then steps back and lets things happen. When things do happen, first comes asset acceleration followed by asset leverage. As most parents are aware, knowing when to let go can be difficult. Most parents like to keep a close eye on their children's progress and to offer guidance and help when it is needed.

Asset leverage occurs at multiple levels. Similar assets can leverage one another within an industry cluster. Groups of assets can work together on a large scale. As leverage begins, the interactions in different parts and different levels of the ecosystem spill over into other parts and levels. Since the Dubai Shopping Festival was conceived in 1996, it has grown by leaps and bounds. The asset acceleration has been created by good marketing: first within the region, then internationally and all the time within Dubai. Because the festival lasts only a month, there are another 11 months each year during which acceleration can build, to be leveraged when the festival begins. Apart from the retail boom, the spillover effects of the festival are clear: hotels are full almost to capacity, and restaurants, tourist attractions and related services all benefit from the people who come to Dubai for the festival. This success of the festival has also helped launch a range of sporting events during the same period and has spawned the Dubai Summer Surprise, focusing again on the regional Middle Eastern market.

This spillover effect is illustrated by an example Sheikh Rashid used many years ago to explain why the airport was important to Dubai. A man arrives at Dubai airport on his way to a meeting in the city. He buys a pack of gum and gets into a taxi for a ride into town. He pays the taxi driver, who uses the money to buy fuel. When the traveller arrives at his hotel, he orders a cup of coffee. Later, he goes out and finds a present for his wife, and so on.[1] This is basic economics at work, but it goes to the heart of asset leverage. One additional visitor to a country like Dubai will benefit the local economy in a variety of ways. Multiply this effect by the number of additional visitors who are continually attracted to Dubai by the growing asset base and the power of asset leverage becomes increasingly clear.

Mike Simon of the Emirates Group gives another illustration of the spillover effect of asset leverage:

> *Three or four months after we started to fly to South Africa, I was walking round the centre of Dubai and there was a Woolworths. It had just opened. The Woolworths was not Woolworths UK, it was Woolworths South Africa and I thought, this is so interesting because it reflects what we always say in that we bring commercial ties between two countries when we start to fly there.*

Sultan Bin Sulayem provides another good example of two sorts of assets leveraging one another.

> *If you look at the port and free zone, the port definitely makes more money because the free zone is limited as to how much it can make. But the port isn't. But also, the free zone generates business for the port. When you have a port and a free zone, you maximize profit. Because the free zone generates the business, the port handles the business, and you make money.*

This example shows how collaboration between two assets can create disproportionate benefits.

Key components of asset leverage
The key components of asset leverage are:

• The ability to take advantage of asset acceleration, the natural precedent to leverage;
• Timing;
• Understanding how to combine assets for maximum effect;
• The ability of leadership to empower workers;
• The ability of leadership to step back and give market forces a free rein.

Using asset acceleration
As noted in the previous chapter, the value generated by asset acceleration can happen on its own through natural market factors, but the most dramatic effects are seen through the application of a catalyst. Asset leverage can also happen organically, not following on from asset acceleration. In either of these cases, growth will depend on the behaviour of the market and reactions of the assets in question.

Removing barriers to and encouraging trade are big spurs to asset acceleration, which in turn will increase growth, particularly spillover growth, achieved through asset leverage. When a country is open to the world, word of mouth travels faster, the mix in business ecosystem becomes richer and networks expand exponentially. DP World's expansion into the management of foreign ports and free zones is a good example of this. The authority could only have become known around the world as a result of shipping lines spreading the word. The more new firms that come to do business in Dubai, the more innovation among companies there is.

The leadership attributes that are important in the asset acceleration stage continue to be important in asset leverage. Trust and confidence in the business ecosystem and those who inhabit it are crucial as growth continues, and as different types of assets leverage one another. Although freedom of action will also undoubtedly contribute to faster growth, it needs to exist within a stable, controlled environment and be supported by regulations that prove necessary to reinforce of business confidence and trust.

Indeed, the ability to intervene when necessary will become increasingly important as growth slows, opportunities for spin-offs present themselves, or other reasons for intervention emerge.

Timing
Judging when to introduce a new asset into the system, or when to shift from acceleration to leverage, is crucial. Even Dubai will have got it wrong sometimes by introducing the wrong type of business into an existing successful enterprise.

Other decisions have been much better. Mike Simon explains:

1985 was a good time to start an airline. I don't think you could have created an airline that's become as successful as Emirates at another time.

The emergence of Dubai on the international business scene in the 1980s was one positive indication of the timeliness of this decision. Asset acceleration of the airline began almost immediately, allowing a quick transition into the leverage phase as the airline began acquiring its own aircraft and expanding its routes.

Dubai's rulers are well known for their desire to shave time off development and building processes, but the people around them seem to have developed a knack for living up to these expectations. Examples are the one-year development of Dubai Internet City and the fast development of the Palm projects. The rulers seem to have developed a knack for identifying opportunities that need only to be announced in order to generate massive amounts of accelerated value. The first Palm Island attracted a great deal of interest from the earliest planning stages, then sold out in days. Dubai Internet City, too, gained buy-in almost immediately from the likes of IBM, Microsoft, Oracle and others. By making the time these projects take to complete as short as possible, asset leverage can begin while the excitement is still fresh and has not been dulled by a long development stage.

Stepping back

The leaders' role is to set the stage, make sure an asset is in place and functioning well, and show that demand for it exists. Then they should step back and let others take advantage of the acceleration that has built up behind it.

In Dubai the rulers provide a lot of support for new industries, but on a strict 'sink or swim' basis. Mike Simon of the Emirates Group explains:

We're given a free hand and we're run just as an ordinary commercial concern. We're not protected, and we're not given any subsidies. I think that's how Sheikh Mohammed likes all businesses to go, even those in which the government has a big investment. He believes in open skies . . . a good example of where the government is hands-off and it's sink or swim – if it works, good; if it doesn't, close it down.

As the original owners of all the land in the emirate, the rulers often kick off a major project by handing over some real estate, as in the case of the Dubai International Financial Centre. Although the ruling family often invests its own money in projects, developers usually have to fund their projects through local and international banks, as would be expected in most parts of the world.

Similarly, through its holding companies and investment arms, the government creates massive initiatives like the Palms, Business Bay and Dubailand, then steps back while private developers fill in the blanks with their luxury hotels and attractions.

Ahmad Bin Byat (Chairman of TECOM) describes the brief negotiations with Sheikh Mohammed in planning Dubai Internet City:

> *We got the land from the government and we came back with our wish list, which really had a lot of things to do with freedom to do things the way we wanted to do them. His Highness was very keen on giving us this, but also he gave us a bigger challenge. 'Fine,' he said, 'you can have these freedoms, but I'm not giving you any money to do it. And let's see if we could make this work as a commercial project that could stand on its own.' That was really a challenge.*

Because of the success of the project, it has remained free of any government subsidy or support. The entire Technology, Electronic Commerce and Media Free Zone development doesn't cost the government a penny; it has its own police, infrastructure, planning and road construction crews. As Ahmad Bin Byat puts it, 'It's like running a whole country – a tiny little country.'

The government's laissez-faire policies aren't always appreciated, however. Property owners complained when new property development led to rents going down, but the government left the rates to market forces, stepping in occasionally to reinforce confidence, when need be.

Stepping back can also be seen in the actions described earlier for DIFC. In the case of DIFC, leadership steps in early to ensure the right building blocks are in place, and then steps back. But importantly, keeps a watchful eye on the initiative to ensure that the fragile and young ecosystem is allowed to mature and grow smoothly in a sustainable manner.

Empowerment

Giving individuals the skills, confidence and resources to work independently is important in asset leverage. Sheikh Ahmed describes Sheikh Mohammed's tendency to do this:

> *He is the main driver behind pushing everybody. He is pushy, he is aggressive, he wants things to happen yesterday if you decide today,*

but also at the same time, he gives you all the support you need. Not like somebody who asks you for something and does not give you the support – financial, moral, or whatever – you need to make it happen. He will push you to do things, but he will always be there to support you.

TECOM's Abdullatif Al Mulla draws parallels between the empowerment culture in Dubai and his Microsoft's Dubai HQ, where he was previously CEO:

The key to good management is having people you can trust. You empower them because you believe in their capabilities. I'm not going to hire anybody that might hurt my company. I'm going to hire a person to help me, to collaborate with me, to coordinate things with me. So what we do is hire people that we can rely on and people that we trust, that we know will treat the company as their own. The same thing happens in Dubai. They hire people, and the more they trust them the more jobs they give them, the more projects they can handle.

Asset leverage in Dubai
The previous chapter looked at a number of examples of asset acceleration in Dubai. Below we examine the asset leverage phase and how it has created growth, competition and innovation.

Hotel innovation and growth
The effects of the asset acceleration of the hotel industry in Dubai can be seen in the growing numbers of tourists and convention visitors coming to the city, and the influx of leading hotel chains. Mike Simon describes how the government stimulated the industry, then stepped back:

The government gives a lot of support in the comfort zone area. They always encourage people. When they wanted hotels to be built here they came in first and built some. Then local businessmen were encouraged and believed they could afford to invest and make some money.

Dubai has one of the highest concentrations of luxury hotels in the world. By the end of 2004 it was home to 276 hotels with over 26,155 rooms[2] and in 2008 this figure has crossed 300 hotels, with dozens of new hotels under construction and thousands of rooms due to become available by 2010 in stand-alone hotels and in developments like Dubailand and the Palm Islands. Almost six million guests spent around 16 million nights in residence in Dubai in 2007.[3] Interestingly almost half of the guests came from Europe and the United States, with the latter growing faster presumably because of a number of factors including the introduction and increase of direct flights from Dubai to the US and vice versa. But it's not just a numbers game. The government invests in hotels that give Dubai international prominence, and private investors have to compete with those hotels.

The Burj Al Arab was intended to set a standard that's nearly impossible to match. The world's only seven-star hotel, as some describe it, was designed to resemble the full sail of a ship, and at 321 metres, it is among the world's tallest hotels. It is composed of luxury suites, and each floor has its own reception and a staff of butlers. So spectacular is the atrium (also the world's tallest) that many tourists are happy to pay the admission charge just to be able to look at it. The hotel even has an underwater restaurant that's only a short internal "submarine ride" away.

The Burj Al Arab is one of the government-owned Jumeirah's managed properties (part of Dubai Holding). Others include the Emirates Towers (the third tallest hotel in the world, with the world's largest floor mosaic in one restaurant), the Jumeirah Beach Hotel, with its own man-made coral reef and the Jumeirah Beach Club complex (which is being redeveloped).

Jumeirah opened the Madinat Jumeirah Arabian Resort in 2003 to complement its other properties in Dubai. Its flagship properties are the Al Qasr and the Mina A'Salam hotels, which are modelled on traditional Arabian architecture, complete with wind towers, an ancient equivalent of central air. The resort also has a private beach, extensive landscaping, waterways, its own souk style shopping centre and top-quality restaurants and bars. In 2006, it opened the Bab Al Shams resort in the desert with a distinctly Arabian feel to it with its own Arabian desert shows. Already, this hotel has proved to be very popular with tourists as well as corporate retreats (including Dubai Holding and Sheikh Mohammed's own cabinet). As Gerald Lawless, Chairman of Jumeirah Group, notes the growth of the group will be to have 57 hotels by 2012 (from 30 hotels in 2007) and to grow its employee number from 12,500 employees in 2007 to over 75,000 employees in 2012. Growth of this nature can only come about through the leveraging many relationships and skills that were developed in Jumeirah's first few highly successful hotels; or of course to speed this process externally it can be done by acquisition.

Jumeirah has also founded the Emirates Academy of Hospitality Management in association with the Ecole Hôtelière de Lausanne, a leading Swiss school of hotel management. The academy offers a four-year BSc in International Hospitality Management, which includes study abroad and work experience at Jumeirah's properties.

The Royal Mirage, operated and 50 per cent owned by Kerzner International (previously known as Sun International Hotels), a leading developer of resorts, hotels and casinos, was extended in 2002 after opening only three years earlier, more than doubling the size of its beachfront grounds. The new buildings at the resort, designed to look old and traditional, were constructed using largely local materials. The same developer opened in September 2008 a flagship 1500-room property, known as Atlantis, on the Palm Jumeirah. Based on a 120-acre plot at the apex of the Palm's crescent breakwater, the luxury resort will have numerous water attractions, including an aquatic habitat with 65,000 sea creatures.[4]

There is indeed a seemingly endless list of top hotel chains announcing properties in Dubai which boast all manner activities, luxuries, and firsts. In addition to the ultra-luxury properties and themed hotels, Hydropolis is a $500 million hotel being built underwater in the Arabian Gulf.

The development of the hospitality industry in Dubai has been the result in large part of government initiatives in promoting Dubai and upgrading facilities. These helped to create asset acceleration, which, in turn, resulted in asset leverage: more hotels and more innovation.

This shows how the strategic vortex works at several levels. Dubai's portfolio of hotels is an asset that has been created, accelerated and leveraged with the help of government incentives. The acceleration happened because increased demand was created through development of the tourism industry, and then asset leverage happened when additional competitors entered the market and helped spur innovation and growth.

The hotel sector is a good illustration of the strategic trajectory model. Hotels are built, demand is created through external (tourism, conferences and other attractions) and internal (design, unique attributes and shops) means, and the asset is leveraged as occupancy increases. The facilities need to be constantly monitored and evaluated, and reinvested (maintenance, upkeep, renovation), reinvented (expanded or adding different types of hotels – for example boutique hotels or three and four star hotels, not just more five star hotels) or harvested (completely redone or rebuilt). Once there are dozens or hundreds of hotels going through this cycle in a developing market, the combined effects of the strategic vortex can be clearly seen.

Looking at these assets in the context of the strategic vortex of Dubai, it is easy to see how further acceleration and leverage are created by their interaction. The airport, Emirates airline and the tourism industry have grown in tandem, as part of the leadership's vision for Dubai. As one element grows, it allows and even encourages others to grow. The spillover effects create opportunities for investors in tourist attractions, restaurants and retailing. So as this part of the ecosystem develops, it creates leverage on a higher level that has contributed to the overall growth of the emirate and its economy.

Dubai Internet City and Dubai Media City

Sheikh Mohammed's analogy, likening Dubai Internet City to a virtual Dubai Creek, seems all the more apt when considering the asset leverage of the Technology, Electronic Commerce and Media Free Zone as a whole. The growth of cargo traffic in the Creek transformed Dubai. Similar growth in the free zone may have as great an influence on the economy of Dubai as the Creek once did.

The effects of asset acceleration in Dubai Internet City and Dubai Media City should be manifested in the asset leverage phase – perhaps with fast growth as a result of increasing demand for office space or corporate synergies and networking opportunities, and innovation stemming from competition between companies. When Dubai Media City celebrated its second anniversary in January 2003, there was a great deal to be thankful for. The venture had grown far beyond expectations, having attracted over 620 companies by early 2003. After the initial building phase that created space for 96 companies in three buildings, two further phases were completed, with more than 600,000 square feet of space in eight new buildings.

Dubai Internet City and Dubai Media City have attracted companies large and small, and few of the major players in the technology and media industries are not represented. Compaq, Cisco, Dell, IBM, Logica, Microsoft, Oracle, Sun, Sony Ericsson, Canon and Hewlett-Packard, but to name a few, all have offices in Dubai Internet City. Sun Microsystems supports over 90 countries from this office, including all of Europe. Major players such as CNN, Reuters, Bertelsmann and several regional broadcasters are represented in Dubai Media City. In all, around 20 TV and radio broadcasters operate out of the city.

After its first two years, half of the companies in the in Dubai Media City were in marketing services or publishing – these companies may now choose to move to zone Dubai International Media Production for more dedicated support facilities and greater synergies among companies.

Asset leverage unleashes pent-up demand, as has happened in Dubai Internet City and Dubai Media City. Companies inside the zone should also benefit from synergies. In its early days, Tejari.com took advantage of the range of services provided by other companies inside the DIC and DMC. One of the principal drivers of the company's success is its ability to find providers for training, value-added hosting services and any number of other services at arm's length. Recalling her time as CEO of Tejari.com, Sheikha Lubna says that the growth of Dubai Internet City and Dubai Media City has been largely organic, and she attributes this growth to the evolution of the network of companies and their interrelationships. These relationships are created and strengthened by a range of activities organized by the management of the two cities, such as regular breakfasts and networking events. One regular event in Dubai Media City is the Media Majlis, which, according to the city's website, provides 'an opportunity for partners to share ideas, suggestions and concerns with the senior management team of Dubai Media City'. It is 'great for networking too'.[5]

Microsoft works hard to cultivate a network of suppliers, and having many of them based in Dubai Internet City makes this much easier. The combination of large companies like Microsoft and smaller, more specialized providers helps to create a value network similar to the Silicon Valley model. The structure of the media production industry in Dubai Media City also encourages this, cultivating a diverse group of production, post-production and other creative services like those found in media districts in New York or London.

Dubai Media City has taken the idea of the small, specialized provider one step further by creating the Media Business Centre, which is home to 165 independent media workers with a wide variety of skills. Because employment law prevents self-employed foreigners from working in the UAE, the centre provides a unique opportunity for this group. It also gives companies within the free zone access to their talent. This is another example of leverage, with the demand for the services of these people acting as a spur to the innovative solution that allows them to work.

It is early days for innovation to emerge from competition among the companies operating in the Technology, Electronic Commerce and Media Free Zone. But Dubai Internet City and Dubai Media City have been leveraged beyond the zone in the strategic vortex of Dubai Inc. Their success has paved the way for further free zone developments focusing on industries as diverse as finance, healthcare and semiconductors. Their public relations value in the international business community adds to the image of Dubai as fast-moving, progressive and technically savvy, paving the way for further growth.

Residential property

Another example of asset acceleration and leverage in Dubai is the market for residential property as a result of the initiative of developers and the enablement of the government. In 1999, new residential and mixed-use developments were announced that allowed foreigners to buy freehold or leasehold property along with an assurance of residency visas. Until that time, only nationals of the Gulf Cooperation Council countries could buy property, and it was almost impossible to reside in the emirate if not employed. While early laws and regulations in this area were ambiguous, the government of Dubai (along with an army of real estate developers, sales agents, and the media) made great efforts to clarify the rules early on to pave the way for robust sales. It wasn't until March 2006 that the government issued the law allowing foreign ownership of property in certain areas of the emirate – a full four years after the initial property boom of 2002.

Any early ambiguity regarding property ownership or visas does not seem to have had a detrimental effect on the market. The residential property boom began with the launch of the first phase of Emaar Properties' Emirates Hills development. As the first development open to expatriates, take-up was fast and furious, with the initial phase selling out in hours. Demand increased further in May 2002, when the government announced that properties in selected developments would be available to buy freehold. This was at the time that the first houses and apartments became available on the Palm Jumeirah, prompting a sell-out in the first couple of days. Strong demand for properties continues, with buyers signing up on the spot the moment new developments are announced.

Ian Fairservice is founder and managing partner of Motivate Publishing. He emigrated to Dubai in the late 1970s and launched the local *What's On* magazine in 1979 (the Gulf's first English-language magazine) and now produces a range of magazines, books and custom publications covering the entire Gulf region. He was at the head of the queue when the Palm project was announced and bought a detached house on Palm Jumeirah. That same day, he made the decision to launch *Identity*, an interiors, design and property magazine aimed at property buyers like himself. The first issue appeared within four months, with features including the logistics and benefits of buying property and overviews of many of the developments on offer.

The growth in residential property and the relaxation of ownership restrictions will result in considerable economic and social change. By allowing anyone to buy property, the government is telling foreign investors that it wants not only their money but also themselves. Inevitably, services and related industries will grow to support this new group of permanent residents. Indeed, this is already happening as healthcare and educational institutions are developed.

All this will help attract families to Dubai and allow retired people to stay. The developers, meanwhile, are vigorously marketing the physical attractions of their developments together with the services included, ranging from pet sitting, landscaping and cleaning services to a residency visa with automatic renewal. Expatriate buyers who work in the free zones will recognize the convenience of the one-stop shop approach. However, some in Dubai believe that allowing foreigners to buy property puts UAE nationals at a disadvantage. A similar argument was used to oppose the free zones.

As one might expect, the government has a stake in each of the major property developments open to foreigners. Nakheel Corporation is the developer of the Palm Islands, Dubai Waterfront, and several other mega-projects. The corporation is run by Sultan Bin Sulayem, also chairman of DP World and of Sheikh Mohammed's Corporate Office. Emaar Properties was a pioneer in development of freehold Dubai properties, and has now taken on the massive Dubai Downtown property development project, including the Burj Dubai skyscraper. Emaar Properties is a publicly-traded company which is about one-third owned by the government. Dubai Holding is an umbrella corporation that owns a number of the free zones (some of which have residential properties within them), as well as the Jumeirah Group (hotels and resorts), Dubai Properties, Sama Dubai and the Dubailand mega-project. The energetic chairman of Dubai Holding (Mohammad Al Gergawi) is the head of Sheikh Mohammed's Executive Office and a member of the UAE cabinet.

But the government has not taken all this on alone – in many cases (most notably in the mega-projects), the main developer builds the infrastructure and invites private developers to add their own hotels, resorts, and other fixtures – continuing to leverage the existing portfolio of assets and the enthusiasm and wonder of business people and tourists from around the world.

Counterpoint

The examples discussed in the chapter show how the effects of asset acceleration led to rapid growth and development. In each example, growth has happened organically after outside intervention helped to facilitate the acceleration effect. To illustrate what can happen when asset leverage is artificially stifled, we need look no further than some of the UAE's sponsorship, joint venture and agency laws and practices. Basically, if a foreign company or investor wishes to set up a business in Dubai, outside a free zone, he is required to have a local sponsoring partner who has a majority of the equity. Originally, this was an effort by the government to invite foreign investment while creating the opportunity for UAE nationals to learn from the best.

Although the original aim was to also stimulate entrepreneurs, it can be argued that it has had the opposite effect. In practice, in many cases local partners appear to have little involvement in and little opportunity to learn from the partnership/joint venture. It seems that often there is a side agreement which specifies the true conditions and rights in the partnership/joint venture and that the local partner is in effect being paid a service fee to allow small or medium-size enterprises (SMEs) to establish themselves in Dubai.

In addition, and in contrast to the above, foreign companies that want to trade and sell their products and/or services in Dubai (outside a free zone) must have a local agent-distributor to represent them (there are some exceptions to this requirement, such as some professional services firms). These relationships, subject to whatever commercial agreements that may govern the relationship, may not be exclusive and may be terminated. For example, a large multinational could have a different agent – in effect a distributor – for each product line it sells, such as computers, televisions, etc. This gives some foreign companies more control over their products and services, and the local agent/distributor more incentive to perform because they know that they can be replaced.

In most cases agency practices seem to have worked well. Because a local agent/distributor knows and understands the local market – for example, where to locate a dealership and how to go about hiring and managing local staff – the risk to a multinational entering the market is reduced.

Overall, such sharing of activities has been an effective means of accelerating the internationalization of trade in Dubai and the surrounding region. Many local agents/distributors have been active in their businesses, investing and expanding, and providing top-quality levels of service and a high degree of integration with, and sensitivity to, the local community. On the other hand some local joint venture sponsors appear to have taken their position for granted and put relatively little into the businesses they are involved in as sponsors. However, 'sleeping' or 'silent' partners may now find themselves expected to do more than they have been doing or they may find their joint venture or agency being taken away from them and given to someone else.

The agency and sponsorship practices that Dubai has adopted are common throughout much of the Gulf region. However, it is important to realize some of their shortcomings, particularly of the need to have a majority local joint venture partner. SMEs, the foundation of much economic growth, may have been held back by these requirements, which raise the cost and increase the complexity of doing business in Dubai and thereby deter investors from entering the market.

At the same time, many question the usefulness of the majority shareholder requirement now that competition is thriving within the free zones, albeit not for trade in the local market. If the regulation was to be relaxed, it could open the market to yet more competition, but it could also remove one of the biggest incentives for companies to locate in the free zones – although the one-stop shop advantage would remain. Thus, as rules and regulations evolve, Dubai must achieve a balance that allows it to create greater economic growth and prosperity for its people.

Conclusion

This chapter has shown how the effects of asset acceleration can lead to asset leverage on many levels, given empowering leadership with a good sense of timing that isn't afraid to step back and adopt a hands-off approach. Asset leverage can mean rapid growth innovation, competition and collaboration among players involved in the strategic vortex.

As happened in the hotel industry, the airline, airport, ports, the Technology, Electronic Commerce and Media Free Zone, the commercial and residential property markets, and new initiatives such as financial services (DIFC), the resulting growth and innovation can be dramatic. But, as in the case of stifling sponsorship practices, complacency and sub optimization can result if asset acceleration is not allowed to move on to its logical next step.

Asset leverage can create significant value within groups of assets or within the strategic vortex as a whole. In order to manage this optimally, leadership has to keep an eye on things, maintaining agility and taking action as and when required.

ENDNOTES

1 Related by a Dubai leading business man to the authors
2 From *Emirate of Dubai Socio-Economic Indicators 2005* and accompanying CD-ROM
3 Source: Department of Tourism & Commerce Marketing
4 http://www.atlantisthepalm.com/
5 From Dubai Media City website at www. dmc.ae

CHAPTER 8

CLOSING THE LOOP

Our greatest glory is not in never falling, but in rising every time we fall.

Confucius

We have seen how assets in the Dubai have been created, accelerated and leveraged to form the basis for the growth that the emirate has experienced in recent years. As we've implied, this process is by no means linear, with a set beginning and end. It's cyclical, with the strategic vortex growing exponentially as a result of interactions between individual assets and groups of assets. The asset leverage stage, as we've seen, is where much of the inherent value of an asset can be unleashed, with little outside intervention required at that point. But this growth can continue only for so long before it needs some attention. When that point is reached, how should you proceed?

There are four options available to decision-makers once an asset stops developing optimally: reinvestment, reinvention, globalization and harvesting. Brief explanations of each of these options follow.

The strategic trajectory

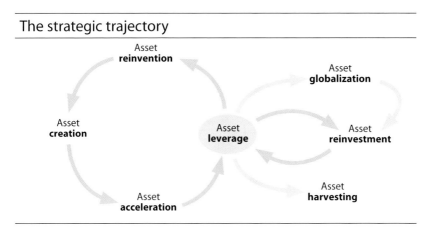

At its most fundamental level, asset reinvestment involves maintenance, upkeep and further development of an existing asset or group of similar assets. When the data indicate that an asset is being fully and efficiently utilized, it will need maintenance to keep it functioning properly. Often, additional resources will need to be allocated to ensure that the asset is able to change to meet growing or changing demands on it.

In the context of the strategic vortex, this step is crucial for establishing an ever-developing core to which future assets can be added and grown. Both infrastructural assets and revenue-generating assets need to be developed to ensure that the integrity of the strategic vortex is maintained and strengthened to allow for future growth and increases in momentum.

Asset reinvention is the second option. After experiencing the growth of asset leverage, it may be that additional uses for an asset have emerged, or that the main utility of the asset has been exhausted, but another use presents itself. So when it's clear that an asset can be used in a different or additional way, it's time to consider reinventing that asset. This ultimately leads back to the asset creation phase for the strategic trajectory cycle to start all over again. Then, whether the asset starts with a new use, or carries on as before with a new spin-off, reinvention integrates accumulated learning to add exponential amounts of value to the strategic vortex as it begins again.

The third option is asset globalization. An asset can be taken global when its value in the local system has maxed out and the business model, operations, and management are solid enough. Since the first edition of this book came out, there have been many examples of this in Dubai, but very few before that.

The fourth option is asset harvesting. When an asset has no further useful life, it should be retired to avoid becoming a liability to the system. Its resources can then be redeployed to support new or existing assets, set aside for future use, or disposed of entirely.

Success factors
Effective decision-making depends on having the information necessary for a decision to be made and there being appropriate and well-oiled channels to ensure the decision is communicated and implemented. In Dubai, commonly accepted project appraisal techniques are often used to provide the information that the decision-makers need. For example, the Palm Island development was the subject of reams of studies by numerous individual consulting firms before it went ahead; in fact, the government of Dubai appears to have enlisted the help of every major management consulting firm in recent years. Although a project like the Burj Al Arab might be unlikely to satisfy any publicly traded company's

project assessment criteria, it made sense for the government to invest in it because of the buzz it would create and the boost it would give to Dubai's unique image and, in turn, the tourism industry. As the unwillingness of the merchant community to develop the Dubai Marina showed, if Dubai is to drive towards its own ambitious vision, the government has to decide the criteria for major asset creation. In short, strong, visionary and experienced leadership is at the heart of successful decision-making in the emirate today.

Accessibility and visibility

The accessibility of Sheikh Mohammed is a key factor that allows two-way communication and keeps his office abreast of everything that's happening in Dubai. The more structured forum for consultations with the rulers, the *majlis*, is another important mechanism.

Many of Dubai's senior executives have said to the authors that 'Sheikh Mohammed is accessible. The problem with a lot of CEOs is that they aren't.' Thus they reinforce the often-used metaphor of Sheikh Mohammed being the man running 'Dubai Inc'.

There are many stories about Sheikh Mohammed, his accessibility and how he goes out of his way to learn about the needs and concerns of the people and local businesses, by way of example:

> *Two days ago, he was in the old city. He talked with every store owner there. It took three and a half hours. You see him at an exhibition, he doesn't come just to be seen there, he really talks to people. He understands them. And if he wants to know more, he invites companies to come to him with presentations on what they do. He's very much involved.*

The accessibility and visibility of Sheikh Mohammed also makes a significant contribution to the trust that individuals and businesses have in him and his office. By having lunch with few attendants in bustling public restaurants and strolling on his own through shopping arcades, he at once communicates that he is aware of what happens in daily life in Dubai and that he is part of it.

There is similar accessibility to senior management in government departments as well as in private companies. Khalid Bin Sulayem of the Department of Tourism and Commerce Marketing explains how this happens:

> *Any employee can come at any time and meet with me or call me. Not only in working hours, even in evenings at home. Every day people do this. After I have dinner at home people come. Even until midnight or one o'clock in the morning.*

Raja Easa Al Gurg echoes this statement in the context of her large family-owned company, the Easa Saleh Al Gurg Group:

> *I believe that an open-door policy is a very important thing. It makes people feel that they are working from their heart, that this is their business and they want to improve it.*

So when decisions need to be made, these managers clearly have more to work with than their weekly reports and dashboards.

Accessibility and visibility are important, then, not only for their practical application – conveying individual concerns, opinions and options to the decision-makers – but also because they instil confidence and a sense of self-worth and value in others.

Management by majlis

A close, almost symbiotic relationship between the business community and the government works in several ways. Shehab Gargash describes the codependence of these two groups:

> *The business community cannot live without government, and the government cannot live without the business community – both of them recognize this. It's a very flat society, so the distance between the bottom and the top is very small. Word gets to the ruler or the crown prince very fast through his own team of department heads within the government or through the business community. He also holds a lot of meetings throughout the year with various groups.*

Many of these meetings are held in what is commonly known as a *majlis*. The *majlis* is an Arab tradition, usually involving a community leader gathering a group to address people's concerns, hear ideas, communicate plans, or simply as a social forum to gather friends and family. It can take many forms.

In Sheikh Rashid's time, his *majlis* consisted of a set group of leaders which functioned in place of a formal government organization. More recently, the term has taken on a broader meaning in the emirate, ranging from the informal sessions at which virtually anyone is welcome to exclusive meetings among senior government officials and/ or business leaders.

Many business and community leaders have a *majlis*, and many homes have a room or area dedicated to hosting these sessions. At any *majlis*, guests discuss current events and business, watch television (invariably programmes on news or current affairs), have tea and sweets, and make deals. The enduring popularity of this phenomenon guarantees that news travels fast from one *majlis* to the next, eventually reaching Sheikh Mohammed's *majlis*, where the most important strategic decisions regarding the emirate are often made.

Ahmed Al Banna at the Dubai Chamber of Commerce and Industry, explains:

> *Let's say I have a problem I know cannot be sorted out. I know that Sheikh Mohammed will be in his majlis for lunch around one o'clock. I go and explain the issue to him, and he gives me his feedback. I have lunch with him and I leave. That's what happens with all government departments, all the leadership.*

Abdulhamid Juma elaborates:

> *The majlis closes the gap between him and his CEOs and managers. He said to all the directors general, 'If you have an idea, you come straight to me.' He loves ideas. 'I know your boss, I see him every day. I want to see you once in a while.'*

Sheikh Mohammed's *majlis* isn't only for ideas and problem-solving, nor is it only for UAE nationals. Raja Trad, a Lebanese advertising executive, explains:

> *Sheikh Mohammed's office will pick up representatives from each industry, and they will call us into the majlis. We'll be around 100 people and Sheikh Mohammed will say, 'No taboos. You represent Dubai. Dubai is not just for the nationals, Dubai is for you. You contributed to the success of Dubai.' And then he will invite people to stand up and talk about anything.*

Both good news and bad news are conveyed in the *majlis*. This helps problems to be addressed as soon as they arise. In the rulers' *majlis*, the rulers learn what's important to the community, and the members of the community learn the rulers' perspective, as well as those of their peers. Key people come together, pool their knowledge and come up with solutions that they will all endorse.

For example, visiting Dr Anwar Gargash's *majlis* (usually held in the evening, from around nine to just before midnight) in a venerated old family house across the road from his own family home, there is invariably a mixture of government and business leaders, some family members (often including Anwar's young sons) and a few friends. Unless you are in the know, one is never sure who is sitting next to you. One of the authors recalls an imminent British economist and member of the House of Lords visiting the *majlis* and discussing monetary policy with someone to his right, when very politely the senior government official to his left answered a question and said that the other person he is talking with is the local school's Arabic teacher who doesn't speak English! However, in these weekly gatherings it is not uncommon to have two or three cabinet ministers, a couple of heads of the largest family businesses, CEOs and entrepreneurs with almost all locals dressed in Dubai's national white dress, called a kandora (although it can be colourful too), comfortably talking, eating, and even watching television. There is usually an ante room/office for those wishing to discuss a business issue in private. During the fasting month of Ramadan, the *majlis* is open daily and is usually full and lively.

So the *majlis* provides a forum for socializing, problem-solving and debate at many levels of the community. It's also a means for communication in every direction among stakeholder groups, extending right up to the rulers, who are known to ring senior officials during the *majlis* to draw their attention to issues that have been raised and to get them to take action.

Management wearing many hats

Another way in which the government and the business community work together is by combining leadership roles in a way that rarely happens in the West. Senior government officials head a variety of public, private, semi-private and independently managed government-owned companies. This ensures a mutuality in the interests of business and government. Members of the inner circle of leaders who are involved in many private and governmental organizations are thus in a position to feed information back to the rulers on practically any subject. In effect, they appear to take the place of governance boards or consultative bodies.

The system is based on a sort of government patronage, which has to be benign and intelligent if it is to work to the advantage of the emirate as a whole. A Dubai senior executive explains:

> *They choose the best people, the people that can be trusted, the people who can contribute without looking forward for a return – eventually they get rewarded, but this is not their first consideration. Not everyone is looking for financial compensation, some are looking for recognition not only in Dubai or the United Arab Emirates, but also across the region. If anybody has a very successful initiative, he will become well known in the Arab region.*

The range of high-ranking jobs someone may hold is illustrated in the following examples:

1   Sheikh Ahmed is the Chairman of Emirates Group (which
    includes Emirates airline) and President of the Dubai
    Department of Civil Aviation and also chairs and sits on
    the board of many other organizations, including Dubai Aerospace
    Enterprise and the new government investment company,
    Investment Corporation of Dubai. He is also Vice Chairman of the
    Dubai Executive Council.

2   Mohammad Al Gergawi is a UAE cabinet minister, head
of Sheikh Mohammed's Executive Office, Chair of Dubai Holding
    (whose principle assets include: Jumeirah group, Dubai Properties,
    Sama Dubai, and the investment companies Dubai Group, Dubai
    International Capital and Dubailand – part of Tatweer) and Chair
    of the Mohammed Bin Rashid charitable foundation.

3   Sultan Bin Sulayem is the Chairman of Dubai World (whose key
    assets include: DP World, Jebel Ali Free zone, Nakheel, Tejari, The
    World, The Palm, and the Istithmar investment company), and
    head of Sheikh Mohammed's Corporate Office.

When asked how he manages to do so many demanding jobs,
Sultan Bin Sulayem explains simply that he likes it, and that he gets
bored when not working. He also says that he goes out of his way to
communicate with all the people under him, with a regular programme
of training schemes and management feedback sessions.

The multiple roles of many of these figures also come from a long-
standing Arab tradition: when someone succeeds, he – or, increasingly
frequently, she – is rewarded with more responsibility. Sheikha Lubna
was part of Sultan Bin Sulayem's team at Jebel Ali port before being
asked to head the e-government initiative and then, soon after, to
start up Tejari.com. Her next post – and a significant promotion – was
Minister of Economy in the UAE government. Her next move was to
Minister of Foreign Trade.

But some question what's often called the 'Superman syndrome'.
They believe that some high-ranking government officials remain in
their positions too long, with the result that their effectiveness may
decrease and that they may become less good at adapting to changes
in the evolving business environment. However, in view of the pace of
change and the constant need to adapt, there appears to be little room
for laggards and the system does appear to have created some natural
efficiencies. A good example is when Sheikh Mohammed reshuffled
his cabinet in early 2008. One cannot argue with the success of this
system to-date. However, the key issue for Dubai to think about in the
longer term is "growth fatigue" and how long these amazingly talented

executives can continue this pace, and will the next generation of leaders and managers in Dubai possess the same drive, enthusiasm and understanding as these titans.

It is clear, the authors have experienced this first hand, that there are many talented individuals across Dubai, it is also fair to say that the talent pool, although getting deeper is not deep enough to meet the aspirations that Dubai's senior leaders wish to achieve. There are many who have been 'entusted' in positions of responsibility and/or have been given added responsibilities where they may not have entirely been able to live up to expectations, possibly because of added pressure of new responsibilities and/or what we have referred to as "growth fatigue". As more and more talent locates to Dubai this will raise standards and deepen the talent pool, which in turn will enable more structured succession procedures and processes; an encouragement by the leadership to hire the best, either locally, from the region or beyond will be important.

Other conduits

As Dubai grows, there is always a danger of the government becoming bigger and more bureaucratic. But Sheikh Mohammed's distaste for new layers of government suggests this will not happen. Anita Mehra Homayoun describes the importance of maintaining the traditional practices:

> *As Dubai gets bigger and bigger, and the number of merchants gets bigger and bigger, the government losing touch becomes a danger. Then we'd become like many Western democracies. In Sheikh Rashid's days, someone would come to the majlis and say 'I've lost five camels', and the Ruler would give him replacements. Things are different now, but the same kind of thing happens on a larger scale.*

To ensure that the government is able to keep up with people's needs, decidedly modern initiatives have been developed. One is the e-government portal launched in 2002. The objective of the portal is to facilitate interaction between the government, the public and the business community and to contribute to turning Dubai into a leading economic centre. By 2005, 1,600 services were available via the portal, involved in providing information and assisting transactions in such areas as business, health, education, housing, law and the judicial system, and tourism. Users can pay fines, apply for and renew a variety of licences and permits, and find out about a wide range of government services. The same year, Dubai launched the first portal for mobile phone users to access e-government services.

According to Sheikha Lubna, whom Sheikh Mohammed trusted

with developing and launching the portal:

> *He wanted more transparency in the government itself. He wanted to demonstrate the government being customer-centric.*

This transparency should allow more accurate and more timely information to be available, as one government official says:

> *If Sheikh Mohammed wants to sit at home or in his office and know how many visas were issued on that day, that information should be on the portal.*

As it grows, the portal should be able to provide a valuable amount of quantitative data that will aid effective decision-making.

Another means for Dubai's leaders to learn about what's going on in government departments is the Dubai Government Excellence Programme, which is run by a private company and was established to improve efficiency and innovation in government. Government divisions, departments, teams and initiatives are ranked according to a comprehensive framework, including financial performance. Feedback from 'mystery shoppers', who approach government departments in a variety of guises, is also incorporated into the assessment criteria.

Results of the rankings are made public and those whose performance is relatively poor are made aware that they must improve. This programme is crucial in creating government transparency and also provides an incentive for every part of government to perform well. The extensive data-gathering and analysis involved in the programme provides further information for the government to use in its decision-making process. It also provides opportunities for benchmarking and learning across the government. One government official explained:

> *The government has implemented the quality programmes so that departments will learn from one another and improve. This has improved our customer service by a tremendous amount.*

Some of the programme's methods have been adopted by Sheikh Mohammed's office, which has been known to send mystery shoppers independently to different parts of the government. One official told of an excitable character who turned up at his office looking for a job, and who was suspected of being a plant from The Executive Office. The official later discovered that this was not the case, but awareness of the possibility exists throughout the civil service.

Still room for improvement

There is no shortage of information available to the government, but it has been suggested that the accuracy and timeliness of some data need to be improved, which may prove to be an increasingly important issue as the emirate develops. Sheikh Mohammed referred to the 50 weather stations around Dubai that provide real-time data, and said that he would like to see business information with the same immediacy. The data exist but are not always shared between departments let alone available electronically in real time.

When trying to collect data for this book, the effort required was greater than in some other jurisdictions. In some cases the data was not available, in others it was, but difficult to obtain. Having said that there has been a noticeable improvement since 2002–2003 when the first edition of the book was written. In all cases everyone was exceptionally willing and helpful, especially at the senior levels of organizations, but as we have also observed what they are willing or want to deliver is not necessarily what occurs! We were not entirely surprised by this – it is often the case in many fast-growing organizations. However, this time lag needs to be addressed in Dubai because it is critical to attracting and developing an international talent pool as well as empowering the next generation of managers. When the authors got stuck, they were fortunate in being able to approach Sheikh Mohammed's Executive Office who were always both willing and able to assist (thank you!). This is encouraging since presumably this is a very important source of information for Sheikh Mohammed himself and his senior team.

As many have indicated, a major challenge for Dubai will be maintaining the close contact between the ruler and the community. Better information and better information flows will help do this and will also maintain the effectiveness of the decision-making process.

Options in practice

Asset reinvestment

Examples of asset reinvestment are rife in Dubai, as many of the infrastructural assets and other large core assets were created in their initial form decades ago and have had to develop to sustain the pace of growth.

The road network is constantly under construction, particularly outside the old town centre where new roads are being built. The mushroom-like construction of office and apartment buildings along Sheikh Zayed Road causes tremendous traffic congestion at many times during a typical day. The layout of the road means that it can take over half an hour to get from a building on one side of the divided road to one immediately opposite.

The pace at which the roads are being built is startling, even for Dubai's residents. Everyone seems to have a story to tell about getting lost because the road layout has changed. One man who went on a short business trip returned to find that the airport lot where he'd left his car only a few days before had been moved to make way for more building. His car was safe and sound in another lot.

In 2005, the Roads and Transport Authority was set up by the government to plan and execute transport in the area. This includes a responsibility for the Dubai Metro train system, roads, public transport, taxis, and marine transport. The RTA has set about creating an integrated transport system that will provide 'safe and smooth transport for all.'[1]

By late 2009, the first phase of the fully-automatic Dubai Metro should be complete. On every visit to Dubai, the authors have noticed the amazing speed with which the metro is being built and towards the end of 2008 it looked almost complete. The system will ultimately total 70 kilometres of lines and 42 stations, making it one of the longest metropolitan transit systems in the world. The system is planned to absorb 34 per cent of trips in Dubai by 2020.[2] We would not be surprised to see, ultimately, a number of the emirates being linked by a metro/train system. It makes ample sense to have a link from Abu Dhabi to Dubai and on to Sharjah, linking all three emirates and perhaps even countries in the region, which will of course spur even more growth.

Further major initiatives to expand the capacity of both electricity generation and water provision were undertaken early in the 21st century to meet the rapidly growing demand. As roads, offices and residences threaten to overwhelm the city; the development of several parks and green spaces is also under way, including expansion of Dubai Zoo, which is moving to a new site and being significantly upgraded. Each of the mega-projects also includes large swathes of outdoor space, many with significant water features like navigable canals.

This isn't being done just to maintain the status quo, however; there's a strong competitive element to asset reinvestment as well. The ports, airport and Emirates airline have also undergone frequent expansion over the years, each helping to fuel the growth of tourism and make life and business more comfortable in the emirate. The combined effect of these assets within the strategic vortex is important, even if they are merely being grown and expanded over time.

One government official explains how he sees asset reinvestment working in Dubai:

> *It's important to continually update your operations. The government of Dubai recognizes this and takes risks to keep improving. This is why Dubai is one of the only places in the world where the public sector moves faster than the private sector.*

This is consistent with the government's vision, which involves the creation of superlative assets at high speed.

In the hotel industry, standards are being raised constantly by new entrants with increasingly spectacular offerings. This forces existing hotels to implement renovation programmes and continue to improve in order to stay competitive. The retail sector has seen similar growth in recent years, but, as ever more spectacular shopping venues are created with built-in entertainment and restaurants, some of the older malls look tired and can start to become less popular, although some have seen these challenges coming and have reacted by rejuvenating their shopping centres, by expanding and modernizing them. Those who did not do this have lost out to the new developments.

Much the same is true in the commercial property market. As the city has expanded beyond the centre, better and better office buildings have become available. The World Trade Centre (WTC) was once on the outskirts of the town and a highly prestigious address; now it is the first of many newer and taller high rise towers, not the least of which is the Emirates Towers virtually next door. Several of the buildings in the same area along Sheikh Zayed Road are beginning to seem slightly downmarket compared with some of their newer neighbours, even though almost none of them are more than a decade old. And an increasing number of businesses are moving from their existing office space to offices in Dubai Internet City and Dubai Media City, forcing some buildings to undergo refurbishment just to stay in the game.

Hence the need for continuous investment so that hotels, shopping centres, commercial and residential buildings stay ahead of the game or at least keep up with the fast pace of change. This is already happening in many of the earlier developments mentioned above. In particular, it should be noted that in the case of the WTC, it is being replaced by the newer and bigger WTC with the goal of becoming one of the world's major event and exhibition venues.

In many cases, such as the facilities in Dubai's ports, international competition drives reinvestment. Sultan Bin Sulayem describes the constant upgrading of Jebel Ali Port to keep up with Singapore.

Whatever you see in Singapore, you see here. Sometimes we are more advanced than them, sometimes they are more advanced than us. We invest in different things. For example, Singapore invested in a single crane that carries two containers. We decided to get a faster, more advanced crane that worked better and was less expensive. Later, they came to see ours and decided to change. Sometimes we are better, sometimes they are better, but we are very, very close.

Asset reinvention

Asset reinvention can involve repositioning an asset that has outlived its original purpose, although it is early days for this to have happened in Dubai. It can be like brand extension: developing a new use for an existing asset. There are many examples of this in the emirate.

The Dubai Police Academy was set up by Sheikh Rashid in 1968 to help train local people to supplement the Trucial Oman Scouts, a regional force funded and armed by the British. Since that time, the academy has been reinvented many times, taking on its present form in 1987 and becoming independent in 1998. Over the years, it has retained its affiliation with the Police Department, but has reinvented itself as an institute for higher learning, offering a variety of law degrees and evening programmes in addition to its cadet training. The academy is also now recognized as a centre for excellence in the region, accepting recruits from other Gulf Cooperation Council countries. Women are also eligible to take part in academy programmes, including a combination of police sciences and military training.

The Dubai Ports Authority has pursued a similar model, having developed such an expertise in port and free zone management that it could begin to apply them in other countries. The newly formed Dubai Ports International more than doubled productivity in the first three years of a 20-year contract it signed in 1999 to manage and operate Jeddah's container terminal with a local partner. The following year, it invested in Djibouti's port, this time doubling productivity in the first year of managing its operations.

The Dubai Shopping Festival is another asset that has undergone multiple reinventions. Inspired by the Great Singapore Sale, it was started in 1996 to create an attraction for visitors from around the region and stimulate retail trade. By 2005, the shopping festival was attracting 3.3 million visitors, and more than $1.8 billion was spent. Hotels, transport, shops and restaurants all benefit from the event; some earn more during the festival than during the rest of the year.[3]

The Global Village is a reinvention spin-off from the Dubai Shopping Festival. It began as six pavilions representing different countries on a plot next to the Creek for the duration of the festival. By 2007, there were 39 pavilions, 2,000 stalls, and 44 restaurants from all over the world.[4] The Dubai Summer Surprises is a reinvented Dubai Shopping Festival in the heat of the summer, focusing on family activities for the regional market, with a different theme each year. The Dubai World Cup horse race used to coincide with the shopping festival, taking advantage of the influx of visitors. Starting in 2003 the race took place afterwards because the shopping festival was moved to take advantage of school and religious holidays. Early indications were that the race is well able to stand up on its own and it has.

One example of reinvention is at the personal level. Dubai International Airport was one of the first airports in the world to implement an electronic pass system called e-gate. This allows registered users to bypass immigration and enter the country with just their e-card and a fingerprint scan. The programme is open to all UAE residents, as well as citizens of 34 countries that are eligible for on-the-spot visas. The programme has had a remarkably fast take-up, with 3,500 citizens from 45 countries signing up in the first month. When an immigration attendant was asked if such technologies made him fear for his job, he replied that if this job disappeared, he was confident that he would be given a new job. This speaks volumes about the mindset of people in Dubai. This man had complete trust in the government and his employer to do right by him. This belief, in turn, gave him the confidence to do his job well and indeed convinced one of the authors to get an e-gate card.

In each of the examples of asset reinvention described above, changes were made with careful consideration, based on the best information available and guided by the asset's place in the vision of Dubai. In terms of the strategic vortex model, spin-off assets start the cycle anew at the asset creation stage, while upgraded assets remain in asset leverage, still growing and interacting with other elements.

Asset harvesting

One example of asset harvesting in Dubai was created in the Technology, Electronic Commerce and Media Free Zone at the same time as Dubai Internet City. The Dubai Ideas Oasis, a dotcom incubator, was a short-lived initiative, and it seems to have been easily forgotten in the light of the successes of Dubai Internet City and Dubai Media City. The government provided seed funds, but further venture capital didn't emerge. But in the end, according to one of those interviewed for this book, there just weren't enough good ideas to sustain the project. The Dubai Ideas Oasis was put on hold indefinitely, although several of the original start-ups that participated are continuing to manage their businesses in Dubai Internet City. The facilities and resources of the Dubai Ideas Oasis have since been taken over and put to use there.

There will be many candidates for asset harvesting if the agency laws are changed. As already discussed, these laws provide the prominent trading families with monopolies in many areas, thus in some cases preventing competition and asset leverage, though it is clear that some monopoly businesses are very well managed and customer focused, reinvesting regularly to keep up with changing market requirements and to take advantage of new opportunities. It is unclear whether such changes may happen in the foreseeable future and what the effects would be. But as the economy grows and attracts more skilled workers with disposable income, it is reasonable to expect that the demand for luxury cars, for example, will also grow. Either the existing sole sellers of each brand will reap the benefits, or, if competition is allowed, the benefits may be shared and buyers may also enjoy lower prices. If this happens, the incumbents may continue to prosper, but some may be unable to compete and may have to harvest some of the assets that currently seem so prosperous. Asset harvesting should not be equated with failure; some projects simply have a limited useful life and must at some point be retired. Nevertheless, there is an aversion to failure in Dubai that may help to explain why few projects seem to have reached this stage. As a government official puts it succinctly:

We don't have projects that fail here. If it's going to fail, we'll change it.

The pride that many people feel in their work is a strong disincentive to perceived failure. Even in the face of extreme risk, failure is never considered to be an option by some, as Sultan Bin Sulayem says:

Even if a project is barely able to be done, there are people who will never accept failure. If they fail, it will be a big embarrassment. I would be very embarrassed if the Palm didn't work, even though the risk of failure is very high. They manage, and they do it. This is what we try to promote.

He is a good example of a senior executive who stays involved with his projects at every level, making adjustments and changes whenever needed so that they never approach the point of failure.

This perspective is shared by many business leaders in the West, particularly successful entrepreneurs who aren't shy about reallocating resources when signs of failure begin to loom. As development in Dubai continues, it is inevitable that there will be failures; accepting this fact may prove a challenge for government and business community alike.

The cycle described above applies readily to much of the development happening in Dubai, but increasingly, the expertise developed locally is being leveraged elsewhere in the world. This additional option is discussed in the next chapter.

ENDNOTES

1   http://www.rta.ae/vision.asp
2   http://www.ameinfo.com/81162.html
3   Figures provided by The Executive Office
4   Gale, I., 'Visitor rush brings little business to Global Village', Gulfnews.com, 8 January 2007

CHAPTER 9

GOING GLOBAL

I do not want to be walled in on all sides and my windows to be stuffed. I want the cultures of all the lands to blow about my house as freely as possible. But I refuse to be blown off my feet by any.

Mahatma Gandhi

In the first edition of this book, the preceding three options were sufficient to describe how Dubai was managing its assets in the context of the strategic trajectory model. Since 2003, the most successful enterprises in Dubai have developed such expertise and inherent value that expanding outside of the emirate's borders has been a natural step. By 2008, Dubai has become more visible than ever before, not only because of its own attractions, but also due to branching out into new international markets. Some of the headlines that have come along early on with this expansion may not have been positive ones, providing some valuable lessons along the way.

This chapter, new in this edition, examines some of Dubai's efforts to expand internationally and relates these examples to the strategic trajectory model, then concludes by exploring how these assets can be managed as a portfolio.

Towards asset globalization
The leaders of Dubai's government and businesses have long been accustomed to working with people from all over the world. As a trading centre, this became a necessity early on. By early in the 21st century, Dubai had mastered the art of enticing the world to visit its myriad of attractions. Luxurious and unique hotels, shopping, beaches, and restaurants, all combined to lure in the tourists; the free zones enticed the world's leading companies to set up regional HQs; conference facilities and large-scale industry events attracted industry groups; and sports enthusiasts flocked to Dubai's sporting venues for pro tennis, powerboat racing, golf, cricket, rugby and horse racing.

148

These developments make it easy to understand how Dubai has enjoyed the successes it has had in recent years. And while there seems to be no end in sight for the further development of groundbreaking attractions in Dubai, it has also become clear that there is demand elsewhere in the world for what Dubai's home-grown capabilities have to offer.

There have been several success stories involving Dubai's brands creating international capabilities using domestic successes as a springboard. In the context of the strategic trajectory model, in each case an existing asset has been moved from asset leverage to asset globalization, taking advantage of the value and appeal already present to launch into new markets with gusto. As we will see, however, having a top-quality product is not always enough to guarantee success.

Dubai goes global

Below are a handful of examples of Dubai going global with some of its strategic assets.

Property development

Dubai's major property development companies (including Emaar, Nakheel, Dubai Properties and Sama Dubai) have developed a myriad of residential and commercial projects in the emirate. Some of Dubai Properties' more recent projects include Business Bay (some 64 million square feet), the Jumeirah Beach Residence (40 towers on 1.7 km of beachfront) and Culture Village (with its newly launched Museum of Middle East Modern Art – a first for the region). Sama Dubai is building The Lagoons, which incorporates the new Dubai Opera House designed by world renowned architect Zaha Hadid, as well as the Dubai Towers which it is building around the world, spreading the Dubai name. The list of major developments in Dubai goes on . . .

However, this is no longer enough of a challenge. These companies are turning their attention to the world and have begun aggressive expansion into the Middle East (including Turkey), North Africa, India, China and beyond. For example, Emaar is developing Saudi Arabia's King Abdullah Economic City on 5.451 hectares on the coast of the Red Sea. Estimated to cost $30 billion, the development will include zones for port operations, financial services, industrial facilities, luxury resorts, residential areas, and a zone dedicated to education.

Emaar is developing the Dead Sea Golf and Beach Resort in Jordan. This development will have 850 residential units, two hotels, the country's first green golf course, and 17,000 square metres of shopping and entertainment venues spread across 400 acres.

Emaar has also entered into joint ventures with local companies in Egypt and Syria to develop large-scale properties in those countries. Emaar has also formed a joint venture (JV) in India, which in 2005 announced projects totalling $4 billion in five cities in India. In Pakistan, Emaar is developing three mixed-use developments at a cost of $2.4 billion.

Additionally, Emaar has set its sights on Morocco, and has formed another JV there to develop a range of properties, including Bahia Bay, with 531 hectares close to Bouznika bay featuring golf, villas and houses, hotels, equestrian facilities, and entertainment, as well as Amelkis II (following the successful Amelkis I) a luxury residential and golfing complex in Marrakech and Oukaimeden a mountain destination. Further properties are being developed in South Africa, Turkey and Tunisia.

Emaar is also aggressively pursuing business in China, with an initial focus on residential developments in Beijing and Shanghai. With Beijing hosting the Olympics in 2008 and the 2010 World Expo happening in Shanghai, these two cities were chosen as strategic entry points.

In the US, Emaar has acquired John Liang Homes, a leading privately-held homebuilder, which 'is consistent with Emaar's strategy of expanding its business on a global basis beyond Dubai.' Similarly, in the UK, Emaar has acquired Hamptons, one of the country's leading property estate agents.[1]

This rapid expansion has made Emaar one of the world's largest property development companies.

Sama Dubai (formerly Dubai International Properties), the active overseas property development arm of Dubai Holding, is undertaking major developments in Qatar, Oman, Morocco and Bahrain.

In the context of Dubai developing the Gulf region, what it is also doing is spreading its own positive mantra. In a meeting with Dubai's senior team, it was said that in Morocco things were "down", people generally "depressed". But that was two or three years ago before Dubai came along to develop much of the country which has fuelled other inward investors. A similar example applies to its neighbour to the south in the Sultan of Oman. Now there is a sense of enthusiasm and positive feelings there – the property market is buoyant, and everyone is clearly a winner. Dubai has assisted a country within the region to grow and at the same time their investments have also done well.

Hotels and hospitality
Dubai Holding's hotel and resort arm, Jumeirah, began expanding outside the borders of the emirate through strategic alliances, acquisitions and developments by some its sister companies, and continues by developing new properties in foreign markets. These

include London's Jumeirah Carlton Tower and Jumeirah Lowndes hotels, and the Jumeirah Essex House in New York City.

Future developments include a private island resort in Thailand, a new London hotel occupying the bottom half of a proposed skyscraper adjacent to the Thames, and a hotel within 52-acre mixed-use development in Shanghai, to name but a few. They are looking at managing some 60 hotels in the next few years and appear on track to do so.

Not to be left out, Emaar Properties has joined forces with Italy's Giorgio Armani Spa to create a series of Armani-branded resorts in top markets around the world, one of which will be in Burj Dubai. Similarly, Nakheel has acquired investments in Africa including the Waterfront in Cape Town, as well as a number of African resorts, and invested in the US, Australia, Asia and Europe, and of course its major investment with Kerzner International in developing the enormous Atlantis (1,500 plus rooms) hotel in the Palm Jumeirah and another venture together in Mexico (where Nakheel has a 50 per cent shareholding of a Mexican resort).

Ports and logistics

Long before Dubai was a tourist destination, though, it thrived as a cargo port, so it seems natural for Dubai to take these capabilities to the global market. Dubai Ports International (DPI) began aggressive international expansion in 1999 to export the expertise that the Dubai Ports Authority had developed running Port Rashid and the Jebel Ali Port. This was a tremendous success, and by 2003, DPI was managing ports across the Middle East, India, and Europe. A major acquisition in 2005 added a strong presence in Asia and South America. And the following year held the acquisition of Britain's P&O, including a portfolio of terminals (ports), plus P&O Ferries and related operations.

Government-owned DP World had a highly-publicized mis-step later in 2006 when attempting to take over operations of a half dozen US ports. The deal was approved by the US government, but popular outcry over security concerns led to Dubai pulling out of managing some of the ports.

Free zone/tech clusters

As the proliferation of free zones in Dubai shows, developing knowledge-based business parks is another strong competency. As of early 2006, Dubai Internet City had signed a deal with the Indian State of Kerala to develop a zone for software companies, and further discussions were underway with authorities in other Indian regions, plus Pakistan, Iran, and Malta about similar projects.[2]

DUBAL

Another long-established jewel in Dubai's government-owned portfolio of companies is DUBAL, Dubai Aluminium. Generating 861,000 metric tonnes of product in 2006, DUBAL is the single largest non-oil contributor to Dubai's GDP.

This capability is also being leveraged internationally. One 2006 deal close to home is with the neighbouring Emirate of Abu Dhabi, to develop a world-class smelter complex utilizing DUBAL's proprietary technologies at a cost of $6 billion.[3] Further afield, the same technology was used to develop a smelter for the Indian state of Orissa in 2005.

Understanding what it takes

Clearly, expanding internationally is a major endeavour for any sort of enterprise; and having the resources to do the job is not sufficient. The key to successful asset globalization based on these examples seems to be breaking all the rules at first, then playing by the rules when going global.

Each of these examples became successful by breaking free of constraints; property developers created increasingly unique luxury developments; hotels and resorts (often managed by Jumeirah) became architectural icons overnight; Dubai's government sunk nearly every last dirham into its ports early on; the free zones were designed expressly to avoid the limitations of local or federal laws and regulations; and DUBAL developed proprietary technologies to propel it to the top of the industry.

Then, when expanding internationally, each recognized that the rules would be different, and that a new way of working on the terms of the new markets would be required. When necessary, Emaar Properties has partnered with local developers. Jumeirah started its expansion by acquiring and developing top-shelf hotels in major markets. Dubai Internet City has recognized that free zones may not be desirable or feasible in some markets and is therefore concentrating on the infrastructure and local synergies; and DUBAL works cooperatively with government to ensure a good fit.

DP World has, of course, been successful in its asset globalization, both through acquisition of major port operators and through working with governments to manage terminals. Its only mis-step involved an arguably forgivable failure to sense the zeitgeist in the US market that would be so resistant. The deal was approved by the US government, but the outcry only occurred when it became public, and Dubai had to pull out of managing US ports shortly thereafter. The lesson may be that, when contemplating asset globalization, there are indeed many rules to be conscious of – written, unwritten, and cultural – that will differ from one context to the next.

However, there are challenges in going global. As the above examples show, there are clear synergies when Dubai is building on existing strength such as property development, port management, hotel management, airline expertise, etc. It is however unclear where some overseas investments are being made how Dubai can add deep expertise, but rather seems to contributing value more as a financial investor. Of course it may be that in these cases this is all part of Dubai's overseas investment portfolio to develop a more diversified asset base. Or it may be part of a future strategy that is as yet unclear about developing new types of strategic capabilities. Observers of Dubai must watch this area carefully as it will be one of the key determinants of Dubai's global impact.

Asset globalization in context
As another option in the strategic vortex model, asset globalization presents an opportunity to take a strategic asset to a whole new level, but in doing so, it is clearly still necessary to recognize the other steps in the model, and reinvest or reinvent when necessary – and retire when the time comes. Indeed, at any stage of the model, it is crucial to maintain a holistic perspective and to regard assets as a portfolio. This topic is discussed below.

Managing the portfolio
The strategic vortex model is a fluid one, and can be applied at several different levels. An asset can be a company, an organization, a facility or a bundle of related entities. When you put multiple assets together and manage the portfolio strategically, you begin to see radical growth on a large scale. This is what has occurred in Dubai.

Initial assets were created to build on existing strengths: the Creek was developed and ports were built. To supplement the flow of goods in and out, industrial free zones for businesses to set up operations were created. Then, anticipating increased demand for air passenger and freight traffic, Emirates airline was created. The airport was expanded and the Airport Free Zone was created to supplement the existing free zones. To diversify the economy into high-value-added knowledge-based industries, the Technology, Electronic Commerce and Media Free Zone was created. The influx of companies and workers led to a demand for world-class facilities such as education, healthcare and housing. The Dubai International Financial Centre was conceived with the intention of making the emirate an internationally recognized institutional finance hub and a gateway in the region for capital markets and investment. Throughout this process the infrastructure has been built and upgraded to support the needs of the growing system, although it has occasionally fallen behind, as the level of traffic congestion makes all too clear, largely because demand/ growth far exceeded the most optimistic expectations.

Each new asset has taken advantage of the business ecosystem into which it has been introduced. For example, the development of Port Rashid benefited from Dubai's existing reputation as a trading port, and the Technology, Electronic Commerce and Media Free Zone was developed as a result of knowledge and experience from Jebel Ali. The Dubai International Financial Centre is the next natural step, albeit a large and risky one. Its success is in large part thanks to the size and momentum of the asset base that's already been established, and the leadership's understanding of what the customer base wants. Essa Abdulfattah Kazim, Chairman of Borse Dubai (which owns the Dubai Financial Market, and parts of DIFX, NASDAQ, OMV and the LSE) describes the readiness of Dubai's financial activities in 2007:

> *We have the critical mass now. We can capitalize on the name of Dubai. If you ask anyone in finance today where the centre for finance is in the region, he would say it is Bahrain. But because of the reputation of Dubai, we believe that this is the right time for developing the Dubai International Financial Centre and the financial sector here.*

Today, many will agree that Dubai has been able to very quickly establish itself as the alternative to Bahrain, and it seems, based on growth to date, that once the DIFC is largely built by 2010, that Dubai might have by then overtaken Bahrain as the main financial centre in the region. This sort of strategic thinking and decisive action can only be possible when leaders are well informed and surrounded by like-minded executives who are in touch with a wide range of stakeholders. With this sort of group at the helm, the right assets can be created at just the right time, and their growth can be managed optimally within the ecosystem. As we've seen, initial assets require bold, risky moves – think of Sheikh Rashid's early initiatives or, more recently, the islands developments and Dubailand – so they need to be chosen with care. They will form the foundation on which other assets will grow and develop. They'll need to be solid and scalable like the airline, the airport, the ports and free zones have been. (If it seems easy, think of the problems many other airports have had in expanding to meet demand over recent years.) Unless these assets are the right ones, created in the right way, they won't be able to support the momentum of assets that are added later.

Once you've got these assets right, though, additional assets should present decreased risk because of the momentum already built up, and because you're building on existing assets and knowledge. This is why it's important for leadership to be able to step back and regard the ecosystem as a whole, as well as the detailed components that interact within it. A winning strategy, then, is able to leverage past successes (and what you have learnt from failures) to determine which assets to create and when, so that they have an optimal effect on the rest of the system. The principal factor is being able to understand what the ecosystem wants and needs, based on external factors (the economy, markets, customers, competitors) and internal factors (other assets, available resources), and then put the strategy into action rapidly. When it starts to make sense to go global with an asset in the portfolio, it will remain important to maintain perspective, since the stakes become higher with the increased visibility.

ENDNOTES

1   From Emaar Properties website at www.emaar.ae/International/
2   "The Circuit", DIC Newsletter Issue 2, December 2005
3   From DUBAL website at www.dubal.ae

CHAPTER 10

CORPORATE IMPLICATIONS

The speed of the boss is the speed of the team.

Lee Iacocca, former Chrysler chairman

In the dramatic transformation of Dubai many themes stand out – leadership, vision and strategy – all of which are commonly covered in business books. But it isn't often that they are associated in business with governments. It is the innovative application of these themes in Dubai that makes it such an interesting example, from which can be drawn a range of lessons for use in today's corporations and other organizations.

This book has sought to explore the fundamental issue of how organizations can achieve large-scale, rapid growth. Expanding current business operations through the extension of existing products or services or entering new markets is one way. Others include mergers and acquisitions, attempts to innovate outside the current product-market offerings and reorganizing around multidisciplinary 'skunk-works' project teams. But each of these methods has potential shortcomings.

Over half of mergers and acquisitions fail because they don't achieve the much-trumpeted synergies they were supposed to, or because of culture clashes or a host of other reasons. The failure is all the more painful when the acquisition was made at a price that included a high premium. The problem with skunk-works is that it invariably takes longer than expected to produce results.

As is the case with many if not most corporations, the emirate of Dubai was not blessed with abundant resources when its rapid development began in the mid-20th century, so its rulers had little choice but to build on their existing strengths. This is what Sheikh Rashid did, beginning with the development of the Dubai Creek and building the airport back in the early 1960s, adding to the region's value as a port and a hub. With these small steps he set Dubai on a path that has led the emirate to where it is today, with a lot of care, attention and adjustment on the way as well as enormous drive.

This chapter considers how Dubai succeeded in order to draw lessons that can be applied across a wide range of organizations. Four broad themes are covered: active, creative leadership; asset creation, acceleration and leverage stages of the strategic vortex model; the strategic vortex model itself; and some of the principal considerations in managing a portfolio of assets to enable rapid growth.

Active leadership

One of the crucial components of a successful strategy is active leadership. Dubai has proved this through its own distinctive style of active leadership, which fosters innovation, breaks through boundaries, involves taking risks and instils confidence among stakeholders – in stark contrast to many business and government leaders today and in the past.

Active leadership is important at every stage of the strategic trajectory model. There will almost always be multiple assets in their own strategic trajectories interacting within the larger ecosystem. While one asset is being created another may be being accelerated and yet another being harvested, and so the leadership characteristics required at each phase need to be demonstrated.

Set the vision

Vision is frequently cited as an important element of leadership. Indeed, the authors' experience in Dubai reinforces this view. But vision in Dubai is more than just an expression of where it is meant to be going. It also has a multidimensional, cascading effect, providing inspiration and goals for senior managers and civil servants alike as they consider what the vision means to them and their own domain within greater Dubai Inc.

Just over half a century ago Dubai was little more than sand. The cornerstone of its economy, pearl diving, had been decimated. Out of this adversity, the vision to create a major economic centre was born. Much of the ensuing development has occurred in the last 30 or so years, but the vision of stretching to new levels is seen in all aspects of Dubai – its airports, seaports, real estate and other developments – and its facilities are virtually without parallel.

Part of the strength of the Dubai vision is its flexibility. Everyone seems to have a different idea of exactly what the vision is, so the leadership has succeeded not only in creating a widespread understanding of the emirate's priorities, direction and values, but also in encouraging a climate in which different stakeholders can create their own impression of the vision and determine how best to achieve it. This flexible type of vision is more effective than a static vision statement, reproduced in corporate literature and promptly ignored or forgotten until the next internal strategic realignment.

The Dubai vision is a living vision, one that has as many meanings as there are stakeholders. It can only be accurately expressed as the sum of all of its constituents' visions, but that nevertheless serves as a set of guiding principles for all activities. It does incorporate quantifiable targets – for example, so many tourists by 2010 and so many airline departures by 2020 – but these figures serve to add depth to the greater vision of Dubai becoming a leading hub for visitors and businesses, with all the amenities and the high standard of living that go with this.

It is an all-encompassing vision that guides all stages of the cycle of asset creation, acceleration and leverage. The first step is for the leadership to decide on its vision, which must be one that can be understood, interpreted and applied at every level of the organization, but must also have a depth that conveys the true meaning of the intended messages. Once the vision has been set, the most effective way for the leadership to communicate and reinforce it is by example.

Lead by example

The government and its leadership in Dubai takes tremendous risks by investing in infrastructure and commercial development projects which in most cases no private business would consider, but which private investors invariably follow. It appears to be reasonably transparent and intolerant of corruption. Government departments are customer-oriented, striving to provide truly excellent service. The government is constantly seen to be striving for the best in everything it does, all seemingly focused on the realization of the Dubai vision.

It also presents a consistent message, constantly reinforced by its actions and by self-examination through programmes such as the Dubai Award for Government Excellence. By holding up high-performing government departments as exemplars as well as reporting on those whose standards of performance need improvement, the government shows its commitment to high standards and, at the same time, sends a strong message about the standards it expects from the private sector.

For a vision to be achieved it must be supported by active leadership. Seeing your leader working harder than you do is bound to be inspiring. Government leaders in Dubai talk enthusiastically about their 'open-door policies' and their habit of seeing workers until late in the evening, and it is clear that the same practices are catching on among managers of private companies.

Leadership by example is a simple concept that can be easily adopted in any organization. When leaders constantly strive to embody the organizational vision, it is much easier for others to follow.

Instil confidence
Another important element of Dubai's leadership is the ability to instil confidence. Many huge projects, most recently the Palm Islands, involved daunting deadlines on top of already ambitious objectives. But in each case, the project managers describe how Sheikh Mohammed gave them the confidence to get the job done. In turn, that confidence was passed on to members of their teams. We and many throughout Dubai have noticed that Sheikh Mohammed has an admirable ability to instil confidence, reminding us of a 19th-century Austrian proverb "instilling confidence is proof of courage".

Clearly this is partly due to the leadership's ability to provide latitude to get the job done and the understanding that the necessary resources and support will be provided. By setting ambitious goals and ensuring that the resources are in place to achieve them, Dubai's rulers have created what many of the interviewees call 'an army of leaders', all taking responsibility for building Dubai and achieving the vision.

Showing confidence in managers and building their confidence is an important leadership role in any organization. If leaders communicate and live the vision, and then enable others to take part in achieving it, everyone will gain confidence in themselves and the enterprise, reinforcing the vision in the process. An example of this is when Sheikh Mohammed told one of the authors recently in the presence of two of his most trusted lieutenants, "I have reared my lions (referring to his two most senior executives) well – I trust them and their judgement."

Manage through trust
The morality of the traditional trading culture of Dubai combined with the governmental structure has created a society in which, to a significant degree, trust takes the place of formal rules or regulation. Just as gold traders on the Creek took each other at their word, many of the freedoms enjoyed in the current business environment exist because of a sense of trust between business and the government. Instead of issuing regulations that impinge on everyone, Dubai's government prefers to focus on detecting the small number of wrongdoers and excluding them. But it is accepted that regulation is necessary in some circumstances to create trust and, reinforce confidence in the system as, for example, in financial services.

In the West, particularly in the USA, there has been a shift towards a more regulatory approach and a reliance on legal mechanisms such as highly detailed contracts to govern business relationships. The practical lesson from Dubai is that governments and firms alike would do well to strip out unnecessary regulations, restrictions, red tape and procedures, and to put more emphasis on building a value system founded on trust. This will, as it does in Dubai, allow greater flexibility, encourage more effective communication and teamwork, and enable faster adjustment to change. It may not be easy to do, but it is surely worth a try.

However, it should be noted that there appears to be a greater degree of documentation done, often on a voluntary basis. It seems this is done for two reasons. First, because out of necessity as projects become larger, and second, as the stakeholders backing many of the ventures change with an increasing mix of international investors. As a young leading Dubai business man said, "we need to better document agreements and understandings because firstly projects are now much more complex and areas for misunderstanding and reliance on memory (as our fathers did) are more prevalent and also because we are no longer dealing only with friends and family. What we need to do is not allow legal procedures to create unwanted complications; although we understand the need to properly document agreements, quickly and pragmatically. At times we ask for things to be done within 24 hours even when they involve hundreds of millions of dollars".

Be visible and accessible

Another element of effective leadership is visibility, being seen as an ever-present part of the system. Sheikh Mohammed is always out and about in Dubai, mixing with his people in restaurants or in the mall, or driving around on his own. He also pays attention to detail, as any good CEO would. He is frequently seen checking on the progress of projects or meeting local workers. Despite his position, he is an active and visible part of Dubai Inc., (this was also the case with his father Sheikh Rashid). Contrast this with many of the Western CEOs who have recently departed, who seemed more concerned with stock options than with building a business. Today, people are too well educated and well informed to be led by passive, hollow vision statements. The CEO must be visible to the entire organization as being an active agent of change, not an invisible demigod espousing an unattainable ideal.

Related to this is how a leader can learn from people at all levels, not just a few elite workers or influential figures. This comes down to accessibility. Dubai's open-door policy enables business people to meet Sheikh Mohammed and express their thoughts about the implications of new government initiatives on their business.

Many corporations have open-door policies, but few work like this. Instead of examining and resolving problems, they are referred and disappear into a bureaucratic black hole. With some open-door policies, the door is one that leads to diminishing career prospects as those who raise an issue find themselves ostracized, sidelined or excluded. Sheikh Mohammed recognizes that the success of this policy is ensuring that those who confide in him won't be punished for their opinions; he regards it as an opening into a world of information and insights too valuable to risk. Without the perceived safety of this process of information sharing, only yes-men would get through, sacrificing the real-time value and losing many opportunities to improve. When managing large projects that are proceeding quickly, failure to get accurate, rapid feedback can spell disaster.

This technique isn't limited to Sheikh Mohammed's office. Other senior government officials and managers in the private sector embrace an open-door policy as well. One interviewed by the authors said that it is known among his staff that any negative repercussions involving people who come to him will be dealt with severely, but this hardly ever seems to be necessary. Although, there will always be someone that one can point to as only wanting to hear good news! But the goal for any organization is for this to be the exception, not the norm.

Use your majlis

The last element of active leadership is 'management by *majlis*'. As noted in chapter 8, the *majlis* can take many forms, both informal and formal. Here we are concerned with meetings between the leaders and their advisers, in which problems are discussed and visions are created and shared. Management by *majlis* particularly focuses on creating a common understanding among the senior policymakers within an organization. It is a process of information sharing as well as reflection, a time to think out of the box as well as to build the box. It provides an opportunity for leadership to be truly active and creative.

Think about your own organization. Do you know your CEO's goals and key issues? Do you know your manager's goals and key issues? Do you actively and quickly share new information with senior leaders on their key issues? In Dubai, the answer to many of these questions is invariably yes.

One example illustrates the effectiveness of the *majlis*. The Al Maha Desert Resort is an eco-tourism resort in the desert near Dubai. It's set within extensive desert grounds, enclosed to protect the endangered *al maha* (Arabian oryx, resembling antelopes) that roam freely on the grounds. Friends of the authors who were staying at this resort went on a guided wildlife tour. During the drive the guide noticed a hole in the fence and got on the radio to report the problem, suggesting that they had probably lost at least one *al maha*. Within 15 minutes of the call, Sheikh Mohammed himself was on the radio to the tour guide, asking questions and suggesting where to locate the animal. The wayward *al maha* was found where Sheikh Mohammed suspected it would be.

Think about the implications of this story. Someone hears about a development on an issue that is important to their leader, and the information filters through to the leader within minutes. What is interesting is not so much that this communication happens, but why it happens. Through the cascading communication that occurs via the *majlis*, the priorities of Sheikh Mohammed are widely known and his values are understood. So when an incident like this occurs, the people involved know that he would want to be informed, and his familiarity with the area allows him to be of immediate assistance.

Compare this with your own organization. Management by *majlis* is one key process for creating this shared understanding of what information to convey, and the other elements of active leadership create the trust for conveying the needed information. The performance implications of such a system are obvious. But think again about your own organization. How often do senior managers meet to reflect on strategy and share information and insights? Daily? Weekly? Monthly? Quarterly? Annually? Never? Can your organization afford not to change its habits?

Manage the cycle

As outlined earlier, the strategic trajectory model represents an iteration of asset creation (see diagram below). Starting with the creation of a new asset from scratch, asset acceleration then acts as a coiling spring, ready to release the inherent value in the asset. Next is leverage, where innovation is spurred by competition among assets. To close the loop and complete the cycle, assets can then be harvested (retired), or reinvested or reinvented, in which case a new asset is created and the cycle begins again.

The strategic trajectory

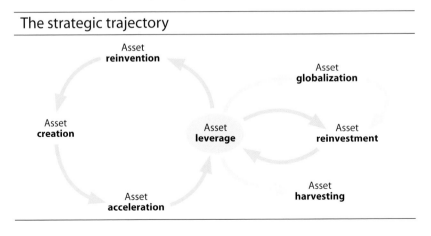

In managing this cycle, there are several imperatives: break free from limits, create assets strategically, set up corporate 'free zones', and know when to step back.

Break free from limits

When Dubai ran out of beach along its coastline, the government set about doubling it by building the Palms – later projects are set to lengthen the coastline many times over. Indeed, as Venice has gone out to the sea on which it has been built, Dubai seems not only to be going out to the sea, but also bringing the sea inland to create an oasis for working, living, and pleasure out of the previously barren desert. Sheikh Mohammed turned the horse-training business on its head by establishing his training stables in Dubai and sponsoring the world's richest horse race. Dubai has filled its hotels nearly to capacity during the most inhospitable hot months of the year by developing attractions and clever marketing. The rulers of Dubai created a dynamic, modern, cosmopolitan city on a site that was desert only 50 years before. In the asset creation stage, starting with a blank slate may be daunting, but it is also liberating. If you can see past the constraints, in terms of resources, finance or available time, it is possible to come up with radical strategies that set the stage for rapid growth. Of course, it's still important to keep the ultimate goals in mind, but if you can focus on what you want to achieve and work towards it, apart from the usual constraints, the assets (whether real or virtual) you create will power you along your strategic trajectory.

Create assets strategically

In order to create assets strategically, there must be a clearly articulated strategy or vision to guide your actions. Remembering that each asset (or initiative, project, acquisition and so on) becomes part of the larger strategic vortex, it is crucial to ensure that each new introduction will add to the overall value and growth of the ecosystem, not languish on its own or, worse still, suck valuable resources from other parts of the vortex.

Dubai is full of examples of how this has been done. The country was already a recognized trading centre early in the 20th century, so it made perfect sense to build on that awareness using the expertise and resources of the local population and visiting traders. Thus the Creek was dredged, Port Rashid was built, Jebel Ali was created and other assets followed to further support this strategy. The strategy changed over time, branching out to create local bases for traders in the free zones and developing intermodal transport facilities as air travel became economically attractive. The addition of each asset in this group has been highly strategic, each focusing on furthering Dubai's position as a trading hub. Within the context of related aspects of the vision, other examples include the development of tourism and the transition to a knowledge-based economy. All of these strands of the vision work together and play off each other. As a result, there are few businesses in Dubai that seem isolated from a commonly recognized vision and that provide little economic value added.

The lessons from this are clear and readily applicable elsewhere. First, make sure the vision of your organization is clear and commonly understood. Then be certain that every major new initiative, project or acquisition is making a solid contribution to that vision, driving the organization in the right direction. Failure to do this can lead to the business becoming fragmented and unfocused, a position from which it is difficult to get back on track.

Set up corporate free zones . . .
The free zone concept, under which investors who set up inside the zones enjoy substantially more freedom to trade and manage their businesses and finances than they would anywhere else in the region, is not a new idea in Dubai.

The largest free zone, Jebel Ali, was set up in the 1980s, but it can be argued that the airport was the first when it was established with an open-skies policy in 1960. The free zone model has more recently been extended to Dubai Internet City, Dubai Media City, Dubai Silicon Oasis and Dubai International Financial Centre. It is a beautifully simple concept and an important part of the asset acceleration phase in the strategic trajectory model. In a corporate context, though, can you create an environment within your company where there is minimal bureaucracy, where you invite the world in and where you actively benchmark the rest of the world? Or do you continue to compare yourself with the same five companies at arm's length, doing the same things every quarter?

When a state opens itself to the world, the resulting interaction works as a supercluster, a supercharged microcosm of global competition. This competition sets representatives from all corners of the globe against one another, not just one primary industry in one area as you see in Silicon Valley or Solingen, a region in Germany where many of the world's best knives are made. When this happens, the amount of innovation increases by orders of magnitude because of the sheer diversity and range of inputs. And everyone's a winner: the innovative companies, their customers, the industry and the host that brought them all together and turned up the heat.

. . . and one-stop shops
Another important element of the free zone concept is the idea of the 'one-stop shop'. This term may be a cliché, but it's exactly how the

managers of the free zones in Dubai describe it. It's a single point of contact within the zone, where any and all questions, support issues, administrative needs and other problems can be addressed. In a business environment, the equivalent might be a 'corporate concierge', which can serve the same function on an organizational level when enabled with a charter or clear understanding and guidelines from the central office or parent corporation.

Global clusters

The idea behind economic geography or clustering is that when competing firms locate in a small geographic area, innovation increases and results in more efficient transfer of knowledge and continuous improvement in best practices.

Examples of clustering include the high-tech firms of Silicon Valley, mechanical watch making in Switzerland and clothing manufacturing in northern Italy. The basic idea behind clusters is that when competing firms locate in a small geographic area innovation increases because of increased competition and the more efficient transfer of knowledge and best practices through employee turnover.

Dubai has taken the concept to another level as part of the process of asset acceleration and leverage. In creating free zones, Dubai announced that it was an open house to the world. So instead of creating regional clusters, it created global clusters, with the entire world competing in a small space. This enables even greater innovation because more firms are competing. And because UAE nationals work alongside skilled expatriates in the zones, the local workers benefit from the knowledge and best practices that companies from all over the world have to offer.

The lesson for corporations is clear. When establishing major new initiatives, learn from the world, not just a few local or usual competitors. This is the only way to ensure long-run globally competitive businesses.

Corporate concierge

For virtually any problem, question or requirement that comes up for a company inside one of the Dubai free zones, there is a single point of contact within the zone that can address it. This bundle of corporate concierge services is the catalyst that has provided much of the accelerated value in the free zones.

In the development of Dubai Internet City and Dubai Media City, the concierge service guaranteed the procurement of work permits within 24 hours. In addition, it resolved any business or logistical questions. To further enhance customer service, the corporate concierge handles non-business issues, embracing total customer care through providing contacts for relocating employees seeking housing and schooling for children. And, taking the corporate concierge concept yet another step further, the management of these free zones helps market the companies located there through road trips and trade shows.

Turning to the lessons that can be learnt from this, ask yourself a couple of questions. How easy is it for outsiders to do business with your company? Do you actively facilitate this process or are you a necessary evil that they must work through?

In today's highly competitive business environment, establishing a corporate concierge service for dealing with outside companies may be one way to improve competitiveness through differentiation and better customer service. Corporations must identify the services that their customers want, and then explore the cost/benefit ratio of providing these services. A single point of contact – a corporate concierge – can be of immense value in getting close to customers and in learning what their needs are.

As seen in the free zones of Dubai, much of the value created by the corporate concierge service was focused inwardly, providing value to the companies within them. In a business environment, this concept may be reminiscent of the shared service centre, but it is really much more. Shared services in corporations rarely exhibit the proactive spirit that Dubai's corporate concierge services seem to. They want companies to succeed and thus do whatever they can to enable that, whether that means engaging in marketing activities or taking on responsibility for administrative tasks and red tape.

Instead of becoming a backwater of back-office tasks, the corporate concierge inside a business can be a strong enabler, allowing managers to focus on their business. Such a service can also become a powerful catalyst for cross-pollination, helping to create synergies between business units and building bridges between silos.

Know when to step back

The asset leverage phase of the strategic trajectory model in Dubai has been successful largely because the leaders know when to step back and let competition flourish, thereby encouraging innovation and rapid growth. At the same time, however, it's important to keep an eye on things to know when adjustments or even major changes are needed.

There are many examples of how the leadership has stepped back in Dubai. In the hotel industry, for example, new hotels are constantly being built, each with its own innovative qualities and superlative characteristics. The exploding demand for office space in Dubai Internet City and Dubai Media City is another good example. Demand has exceeded all expectations and has enabled development of a wide range of properties within the Technology, Electronic Commerce and

Media Free Zone, including more offices, residential units and leisure facilities. The same applies to the Dubai International Financial Centre, where demand for space has far outstripped supply and it is inevitable that the area will need to be expanded to meet demand.

It can be difficult to loosen your grip on a project, particularly when you have been intimately involved in its development. But an active leader should be confident that the vision that's been communicated is sufficient to guide free growth and development with little intervention. Timing matters, of course. When is the right time to step back? There is not a simple answer to this question. In order to make an informed decision, managers must have access to a range of timely, accurate and complete information. Access to this information is crucial throughout the strategic trajectory. Ways to make this happen are addressed in the next section.

Lubricate the system

Once asset leverage has taken place, choosing whether to reinvest, reinvent or harvest will be based on an organization's project assessment criteria, which will encompass elements of its vision and strategy, financial performance indicators, and systems.

We have looked at several examples of how leaders in Dubai have 'closed the loop' by reinvesting, reinventing or harvesting assets as part of the strategic trajectory of individual assets or groups of assets, while also contributing to the cultivation of the larger strategic vortex. Existing centres of expertise in the Police Academy and the Ports Authority have been reinvented as new offerings for customers outside Dubai. We have examined many examples of reinvestment, such as in Dubai's infrastructure, noting in particular how continual reinvestment in commercial office space and other areas has raised standards markedly in the past decade. We also saw that, although there are examples of asset harvesting, there is a tendency to reinvent before the point of harvesting can be reached.

Making decisions on reinvestment, reinvention and harvesting successfully depends on good information flows and effective lines of communication. More fundamentally, it depends on maintaining focus on the vision and its key objectives. The implications of some of these success factors as they can be applied in any organization are discussed below.

Keep it simple

Organizational structures in Dubai, both in the government and in the private sector, are remarkably simple. One reason things can happen as quickly as they do is that there is little distance between the bottom and the top of organizations. Open-door policies give every employee direct access to senior managers, who invariably have direct access to the rulers. This openness and few levels of hierarchy, combined with the tendency of managers to get involved in the daily lives of their subordinates, paints a clear picture of how communication happens and how things get done.

Simplicity is at the heart of Dubai's approach that 'what's good for business is good for Dubai', down to the micro level of a single business traveller and the spillover economic effects that he creates during his stay through the money he spends in hotels, restaurants and shops, and through the business he does.

One reason Dubai's ruling family has been successful is that even with the rapid development of recent years, government has been kept lean and lines of communication open. In the corporate context, better communication can be achieved by flattening layers of management and ensuring that leaders are visible and accessible, both for the reasons already outlined and to ensure that they keep abreast of what is happening. The less complex the organizational structure, the easier it will be for management to become aware of problems and strategic issues and to take appropriate action. It also makes it easier for management to recognize the true strengths of the organization and to exploit them.

In Dubai, massive projects have been conceived, planned and built in a seemingly impossible timeframe. This hasn't been achieved by cutting corners; the unusually high standards in Dubai are a result of the country's ability to attract the best minds and hands. Time is usually saved in the planning process. As long as the feasibility has been proven, there's nothing wrong with starting before it's clear how everything will be done. But this does require careful attention to detail and frequent monitoring, so that potential problems can be identified and avoided or corrected before they do any damage.

For most organizations, one of the biggest difficulties in the planning process is in getting decisions made, particularly about allocation of resources. The question for most organizations is can the process be speeded up? This generally comes down to how can the corporate culture be made freer and more trusting? Returning to one of Sheikh Mohammed's favourite analogies: as long as you're running, even if you fall you'll fall forward, and when you get up, you'll still be making progress. And if you're running along with your colleagues, they'll be there to help you get up and keep going.

Stick to the vision and core values
An uncomplicated organizational structure and clear lines of communication allow action to be taken quickly, which is particularly important when problems arise or things become tricky. But how do

you decide what action to take? In Dubai it has been shown that it usually makes sense to stick to your original vision despite problems arising. That is the reason Emirates airline decided not to reduce its $15 billion order for aircraft following the slump in air travel after the 2001 terrorist attacks on New York and Washington.

Dubai's leaders have managed to create a sense of confidence in the emirate's innate strengths that has encouraged the belief that Dubai can survive virtually any downturn or slump. Compare this attitude with that of many companies today which make cuts when faced with the slightest hint of trouble. Of course, quoted companies have to keep their investors happy and provide returns in the short term as well as the long term, but a robust, flexible vision can help accommodate their wishes while providing a roadmap to navigate any trouble spots that arise.

Don't be afraid to blur boundaries
Many of the senior government officials in Dubai also run businesses and head other organizations. This has provided a direct communication channel between business and government and therefore enabled rapid and effective responsiveness. This direct communication conduit is very important in the reinvestment and reinvention phases of the strategic trajectory model. Messages get to decision-makers fast, so assets can be reinvented or harvested, keeping to the vision.

In the corporate context, managers often work for head office or for a business unit and not on both sides of the fence. This often results in an 'us and them' culture, when what organizations really need is a straightforward 'us' culture. Managers who can represent the interests of their business units as well as those of the head office will develop the ability and agility to think and act globally, which can only benefit the corporation.

Cultivate the ecosystem
The strategic vortex is composed of multiple cycles of the strategic trajectory (see diagram on next page). Strategies build one on top of the other. Taking a step back, it's easy to see how this has been effective in Dubai. The rulers started with the Creek and some traders. The Creek was developed and an airport was built to bring in more trade and businessmen. Because no one would want to stay in Dubai if there were no reliable roads, or water and electricity supplies, they built those too. Then came oil and some real money, which was put to work improving the facilities. More ports and some heavy industry ensured that Dubai didn't go unnoticed. To satisfy the businessmen who were coming in greater numbers, the World Trade Centre and some good hotels were built. To bring even more people and more

The strategic vortex

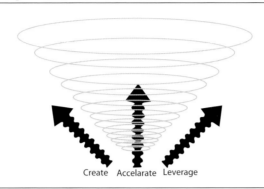

Create   Accelarate   Leverage

freight, Emirates airline was set up. This removed reliance on foreign airlines and made Dubai more self-sufficient, and virtually guaranteed a constant influx of travellers and goods. To help companies using the ports to do some value-added manufacturing, a free zone next to the biggest port was created.

The businesses in Dubai Internet City and Media City are attracting a new calibre of worker, who demands good leisure and healthcare facilities and the right to own property, so projects are being developed to satisfy those needs. For all this to work, robust capital and financial services markets are needed, so the Dubai International Financial Centre is given the go-ahead. Each strategy builds on the base of the previous one, thus expanding the strategic vortex.

In a corporate context, the lesson from Dubai is that you should decide where you're going and pull out all the stops to get there, building on one strength to take you to the next, still monitoring and adjusting at each step.

Use core competencies with care

In recent decades, there has been a shift in how we think about the sources of competitive advantage. In the 1980s, industry structure was considered to be at the heart of competitive advantage.[1] In the 1990s, the essence of competitive advantage was thought to be characteristics internal to the firm, such as resources, competencies, knowledge and capabilities.[2] This transition was caused by two main factors.

• *The pace of change*. Industries are moving so quickly that industry snapshots of the competitive landscape are no longer relevant by the time the strategy based on them is implemented. Increasingly, what is required is continuing analysis or videotape.

• *The blurring of industry boundaries.* An industry-based view of strategy depends on being able to clearly define the industry, but convergence is making this increasingly difficult. This has massive implications, as drivers of profits are often based on the number of competitors, the relative sizes of these competitors and other factors. This sense of convergence increases in industries affected by information technology. Consider the media wars (internet versus print), device wars (cell phones with digital cameras or PDAs) and information wars (retail loyalty cards allow access to vast amounts of customer information, which is often the key to accessing new markets, such as retail financial services).

As a result there has been a massive shift in how firms think about strategy, and many have jumped on the core competencies bandwagon. It's almost impossible to pick up a business publication nowadays without reading about a divestiture or acquisition being justified by the core competencies. Companies are either ridding themselves of 'non-core assets' or 'acquiring core assets'.

However, in reacting to the financially motivated diversification logic of earlier decades, many companies may have taken the idea of core competencies too far. In recent years, more and more firms have entered into outsourcing and alliance relationships as they attempt to streamline their unwieldy businesses in order to be more responsive to turbulent environments. As a result of this streamlining, many firms are now focusing on one or two core competencies as their source of competitive advantage.

But what will happen to those companies that have narrowly defined themselves around a single core competence when the world no longer values that core competence? In other words, are there limits to the applicability of the idea of core competencies?

The limitations of core competencies

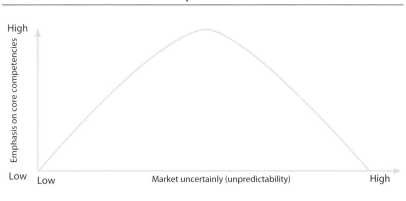

One of the findings of the authors' research in Dubai suggests that environmental uncertainty may be a good reason for firms to expand their core competencies and activities (see diagram on previous page). In times of uncertainty, following a core competence logic may result in missing opportunities, whereas if your range of competence is broader you have more balls to juggle and potentially more opportunities to take advantage of.

Given that the advantages or disadvantages of a core competence focus may depend on the level of uncertainty of the business environment, the diagram above indicates that the 'sweet spot' for companies using core competencies as their primary form of strategic thinking is medium levels of uncertainty. The recent high-tech fallout reinforces this concept. Narrowly pursuing a single skill set is a dangerous and often fatal activity in turbulent competitive environments.

As well as environmental uncertainty, the authors' research in Dubai revealed a second factor limiting the applicability of core competencies: the extent of market development and reliability. Following a narrowly defined business strategy based on one or two core competencies has an immediate result for a firm: all non-core or non-essential activities are carried out externally through contractual relationships (outsourcing) or strategic partnerships and alliances. Such a strategy is only possible if the market in which the firm is competing is reasonably mature and has a host of capable firms to handle these transactions. If not, the firm cannot outsource these activities and must pursue a less narrowly defined strategy.

There is one further dimension to the argument about the limitation of core competencies. In the case of Dubai, it was initially at a competitive disadvantage in respect of more developed countries and some of its neighbours. In order to accelerate growth, it invited the world to compete through its free zones. However, if firms invite other world-class firms into their markets to facilitate long-term growth and learning, how do they survive in the short to medium term? In many cases, narrowly pursuing one or two core competencies may not be the best answer.

Instead, it is advisable to have a superstructure in place to capture the externalities or spillover benefits of those transactions. 'Superstructure' refers to the extended local business ecosystem in which these firms operate. In Dubai, the superstructure that helped these firms thrive included the hotels, restaurants, shops and other service industries that already existed when they set up shop in the emirate.

Dubai's superstructure can be compared to the Korean *chaebol* (large, diversified trading houses) and some of the large family businesses in India, such as the Birla or Tata groups. Why do these hugely diversified conglomerates exist, producing everything from high-tech to white goods to shipping to automobiles? Is there a model here that suggests that in certain types of environments, at a certain stage of industry and country-market evolution, these large, diversified companies make sense? The strategic vortex model of asset creation, acceleration and leverage is evidence that they do reap the benefits of new companies entering.

These companies are not pursuing a strategy of unrelated diversification. Instead, the diversification strategy of the customer interacts within the whole business ecosystem. For example, there is a famous story in Dubai about Sheikh Rashid, who was asked why he was building an airport in Dubai, even if it was only a refuelling centre. He said:

> *If a person lands in Dubai, he will take a taxi, buy a pack of cigarettes, have a meal, and we will benefit.*

This is why Dubai has built the superstructure of activities to facilitate the tourism industry: world-class hotels, restaurants, transportation, safety and so on. For businesses, Dubai has created the superstructure necessary for rapid growth. Innovative projects such as Dubai Internet City and Dubai Media City require many of the same things as the tourism industry, but as the number of companies increases, they also require financial markets (hence the Dubai Financial Market and the Dubai International Financial Centre), healthcare (enter Healthcare City) and eventually a sense of permanence and belonging (foreigners can now own property in certain areas of Dubai). Again, the expanding superstructure captures the set of related activities needed to service major segments of customer needs.

For corporations, this raises a similar question. What set of activities is needed to service major segments of related customer needs? Customer-activity related diversification differs from the traditional definition of diversification in terms of competencies, products or geographic markets. Such customer-activity related diversification is one way non-market leaders or developing corporations – that is, most corporations – may gain a competitive advantage.

Go global
Globalization is nothing new for many large corporations – this has been part of managerial thinking for the last 30 years or more. However, Dubai's recent experiences in going global serve to highlight a few key reminders. First, taking advantages of economies of scale is one of the fundamental ways to increase strategic advantage to a company. Dubai has done this through further expansion of DUBAL (aluminium), DP World (ports) and Emirates (airline). Second, if

traditional economies of scale are not apparent, globalization still presents an opportunity if one can leverage intangible assets – such as skills or branding/image. The international expansion of Emaar, Jumeirah, and the development of free zones around the world are examples of this. Clearly, Emaar has developed a world class capability of managing and implementing large scale construction projects. Similarly, Jumeirah has developed capabilities of managing luxury hotels and a brand that represents luxury and superb hotel standards. These skills, plus the intangible Dubai "buzz" (attitude of achievement, even while attempting what others have said is impossible), and the often iconic style and image that Dubai brings to a project are assets that can be leveraged globally – once they have been developed and proven locally. Finally, Dubai's experience with DP World and managing ports in the USA only serves as a reminder of something every global executive knows – it is impossible to always anticipate global markets no matter how much research you do! Every company competing globally has had similar experiences. The important challenges are to minimize the number of mistakes, learn from the mistakes, listen to sound independent advice and adapt it to their needs, keep trying and continue adapting to changing global markets. Dubai has clearly shown that it has understood this, learned and continues to do so.

Conclusion

It's easy to arrive in Dubai or pick up a newspaper article about the emirate and immediately see evidence of the progress that's been made. The skyscrapers, the airport and ports, the thriving tourism industry and projects like the Palm Islands all illustrate what has been achieved in recent years. Where less than 50 years ago there was little more than sand, silicon chips will soon be produced and distributed all over the world. We have learnt of an old Arabic proverb which so truly embodies Dubai and Sheikh Mohammed, "The bigger the vision, the more difficult it is to articulate."

As we have tried to make clear in this book, the real successes of Dubai are not so much the outward evidence but more the culture and spirit that have allowed the world-class assets to be created and spun into a strategic vortex that can continue to grow and expand. Dubai's leadership has taken the risk of inviting individuals and investors from all over the world to help contribute to this success. In the process, a tolerant, varied culture has been created. Just as the diversified assets within the strategic vortex make it more robust, so too does the diversity of Dubai's culture allow it to continue to develop. It's no coincidence that expatriates in many Middle Eastern countries complete their two- or three-year assignments and then move on, but many of those who are posted to Dubai on a temporary assignment decide to remain. Dubai retains its traditional cultural and religious beliefs, but it also embraces those of the many individuals and groups that make up its population, allowing every resident to feel at home and at ease.

The risks inherent in a population in which four out of every five residents are foreign nationals are significant, but Dubai's leadership has recognized that bringing the world into the emirate will allow it to compete more effectively on an international scale. The social fabric of Dubai has become one of its most valuable resources, and that's not something that can be built as easily as a skyscraper or a luxury hotel. It takes leadership, vision, open-mindedness, determination and patience.

The challenge to organizations is to create a diverse, pluralistic, inclusive culture that can not only support the growth of the concern, but also prove an irresistible attraction to customers and potential employees. We have referred to vision repeatedly in this book: the vision we're talking about must be able to keep people focused on the same strategic trajectory while allowing individual cultures and perspectives to thrive.

When a traveller arrives in Dubai its diversity and multiculturalism is immediately visible, as is the underlying spirit, enthusiasm and positive attitude of its people. After leaving, it is this spirit that remains most memorable. How can you create the same spirit within your organization, one that remains with your customers independently of the products and services you may have offered them? Going global usually means setting up offices around the world. But what if you were to start by bringing the world into your organization instead?

For the creation and cultivation of the strategic vortex that allows rapid growth, this kind of underlying culture is essential, as is a vision that's flexible, inclusive and, ultimately, liberating.

ENDNOTES

1   *Competitive Strategy* (Porter, M. 1980: Free Press, New York) is an often-cited source for this type of thinking

2   In general, this is known as the resource-based school of strategy. Influential works in this area include Prahalad, C.K., and Hamel, G. 1990. 'The Core Competence of the Corporation', *Harvard Business Review* 68(3), pp. 79–91; and Barney, J.B. 1991. 'Firm Resources and Sustained Competitive Advantage', *Journal of Management*, Vol. 17, pp. 99–120

CLOSING THOUGHTS

Life is like riding a bicycle. To keep your balance you must keep moving.

Albert Einstein

As we reflect on the story of Dubai and its implications for corporations and countries, we are struck that even after all the success that Dubai has achieved, many challenges still remain and, indeed, many more will evolve in keeping with the accelerated pace of development.

As we, the authors, debate and discuss the speed of this rapid accelerated growth, a recurring theme is when the speed of this growth could or should slow down. We have come to the conclusion that it cannot, this is the essence of what is happening in Dubai, it is on a fast trajectory that must be fuelled for it to continue to grow. Any time a company or country goes through rapid change, there is invariably a tendency to cling to the past, not necessarily in terms of business practices, but more in terms of culture and practices – this may even be more true for a country with potentially more entrenched behaviour. Thus, we suggest for Dubai, as well as companies that have gone through such a rapid transformation, that the challenges ahead may be as daunting as the ones just gone through.

With Dubai's continuing growth and globalization, we have witnessed several recent and important changes – each presenting additional challenges (as well as opportunities). First, in the past there has been much explicit competition between various parts of Dubai – such as, by way of example, Dubai Holding and Dubai World, and their respective subsidiaries. These are now joined by other government owned or partly owned companies the number of players in the ecosystem has grown both by planning and organically. Often, Sheikh Mohammed encourages competition between his most trusted lieutenants (or "Lions" as he described them in conversation with one of the authors). This strategy worked well in Dubai's early days, particularly when it is just trying to establish itself in the regional economy, and such competition was clearly successful. As we move forward, Dubai has clearly established itself within the region, it seems well on its way to having global impact and as the size of projects continues to increase in size, this strategy of competition may need to be well managed with a different degree of clarity and particularly to those around the world, who are increasingly watching Dubai's every move. In addition to the global monitoring of competition within Dubai, and perhaps more importantly is how this is viewed and construed within the competing Dubai companies – particularly for managers and workers in these organizations. The competition could be misunderstood. At the most senior level, Sheikh Mohammed clearly understands the dynamics of and need for competition, as does his top team – we suspect there is also a sense of camaraderie and healthy sparring that is occurring. As in most organizations, the tension is between competition and cooperation, the challenge must be to ensure that this approach and its message is filtered down throughout the organizations. Similarly, the potentially confusing signal of senior leaders who multi-task between public and private sectors roles must be carefully managed to ensure that those in the broader management team and the outside world understand the logic and benefits of such blending of roles and responsibilities across public and private sectors which have worked well to date.

Another major change is that Dubai is increasingly concerned about the "portfolio effect" of its many projects. In the past, one could argue that much of the focus in Dubai was on the individual project or development. However, as the economic and developed base of Dubai is now much larger, and will continue to grow, one has to not only worry about the individual characteristics of each new project, but also their interaction effects within the existing ecosystem – those familiar with the financial markets will know there is a major difference between selecting individual stocks and managing a stock portfolio. For example, each new real estate development in one area may make perfect economic sense, but the overall interaction effect may have a downside. Thus, we see Dubai and its leadership responding to these challenges and not only worrying about the ROI of each project, but also its impact on quality of life. For example, many of the new developments in Dubai have major areas of land dedicated to water or plants, not buildings. Dubai is developing mass transit and using alternative fuels in taxis and public sector transport to improve air quality, it is providing enlarged pavements for people to be able to walk and exercise as well as cycling lanes and greenery – all expensive parts of urban design, but one that the leadership of Dubai feels committed to as an investment in its people and their quality of life. In terms of fundamental investments in improving quality of life, there is perhaps no single greater initiative than Sheikh Mohammed establishing, in 2007, the Mohammed Bin Rashid Foundation, with a personal endowment of US$10 billion to improve education throughout the region. Sheikh Mohammed realizes that only through education and acquiring knowledge through exposure to the best thinking in the world can the vision of Dubai and the region continue to grow as the leaders of tomorrow are shaped through such endeavours; reminding the authors of a Middle Eastern proverb, "knowledge, lifts those that may otherwise be unable to rise . . ."

Sheikh Mohammed realizes the importance of current, as well as historical knowledge in shaping the minds of tomorrow. One significant indication of this is the Foundations' major initiative of the translation of books and literature in foreign (non-Arab) languages into Arabic and vice versa. This was a very important part of the Arab world's period of great advancement in the 9th Century, when a "movement" of translating works into Arabic was under way starting so the story goes when the then Caliph Al-Ma'mun in Baghdad was visited by a dream. The philosopher Aristotle appeared to him, saying that the reason of the Greeks and the revelation of Islam were not opposed. On waking, the Caliph demanded that all of Aristotle's works be translated into Arabic. And they were. Moreover it wasn't just Aristotle. Over the next 200 years Greek philosophy, medicine, engineering and maths were all poured and sometimes squeezed into Arabic. It was a translation movement of extraordinary depth and scope so that, hundreds of years before Aristotle reached the West, the intellect of Greece was woven into the tapestry of Arab thought.[1]

As Dubai's phenomenal growth continues and its buildings reach to the sky, the sea and the desert, Dubai needs to consider the other elements needed to strengthen the foundation of this success. However, whatever the challenges presented, in order to succeed in the times ahead, it is necessary to remember what enabled this country to change in the first place – desire: a desire to better their current situation or standing, initially regionally, and now within the global economy. In the process of pursuing its ambition, Dubai became a hotbed of ideas and people from around the world, and government-led financing often kick-started these visions into becoming reality. The artful mixing of these elements, and the managing of the accompanying risk, has proved a powerful recipe for success.

Today is no different for Dubai. In order to succeed, it will need to continue to be, albeit more so, a primary market for ideas, people, and capital. The desire to change is often less when the current degree of success is relatively high. The expectations of the new stakeholders in the economy may challenge the pace of change. Social, economic and political norms will need to adapt, as is already happening. The challenges facing leadership in steering Dubai forward will be greater, as the ship continues to grow larger. Crucial will be the ability to minimize bureaucracy, thus enabling both speed and flexibility, while simultaneously ensuring equity is not compromised for the broader set of stakeholders in the new economy, in short maintaining agility.

Again, companies, and indeed governments too, should reflect on the challenges facing Dubai and learn for themselves. Companies are the nexus of ideas, people, and capital – the catalyst in the recipe. Attracting and retaining these elements is the key to success. The challenge for the senior team of executives is to create a culture and leadership style that will keep the organization growing, no matter what its past success. Easy to say, but it is something that few have been able to achieve.

Let us all look to Dubai over the next few years to see, if again, it can provide insights on how to achieve this sustained rapid growth.

May this almost unparalleled journey of sustained rapid growth continue so that we may write the third version of this book in a few years! Until then, we are certain that Dubai will continue to surprise and amaze us all.

To summarize, as it has been said repeatedly to us of late, "Dubai is a phenomena!"

ENDNOTES

1   www.bbc.co.uk/radio4/history/inourtime 02.10.08

APPENDIX 1

TIMELINE – PART I – 1820 to 1995

Year	Event
1820	Britain establishes presence in the Gulf, with the first of several truce agreements, making the region known as the Trucial Coast
1833	Group of Bani Yas tribe settles in Dubai, led by the Al Maktoum family
1892	Agreement is signed giving Britain control of foreign affairs of Trucial Coast
1903	UK steamships begin calling at Dubai
1912	Sheikh Saeed Bin Maktoum becomes Ruler of Dubai
1930s	Worldwide depression and introduction of Japanese cultured pearls starts the decline of Dubai pearling trade
1930s	Population of Dubai is 20,000
1950s	Oil first discovered in the Trucial States
1952	Electricity is introduced
1958	Sheikh Saeed dies, and Sheikh Rashid Bin Saeed Al Maktoum becomes Ruler
1959	First hotel opens in Dubai
1960	Dredging of Dubai Creek is completed
1960	Dubai International Airport opens
1962	Oil production begins in neighbouring Abu Dhabi
1963	Al Maktoum Bridge over Dubai Creek is completed
1963	National Bank of Dubai is established
1966	Oil is discovered in Dubai

Year	Event
1968	UK announces its intention to withdraw from the region
1969	First oil exports from Dubai
1971	United Arab Emirates (UAE) is founded
1971	UAE joins the Arab League
1971	UAE joins the United Nations
1972	Port Rashid opens with 15 berths
1975	Population of Dubai is 183,200
1978	Port Rashid is expanded to 35 berths
1979	Jebel Ali Port is opened
1979	Dubai Dry Docks is established
1979	Dubai Aluminium Company (DUBAL) begins operations
1979	Dubai International Trade Centre is completed (later called the Dubai World Trade Centre)
1980	2.8 million passengers use Dubai International Airport
1981	UAE is founding member of the Gulf Cooperation Council (GCC)
1985	Jebel Ali Free Zone opens
1985	Emirates airline is founded
1989	First Dubai Desert Classic, part of the PGA European Tour
1989	First Dubai Airshow
1990	632,903 people visit Dubai (based on the number of hotel guests)
1990	Sheikh Rashid dies, his son Sheikh Maktoum Bin Rashid Al Maktoum becomes Ruler of Dubai

Year	Event
1990	Five million passengers use Dubai International Airport

PART II – 1995 to date

Year	Event
1995	Population of Dubai is 690,400
1995	Sheikh Mohammed becomes Crown Prince of Dubai
1995	In excess of 100 nationalities are present in Dubai
1996	First Dubai Shopping Festival
1996	First running of the Dubai World Cup horse race
1997	Emaar Properties is established
1997	Department of Tourism and Commerce Marketing is established
1999	Burj Al Arab hotel opens
1999	Residential property developments are announced open to non-GCC nationals to buy
1999	Launch of Dubai Internet City (completed in 2000)
2000	Dubai Financial Market is established
2000	2.8 million people visit Dubai (based on number of hotel guests)
2000	Dubai Internet City opens
2000	Launch of Dubai Media City (completed in 2001)
2000	12.3 million passengers use Dubai International Airport
2001	Dubai Media City opens
2001	First Dubai Strategy Forum meeting
2001	Launch of the Palm Jumeirah (ready for occupation in 2007)

Year	Event
2001	Emirates announce largest order in aviation history for 58 aircraft (US$15 billion)
2002	Dubai Metals and Commodities Centre is established
2002	Dubai International Financial Centre is announced
2002	Dubai's e-government website is launched
2002	Launch of Dubai Healthcare City and association with Harvard (ready for occupation in 2008)
2002	Dubai Silicon Oasis is announced
2002	First sale of land to non-GCC nationals
2003	Launch of Dubailand project
2003	Dubai Executive Council is established
2003	Dubai hosts annual meetings of the boards of governors of the World Bank Group and International Monetary Fund
2004	Dubai Holding is established
2004	DIFC formally opened, with independent Regulator (DFSA) and Judiciary (DIFC Courts)
2004	Begin construction at Burj Dubai – tallest man-made structure
2005	Business Bay launched by Dubai Properties
2005	Dubai School of Government founded in cooperation with Harvard John F Kennedy School
2005	Kick off Dubai International Financial Exchange (DIFX)
2005	Launch of Dubai World Central (US$33 billion), a multi-purpose logistics aviation city development
2006	Sheikh Mohammed becomes the Ruler of Dubai, Prime Minister and Vice President of the UAE

Year	Event
2006	Dubai acquires UK's P&O (US$7 billion) and becomes part of DP World
2007	35 million (approx.) passengers used Dubai International Airport (28 million in 2006)
2007	Sheikh Mohammed launches Dubai Strategic Plan 2015 "Dubai . . . Where The Future Begins"
2007	Some 200 nationalities live in Dubai
2007	Borse Dubai is launched
2007	London Business School Dubai Centre opens at DIFC
2007	Emirates beat previous historic record and order for 132 aircraft (US$35 billion)
2008	New Dubai International Airport terminal opens (capacity 70 million passengers)

APPENDIX 2

GDP

GDP 2000–2002

Economic Sectors	2000			2001			2002*		
	UAE Total	Dubai	%	UAE Total	Dubai	%	UAE Total	Dubai	%
Non-Oil Gross Domestic Product	46,673	15,251	32.7	48,841	16,610	34.0	54,579	20,591	37.7
Gross Domestic Product	70,294	16,985	24.2	69,274	17,991	26.0	74,348	21,933	29.5
The non-Financial Corporation Sector	59,969	14,082	23.5	58,205	14,765	25.4	63,038	18,495	29.3
Agriculture, Livestock and Fishing	2,465	137	5.5	2,415	143	5.9	2,481	148	6.0
Crude Oil and Natural Gas	23,621	1,734	7.3	20,433	1,381	6.8	19.769	1,342	6.8
Quarrying	186	21	11.4	190	20	10.6	198	21	10.6
Manufacturing Industries	9,472	2,749	29.0	9,573	2,871	30.0	10,275	3,214	31.3
Electricity, Gas & Water	1,257	281	22.3	1,332	294	22.1	1,343	379	28.2
Construction	4,593	1,380	30.1	4,754	1,422	29.9	5,852	2,417	41.3
Wholesale, Retail Trade and Repair Services	6,068	2,769	45.6	6,223	2,866	46.1	7,873	3,983	50.6
Hotels and Restaurants	1,369	739	54.0	1,481	811	54.8	1,642	884	53.8
Transport, Storage and Communication	4,699	2,193	46.7	5,339	2,782	52.1	5,924	3,211	54.2
Real Estate and Business Services	5,196	1,650	31.8	5,357	1,714	32.0	6,137	2,271	37.0
Social and Personal Services	1,042	428	41.1	1,108	460	41.6	1,543	626	40.5
The Financial Corporation Sector	4,050	1,686	41.6	4,590	2,048	44.6	4,718	2,178	46.2
Government Services Sector	6,965	1,542	22.1	7,365	1,618	22.0	7,592	1,798	23.7
Household Domestic Services	447	129	28.9	529	154	29.2	553	163	29.5
Less : Imputed Bank Service	-1,137	-454	(40.0)	(5,192)	-595	(42.0)	-1,553	-701	(45.1)

Value in million USD at current prices   * Adjusted figures   ** Preliminary figures
Source: Ministry of Economy & Planning

GDP 2003–2005

Economic Sectors	2003*			2004**			2005**		
	UAE Total	Dubai	%	UAE Total	Dubai	%	UAE Total	Dubai	%
Non-Oil Gross Domestic Product	62,566	25,217	40.3	69,619	28,325	40.7	85,100	36,166	42.5
Gross Domestic Product	87,671	26,633	30.4	103,205	30,151	29.2	132,292	38,202	28.9
The non-Financial Corporation Sector	74,897	22,661	30.3	89,565	25,863	28.9	116,448	32,935	28.3
Agriculture, Livestock and Fishing	2,494	156	6.2	2,752	223	8.1	3,005	216	7.2
Mining and Quarrying	25,314	1,439	16.4	33,812	1,850	16.4	47,443	2,062	15.2
Manufacturing Industries	11,503	3,811	33.1	13,500	4,403	32.6	16,674	6,030	36.2
Electricity, Gas & Water	1,637	390	23.8	1,831	444	24.2	2,162	519	24.0
Construction	7,104	3,259	45.9	7,757	3,671	47.3	9,531	4,486	47.1
Wholesale, Retail Trade and Repair Services	9,662	5,436	56.3	10,540	6,017	57.1	14,441	8,525	59.0
Hotels and Restaurants	1,778	992	55.8	2,001	1,141	57.0	2,438	1,375	56.4
Transport, Storage and Communication	6,728	3,765	56.0	7,429	4,128	55.6	8,894	4,960	55.8
Real Estate and Business Services	6,909	2,666	38.6	8,049	3,195	39.7	9,787	3,878	39.6
Social and Personal Services	1,769	749	42.3	1,894	791	41.8	2,073	885	42.7
The Financial Corporation Sector	5,423	2,540	46.8	6,081	2,860	47.0	7,746	3,728	48.1
Government Services Sector	8,375	1,990	23.8	8,774	2,083	23.7	9,465	2,277	24.1
Household Domestic Services	563	163	29.0	579	168	29.0	649	188	29.0
Less : Imputed Bank Service	-1,587.19	-722	45.4	-1,795	-824	45.9	-2,015	-927	46.0

Value in million USD at current prices   * Adjusted figures   ** Preliminary figures
Source: Ministry of Economy & Planning

APPENDIX 3

POPULATION

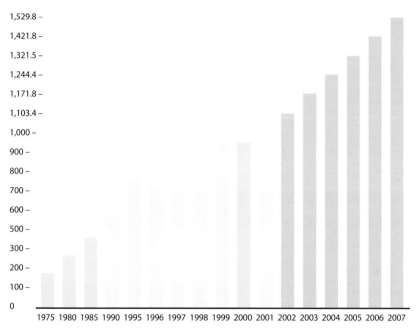

1,529.8 –
1,421.8 –
1,321.5 –
1,244.4 –
1,171.8 –
1,103.4 –
1,000 –
900 –
800 –
700 –
600 –
500 –
300 –
200 –
100 –
0

1975 1980 1985 1990 1995 1996 1997 1998 1999 2000 2001 2002 2003 2004 2005 2006 2007

Final result of population census   Mid-year estimates
Source: Ministry of Planning and Dubai Minicipality

APPENDIX 4

EMPLOYMENT

Dubai: Employment by Economic Sectors

Economic Sectors	2002*			2003*			2004		
	UAE Total	Dubai	%	UAE Total	Dubai	%	UAE Total	Dubai	%
Total	2,176,300	771,978	35.5	2,334,312	859,481	36.8	2,459,145	912,723	37.1
The non-Financial Corporation Sector	1,715,383	637,210	37.0	1,858,039	718,706	38.7	1,967,326	767,524	39.0
Agriculture, Live Stock and Fishing	163,192	9,645	5.9	166,428	10,538	6.3	168,574	10,978	6.5
Crude Oil and Natural Gas	27,197	3,830	14.1	28,073	4,000	14.2	30,015	4,400	14.7
Quarrying	4,505	726	16.1	4,838	790	16.3	5,560	870	15.6
Manufacturing Industries	276,476	104,856	37.9	299,064	115,150	38.5	319,384	123,680	38.7
Electricity, Gas & Water	26,591	6,462	24.3	28,359	7,068	24.9	28,848	7,160	24.8
Construction	420,896	173,150	41.1	473,577	201,111	42.5	497,974	210,800	42.3
Wholesale, Retail Trade and Repair Services	415,974	174,025	41.8	450,208	197,300	43.8	478,716	210,758	44.0
Hotels and Restaurants	94,930	49,648	52.3	98,509	51,225	52.0	73,817	28,380	38.4
Transport, Storage and Communication	130,923	57,860	44.2	142,548	68,057	47.7	109,931	58,710	53.0
Real Estate and Business Services	63,664	22,726	35.7	67,107	24,267	36.2	147,807	69,869	47.3
Social and Personal Services	91,035	34,282	37.7	99,328	39,200	39.5	106,700	41,910	39.3
The Financial Corporation Sector	25,724	13,889	54.0	26,368	14,525	55.1	27,011	14,865	55.0
Government Services Sector	237,368	63,189	26.6	250,174	68,400	27.3	264,568	72,324	27.3
Household Domestic Services	197,825	57,690	29.2	199,731	57,850	29.0	200,240	58,010	29.0

* Approximated Figures

Source: Ministry of Economy & Planning

Dubai: Employment by Economic Sectors

Economic Sectors	2005*			2006*		
	UAE Total	Dubai	%	UAE Total	Dubai	%
Total	2,624,140	962,998	37.0	2,843,643	1,054,045	37.1
The non-Financial Corporation Sector	2,089,974	809,025	39.0	2,297,084	896,097	39.0
Agriculture, Live Stock and Fishing	191,091	11,631	6.1	193,059	11,816	6.1
Crude Oil and Natural Gas	32,864	4,734	14.4	33,127	4,750	14.3
Quarrying	5,439	815	15.0	5,803	868	15.0
Manufacturing Industries	333,180	132,093	40.0	361,766	140,881	38.9
Electricity, Gas & Water	33,861	8,103	24.0	34,142	8,179	24.0
Construction	528,991	227,251	43.0	647,132	281,043	43.4
Whosale, Retail Trade and Repair Services	497,345	214,748	43.2	518,546	225,878	43.6
Real Estate and Business Services	77,070	29,330	38.1	83,923	31,067	37.0
Hotels and Restaurants	115,.435	61,463	53.2	123,995	66,758	53.8
Transport, Storage and Communication	161,122	74,742	46.4	174,489	79,059	45.3
Social and Personal Services	113,576	44,133	39.0	121,102	45,798	37.8
The Financial Corporation Sector	30,701	16,899	55.0	36,525	19,181	25.8
Government Services Sector	283,210	75,779	27.0	284,441	75,835	26.7
Households Domestic Services	220,255	61,295	28.0	225,593	62,932	27.9

* Approximated Figures
  Source: Ministry of Economy & Planning

APPENDIX 5

TRADE

Imports by HS Classification Sections – Emirate of Dubai (2000–2002)

HS Sections	2000		2001		2002	
	Quantity	Value	Quantity	Value	Quantity	Value
Live animals, Animal products	231,752	2863	222,073	388	253,836	428
Vegetable products	2,028,337	938	1,993,842	898	2,077,513	980
Animal and vegetable fats, Oils and Waxes	114,329	66	81,208	44	125,529	70
Prepared foodstuff, Beverages, Tobacco	532,376	495	506,970	558	533,108	657
Mineral products	1,550,611	277	1,167,201	180	1,153,023	170
Products of chemical or allied industries	1,222051	1231	1,518,826	1242	1,581,193	1370
Plastics, Rubber and Rubber articles	482,029	804	518,575	829	589,387	879
Raw hides, Skins, Leather and Articles etc	46,060	120	49,208	132	61,395	142
Wood, Cork, Plating materials and Articles	474,209	226	495,807	228	578,198	237
Wood pulp, Paper products, Waste paper	320,948	315	306,586	275	313,222	277
Textiles and Textile articles	583,145	2661	608,175	2527	693,742	2615
Footwear, Headgear, Umbrellas etc	55,391	224	62,123	239	83,335	265
Articles of stone, cement, asbestos, ceramics	469,630	389	556,192	447	692,698	511
Pearls, Precious stones and Metals	1,845	1661	1,907	4353	1,946	4686
Base metals and Base metal articles	1,722,795	1353	1,993,408	1432	2,341,530	1625
Machinery, Sound recorders, TVs etc	635,201	4641	731,812	4861	918,699	5588
Vehicles, Aircraft, Vessels etc	300,505	2665	334,016	2795	391,972	2651
Optical, Medical equipment, Watches etc	29,241	550	32,384	611	35,210	727
Arms and ammunition, parts and accessories	390	2	280	2	377	2
Miscellaneous manufactured articles	236,145	691	247,522	620	287,315	711
Art work, Collectors' pieces and Antiques	462	4	186	5	105	4
Total	11,037,449	19725	11,428,300	22667	12,713,332	24593

* Difference in total is due to approximation   Value in million USD at current prices

Source: Ports, Customs & Free Zone Corporation

Imports by HS Classification Sections – Emirate of Dubai (2003–2004)

HS Sections	2003		2004	
	Quantity	Value	Quantity	Value
Live animals, Animal products	270 ,676	463	290,858	542
Vegetable products	1,780,524	1,004	2,464,356	1,245
Animal and vegetable fats, Oils and Waxes	139,582	83	163,608	105
Prepared foodstuff, Beverages, Tobacco	1,173,824	1,052	1,770,012	1,334
Mineral products	1,580,867	246	2,115,111	319
Products of chemical or allied industries	1,887,085	1,690	2,301,378	2,179
Plastics, Rubber and Rubber articles	660,306	1,045	804,930	1,411
Raw hides, Skins, Leather and Articles etc	76,092	148	85,332	196
Wood, Cork, Plating materials and Articles	665,086	285	898,092	417
Wood pulp, Paper products, Waste paper	356,870	314	399,335	387
Textiles and Textile articles	819,675	2,849	967,296	3,319
Footwear, Headgear, Umbrellas etc	110,985	286	147,920	353
Articles of stone, cement, asbestos, ceramics	841,508	581	1,136,353	734
Pearls, Precious stones and Metals	2,357	5,513	4,117	9,088
Base metals and Base metal articles	3,140,322	2,097	3,910,617	3,344
Machinery, Sound recorders, TVs etc	1,138,051	6,322	1,422,596	9,169
Vehicles, Aircraft, Vessels etc	491,644	4,071	617,920	4,486
Optical, Medical equipment, Watches etc	40,653	766	45,082	949
Arms and ammunition, parts and accessories	655	3	993	4
Miscellaneous manufactured articles	355,890	807	433,207	1,027
Art work, Collectors' pieces and Antiques	190	3	224	6
Total	15,532,843	29,628	19,979,336	4,0612

* Difference in total is due to approximation   Value in million USD at current prices
  Source: Ports, Customs & Free Zone Corporation

Foreign Trade by HS Classification Sections – Emirate of Dubai (2006)

HS Sections	Imports Quantity	Imports Value	Export Quantity	Export Value	Re-Exports Quantity	Re-Exports Value
Live animals, Animal products	367,079	749	27,539	56	51,154	102
Vegetable products	3,819,793	1,872	174,643	53	1,007,513	635
Animal and vegetable fats, Oils and Waxes	219,353	132	118,878	85	56,146	40
Prepared foodstuff, Beverages, Tobacco	1,941,252	1,630	1,267,544	676	356,017	434
Mineral products	3,547,702	628	434,336	266	87,269	52
Products of chemical or allied industries	2,807,911	3,338	160,451	230	200,293	584
Plastics, Rubber and Rubber articles	972,317	2,023	144,352	203	347,537	720
Raw hides, Skins, Leather and articles etc	99,280	310	4,855	6	43,607	110
Wood, Cork, Plating materials and Articles	1,061,632	597	3,695	6	141,862	112
Wood pulp, Paper products, Waste paper	557,071	586	230,422	119	58,627	78
Textiles and Textile articles	1,027,339	3,759	72,520	253	593,663	1,871
Footwear, Headgear, Umbrellas etc	169,232	481	4,362	8	87,285	214
Articles of stone, cement, asbestos, ceramics	1,823,029	1,034	633,671	284	392,382	496
Pearls, Precious stones and Metals	4,061	12,808	72	1,386	1,997	6,553
Base metals and Base metal articles	6,312,186	6,225	1,201,509	1,124	621,182	857
Machinery, Sound recorders, TVs etc	1,738,838	13,686	25,886	75	714,154	5,292
Vehicles, Aircraft, Vessels etc	839,519	7,368	16,766	38	517,641	2,278
Optical, Medical equipment, Watches etc	53,321	1,257	329	4	22,505	381
Arms and ammunition, parts and accessories	606	6	106	1	201	1
Miscellaneous manufactured articles	518,076	1,407	47,851	100	243,223	520
Art work, Collectors' pieces and Antiques	915	13	40	1	1,729	4
Total	27,880,511	59,910	4,569,825	4,975	5,545,986	21,338

* Difference in total is due to approximation   Value in million USD at current prices
  Source: Dubai World

Foreign Trade by Type – Emirate of Dubai (2000–2002)

	2000		2001		2002	
	Quantity	Value	Quantity	Value	Quantity	Value
Direct Trade						
Imports	11,037,449	19,725	11,428,300	22,667	12,713,332	24,593
Exports	1,347,197	1,489	1,569,617	1,610	2,192,776	1,738
Re-exports	2,372,515	4,812	2,464,973	6,151	3,394,490	8, 070
Free Zone						
Imports	3,866,976	6,587	3,602,689	8,265	5,724,676	10,493
Exports Re-exports	1,756,459	5,102	2,040,125	6,798	3,523,252	8,865

Source: Ports, Customs & Free Zone Corporation
Value in million USD at current prices

Foreign Trade by Type – Emirate of Dubai (2003–2006)

	2003		2004		2005		2006	
	Quantity	Value	Quantity	Value	Quantity	Value	Quantity	Value
Direct Trade								
Imports	15,532,843	29,628	19,979,336	40,612	23,404,292	51,882	27,880,511	59,910
Exports	2,800,385	1,793	3,350,633	2,628	4,156,792	3,059	4,569,825	4,975
Re-exports	3,727,237	10,286	4,544,293	15,542	5,147,993	21,478	5,545,986	21,338
Free Zone								
Imports	4,931,442	13,614	5,200,573	18,743	5,447,422	27,002	6,668,178	30,254
Exports Re-exports	3,107,801	11,264	2,894,003	14,329	3,342,446	21,452	3,029,385	22,512

Source: Ports, Customs & Free Zone Corporation
Value in million USD at current prices

Direct Imports by Country 2002–2005

Countries	2002 Value	%	2003 Value	%	2004 Value	%	2005 Value	%	2006 Value	%
China	2,886	11.7	3,627	12.2	5,001	12.3	6,621	12.8	7,683	12.8
India	1,058	4.3	1,790	6.0	1,766	4.3	6,122	11.8	6,338	10.6
USA	1,593	6.5	1,931	6.5	2435	6.0	3,888	7.5	4,917	8.2
Japan	1,789	7.3	2,626	8.9	481	1.2	3,750	7.2	4,071	6.8
Germany	1,027	4.2	1,150	3.9	1,577	3.9	3,284	6.3	4,071	6.8
UK	1,844	7.5	2,249	7.6	2,864	7.1	3,162	6.1	3,298	5.5
Italy	1,371	5.6	1,195	4.0	1,482	3.6	1,739	3.4	2,303	3.8
Switzerland	1,236	5.0	1,172	4.0	1,753	4.3	1,707	3.3	1,981	3.3
South Korea	1,532	6.2	1,632	5.5	2,372	5.8	1,653	3.2	1,792	3.0
Turkey	1,786	7.3	1,859	6.3	2,576	6.3	1,525	2.9	1,734	2.9
Total Imports	24,593		29,628		40,612		51,882		59,910	

Value in Million USD

APPENDIX 6

TRANSPORT

Arrivals and Departures at Dubai International Airport

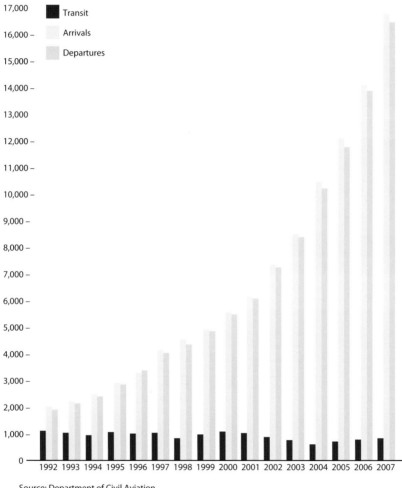

Source: Department of Civil Aviation
Quantity in million tonnes

Air cargo handled at Dubai International Airport

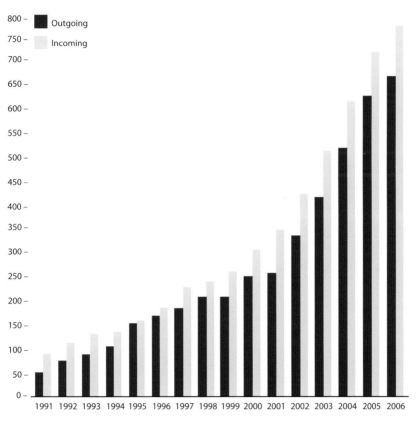

Source: Department of Civil Aviation
Quantity in million tonnes

Vessels calling at Port Rashid and Jebel Ali

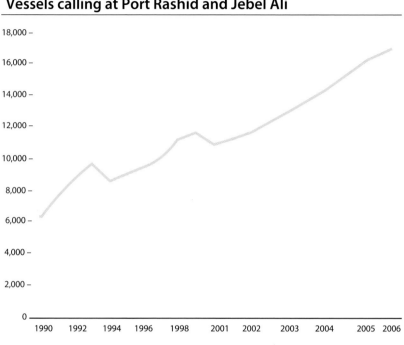

Source: Dubai World & Dubai Ports Authority

Total cargo handled at Port Rashid and Jebel Ali (1990–2006)

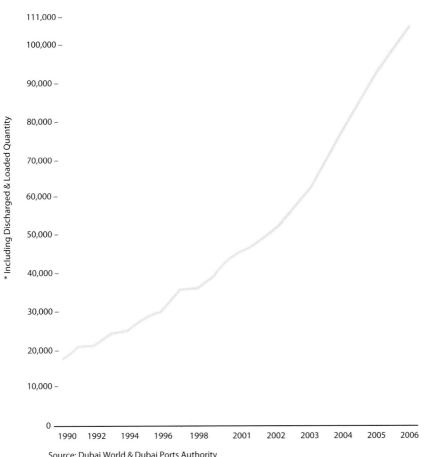

Source: Dubai World & Dubai Ports Authority
Quantity in million tonnes

Motor vehicles registered for the first time at Dubai (1996–2006)

Years	Cars	Buses	Trucks	Motorcycles	Other	Total
1996	29,431	806	4,956	623	602	**36,418**
1997	35,703	946	5,776	660	952	**44,037**
1998	46,094	1,353	6,523	818	1,379	**56,167**
1999	42,382	1,307	6,508	791	1,186	**52,174**
2000	45,662	1,302	5,871	796	714	**54,345**
2001	75,907	3,254	8,235	1,165	615	**89,176**
2002	67,249	1,382	7,810	902	1,362	**78,705**
2003	79,783	1,183	7,391	1,018	1,181	**90,556**
2004	96,762	4,392	13,973	2,583	3,063	**163,398**
2005	136,902	6,877	13,973	2,583	3,063	**212,867**

Sources: Road & Transport Authority

APPENDIX 7

CONSTRUCTION

Dubai: Completed Buildings

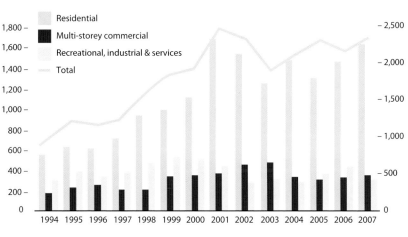

Source: Dubai Statistics Centre & Dubai Municipality

Land Transactions, Emirate of Dubai (1970–2007)

Year	Quantity	Value
1970	630	9
1975	1,607	219
1980	491	82
1985	804	973
1990	1,400	463
1991	1,271	402
1992	1,832	746
1993	2,383	1,279
1994	1,857	1,299
1995	1,541	873
1996	1,897	1,837
1997	2,510	2,223
1998	2,291	2,328
1999	3,558	1,779
2000	2,636	1,564
2001	3,201	2,345
2002	3,707	2,747
2003	3,976	3,425
2004	4,997	6,507
2005	4,816	8,582
2006	5,640	15,290
2007	1,117	33,850

Source: Dubai Statistics Centre & Lands Department
Value in million USD

APPENDIX 8

HOTELS AND TOURISM

Guests and Residence Nights at Hotels by Nationality – Emirate of Dubai

Countries	2005		2006		2007	
	Residence Nights	Guests	Residence Nights	Guests	Residence Nights	Guests
UAE	536,633	297,883	480,555	257,562	481,187	265,072
Other AGCC	1,718,459	783,143	1,781,034	819,310	1,989,274	975,414
Other Arab	1,165,913	476,246	1,162,657	483,074	1,093,643	457,960
Asian & African	4,614,108	1,679,044	3,837,790	1,530,693	3,456,219	1,375,403
European	6,388,640	1,981,720	5,618,720	1,832,372	5,429,877	1,767,901
American	1,044,441	468,366	788,768	388,243	653,353	320,987
Oceanian	397,363	177,107	350,971	162,255	272,231	131,748
Total	15,865,557	5,863,509	14,020,495	5,473,509	13,375,784	5,294,485

Source: Department of Tourism & Commerce Marketing

Hotel Rooms and Occupancy Rates by Type – Emirate of Dubai

	Five -Star	Four Star	Three Star	Two–Star	One–Star	Listed	Total
Hotel Rooms							
2002	8,623	3,686	3,676	2,203	2,203	2,020	23,170
2003	9,966	4,261	4,112	3,164	2,583	1,485	25,571
2004	10,256	4,386	4,369	2,930	2,815	1,399	26,610
2005	10,827	5,425	4,135	3,419	3,503	1,301	28,610
2006	11,806	5,990	4,224	3,856	4,097	877	30,850
Occupancy ates, %							
2002	77.92	72.63	70.87	68.64	47.44	58.66	70.2
2003	76.56	79.23	68.76	64.63	63.77	65.87	72.4
2004	86.12	90.96	80.31	72.7	64.08	66.37	81
2005	89.59	87.87	84.16	77.65	74.02	76.76	84.6
2006	89.2	84.5	80.8	73.8	67.1	79.2	82

Source: Department of Tourism & Commerce Marketing

INDEX